Life between Two Deaths, 1989–2001

POST-CONTEMPORARY

INTERVENTIONS

Series Editors:

STANLEY FISH

& FREDRIC JAMESON

LIFE BETWEEN TWO DEATHS, 1989–2001

U.S. Culture in the Long Nineties

PHILLIP E. WEGNER

DUKE UNIVERSITY PRESS
Durham & London 2009

© 2009 Duke University Press
All rights reserved.

Printed in the United States
of America
on acid-free paper ♾

Designed by Jennifer Hill
Typeset in Chaparral Pro by
Tseng Information Systems, Inc.

Library of Congress
Cataloging-in-Publication Data
appear on the last printed page of
this book.

Every epoch, in fact, not only dreams the one to follow but, in dreaming, precipitates its awakening.

WALTER BENJAMIN, *The Arcades Project*

Historical freedom, indeed, expanding and contracting as it does with the objective conditions themselves, never seems greater than in such transitional periods, where the life-style has not yet taken on the rigidity of a period manner, and when there is sudden release from the old without any corresponding obligation to that which will come to take its place.

FREDRIC JAMESON, *Marxism and Form*

Professor Malik Solanka felt more than ever like a refugee in a small boat, caught between surging tides: reason and unreason, war and peace, the future and the past.

SALMAN RUSHDIE, *Fury*

CONTENTS

ACKNOWLEDGMENTS

ONE OF THE THINGS I discuss in this book is the way in which any periodization emerges only in an act of repetition, or through a form of historical retrospection. And thus while I did not recognize this until early 2004, the period of the writing of this book was a long one, extending back at least to 1991 with the publication of a portion of what is now chapter 3 in the Duke University situationist periodical, *The Missing Link*. Indeed, the final line of that short essay already contains in seed a major conceit of this book: "As in the final image of T2, we still hurtle down a nighttime road, unable to see where we may be headed." Whether this situation be a tragedy or an opportunity remains, I believe, an open question.

Any book this long in gestation is bound to develop a host of debts, far more than I might possibly recognize here. However, there are a few people I would especially like to acknowledge. First, I thank the members of the Summer Institute—Liz Blasco, Susan Hegeman, Caren Irr, Carolyn Lesjak, Chris Pavsek, Michael Rothberg, Rob Seguin, and Yasemin Yildiz (and now Sophie, Owen, Nadia, Mia, Lonso,

Claire, and Madeline)—for offering an unreserved font of friendship, intellectual support, and a true community (and some of the best meals and most memorable hikes I've ever had as well). Our ongoing exchanges mark all the pages of this book. I have been especially fortunate during most of the time of working on this book to have been part of what was a unique and rare experiment in humanist scholarship and teaching at the University of Florida, and I thank many of the colleagues and exceptional students, undergraduate and graduate, that I have had the opportunity to work with over the years. Florida's graduate student Marxist Reading Group and its annual spring conference have provided me with a welcoming forum for presenting my ideas, and I hope this event will continue for a long time to come. Two of my teachers, John Hartzog and Fred Jameson, continue to serve as exemplary models of the committed intellectual and have been inspirations for much of the work in these pages. Tom Moylan and Peter Fitting, as well as many other scholars and friends in the Society for Utopian Studies, have also provided unfailing support and friendship throughout the years. I express my special gratitude to John Leavey Jr. for the leadership, example, and sense of family he has so freely offered to us.

Teachers, friends, and colleagues at the University of Florida and beyond who read, responded to, or otherwise contributed to the various drafts of many of these chapters, sometimes in ways they may not even have realized, include Alex Alberro, Alvaro Aleman, Nora Alter, Apollo Amoko, Don Ault, Raffaella Baccolini, Wesley Beal, Roger Beebe, Marsha Bryant, Richard Burt, Cesare Casarino, Michael Denning, Kim Emery, John Evelev, Stephen Giddens, Pam Gilbert, Brian Greenspan, Michael Hardt, Bob Hatch, Tace Hedrick, Carrie Hintz, Peter Hitchcock, Naomi Jacobs, Raina and Rick Joines, Brandy Kershner, Sam Kimball, Kenneth Kidd, Sheryl Kroen, Jane Kuenz, Amitava Kumar, Nicole LaRose, David Leverenz, Jane Love, Regina Martin, Brian Meredith, Derek Merrill, Carl Miller, Maria Moss, Robin Nuzum, Scott Nygren, Jim Paxson, Aron Pease, Craig Rinne, Bruce Robbins, Ken Roemer, Leah Rosenberg, Reagan Ross, Peter Sands, Lyman Sargent, Malini Schueller, Rich Simpson, Barbara Herrnstein Smith, Dina Smith, Stephanie Smith, Jason Snart, Darko Suvin, Imre Szeman, Csaba Toth, Maureen Turim, Trish Ventura, Shelton Waldrep, Huei-ju Wang, Evan Watkins, Ed White, Jeff Williams, Susan Willis, Julian Wolfreys, and Justin Wyble.

I thank the members of the editorial board at Duke University Press, and especially Reynolds Smith and Sharon Torian, for their help in bringing this book to fruition. I also offer my thanks to the two astute readers for the press. Thanks, too, to Ross Birrell both for permission to reprint an image from some of his recent work and for posing a crucial question that helped crystallize this project. This book benefited immensely from the opportunity to present the ideas contained within it in talks at the University of Florida, Duke University, Carlow College, the University of British Columbia, the University of California, Santa Cruz, the University of Illinois, and the Ralahine Centre for Utopian Studies, University of Limerick; and at the conferences for the Modern Language Association, the Society for the Study of Narrative in the Arts, Rethinking Marxism, and the Society for Utopian Studies. These are all exemplary programs and organizations, and I thank them all for the warm welcome and the chance to share some of my ideas. Summer research funds from the University of Florida also helped provide time to complete this book.

A few months before the idea for this book crystallized there occurred the "two births" of my children, Nadia and Owen. They have given me more joy and a greater sense of hope in these "dark times" than I might ever have imagined. "Do not judge us too harshly." My extended families, Hegeman and Wegner, continue to offer sustenance of every kind. Finally, I was fortunate throughout the entire period of the 1990s and the writing of this book to have had the close company of the best friend, colleague, and reader that anyone could imagine—to you, Susan Hegeman, this book is dedicated.

THE PRESENT AS A MOMENT OF DANGER

Articulating the past historically does not mean recognizing it "the way it really was." It means appropriating a memory as it flashes up in a moment of danger. Historical materialism wishes to hold fast that image of the past which unexpectedly appears to the historical subject in a moment of danger. The danger threatens both the content of the tradition and those who inherit it. For both, it is one and the same thing: the danger of becoming a tool of the ruling classes. Every age must strive anew to wrest tradition away from the conformism that is working to overpower it. The Messiah comes not only as the redeemer; he comes as the victor over the Antichrist. The only historian capable of fanning the spark of hope in the past is the one who is firmly convinced that *even the dead* will not be safe from the enemy if he is victorious. And this enemy has never ceased to be victorious.

WALTER BENJAMIN, "On the Concept of History," Thesis VI

THIS IS A BOOK about our present, but also about another, more distant historical period, that of the 1990s. Throughout this book, I will show that the 1990s represented a moment of heated debate over the direction of the future, and hence of immense historical possibilities for a global left, possibilities that are now, in the aftermath of the events of September 11, 2001, and the emergent global regime of the so-called war on terror, at risk of being forgotten. If this book thus represents a further contribution to the growing body of work exploring the cultural consequences of the event now known simply as 9/11, it does so in an original way by looking at the deep and intimate connections between that event and the cultural, political, and economic developments in the years that preceded it. What unify the analyses throughout this book are two overarching and deceptively simple questions. First, what happened on September 11, 2001? And second, what would be involved in thinking of the 1990s—a span I define for reasons that will become clear shortly as lying between November 1989 and September 2001—as a specific cultural period? My investigation takes the form of careful readings of some of the most interesting work in popular, mass, and genre fiction, film, and television produced in these years. These works are also of special interest in that they shed light on some of the most fundamental issues concerning the nature of narrative: how we recognize beginnings and endings, as well as the networks of relationships that we construct between diverse events. Narrative conceived of in this way is always already deeply imbricated in politics, the forms of the stories we tell shaping the ways we imagine—and in imagining, act—in our world. These issues take on a special urgency in the *Augenblick der Gefahr* (moment of danger), to use Walter Benjamin's striking phrase for the analogous situation of the 1930s, that is our present.

I take my lead in this project from the work of two of the most significant dialectical periodizing thinkers produced by the preceding century. My comments on the differences between our present situation and that of the very recent but already quite distant past are offered in the spirit of Benjamin's monumental ruin of *Das Passagen-Werk*, or *The Arcades Project* (1982). Periodization is itself deeply integral to the methodology Benjamin calls "dialectics at a standstill," the effort to "blast a specific era out of the homogenous course of history."[1] This, Michael Löwy argues, "is the equivalent, at the historiographic level, of the revolutionary interruption of historical continuity."[2] The explicit aim of Benjamin's project is to think the period he names the nineteenth century, whose spatial center was Paris, in terms of the tremendous historical possibilities—technological, cultural, and political—opened up within it. As Benjamin sees it, the nineteenth century was a moment of revolution, invention, experimentation, and utopian schemas of all kinds: "Only in the summery middle of the nineteenth century, under its sun, can one conceive of Fourier's fantasy materialized."[3] The fact that the present can no longer even imagine such radical newness and the degree to which these past experiments are now viewed as naïve are from Benjamin's perspective the most concrete indicators of the immense gulf separating the moment of the nineteenth century from his own. Thus, if there is any judgment to be rendered, it is not on the past but rather on the creative and imaginative poverty of the present.[4]

All this points toward a second, implicit act of periodization that takes place in *The Arcades Project*. Benjamin uses the nineteenth century as a way of coming to grips with the closure of another more recent moment of radical cultural and political experimentation, that of the modernist 1920s. Indeed, as Susan Buck-Morss and others have demonstrated, it was Benjamin's direct experiences in the late 1920s of both the increasing hostility in the Soviet Union toward "avant-garde experimentation" and the last years of radical cultural work in Weimar Berlin that were at the roots of the research that would come to compose the *Arcades* convolutes.[5] In *The Arcades Project* itself, Benjamin accepts Emmanuel Berl's explicit link of surrealism and the period of 1820–40: "And that is certainly no accident. For, on the one hand, we have here elements—anthropological materialism, hostility toward progress—which are refractory to Marxism, while, on the other hand, the will to apocatastasis speaks here, the resolve to gather again, in revolutionary action and in revolutionary thinking, precisely the elements of the 'too early' and the 'too late,' of the first beginning and the final decay."[6] This is akin to what Alain Badiou now describes as the twentieth century's "passion for the real," which I want to suggest reaches certain high points of intensity in the modernist 1920s, in the 1960s, and in the 1990s.[7]

This then suggests another important lesson I take from Benjamin's project. For while to talk in terms of the otherness and closure of the recent past opens up the risk of being misunderstood as engaging in an act of mourning for missed opportunities—will history ever forgive us for our failures to act when we could or should have?—the real aim of Benjamin's project, both in *The Arcades Project* and in its methodological companion essay, "On the Concept of History," is to force its audience to recognize that the sense of catastrophic closure that defined his "moment of danger" was in fact illusory. For Benjamin, every moment is always already "the small gateway in time through which the Messiah might enter," a time of potential "miracles" as Eric Santner puts it, and we must always act as if this were the case, lest the victory of the enemy occur once again.[8] It is this stance, Löwy maintains, that defines Benjamin's original practice of historical materialism: "Against the history written by the victors, the celebration of the *fait accompli*, the historical one-way street and the 'inevitability' of the victory of those who triumphed, we must come back to this essential proposition: each present opens up onto a multiplicity of possible futures. In every historical conjuncture, there were alternatives. . . . In this case, the opening-up of the past and the opening-up of the future are intimately linked."[9] In short, we need to understand the past differently to perceive our present in a new way: history must be used, as Meaghan Morris maintains, "as a source of a liberating certainty that anything could happen."[10] Only in this way can we hope to keep faith with the true radicality of past movements and actors.

The second major inspiration for my book lies in the immense and on-going project of cultural periodization developed by Fredric Jameson, and especially in his work on "postmodernism" as the "cultural logic of late capitalism."[11] An important question thus arises concerning the relationship between the particular periodizing schema I develop here and Jameson's own periodizations. A first provisional answer lies in the matter of scale. As the title of his major study emphasizes, Jameson's scale is that of the economic, of the mode of production itself; mine, on the other hand, is pegged to geopolitical horizons that unfold within this larger temporal formation, the most significant here being the period known as the Cold War, or what Michael Denning has dubbed the "age of three worlds."[12] The relationship is thus akin to that between the economic periodizations of Ernest Mandel (the figure whose work formed the basis of Jameson's periodizing Benjaminian Idea of postmodernism) and those of Michel Aglietta and his colleagues in the French regulationist school of political economics, the latter's more finely tuned periods neatly nestling, as Mike Davis demonstrates, in the larger waves of the former.[13]

However, Jameson's own recent writings on periodization offer us another way of thinking about this relationship. In the first part of his book *A Singular Modernity* (2002), Jameson outlines his "four maxims of modernity," which should also be understood as the fundamental axioms for the production of any successful periodizing narrative. Jameson then develops a number of crucial corollaries to these axioms, of which I find the following to be the most important. First, any "periodization necessarily constructs a frame around itself, and builds on the basis of a subtle interplay between two forms of negation, the contrary and the contradictory, between differentiation and outright opposition, between the locally distinguished and the absolute negation, antagonistic and non-antagonistic, the non- and the anti-."[14] This recalls the distinction Slavoj Žižek draws between the Hegelian negative and infinite judgments, the former "determinate negation" in fact operating within a closed economy with its antithesis, the latter marking a more dramatic dialectical "negation of the negation" opening into true otherness.[15] Second, Jameson points out that whereas a focus on seamless historical change "slowly turns into a consciousness of a radical break," "the enforced attention to a break gradually turns the latter into a period in its own right."[16] Finally, and most significant for my purposes, "each break officially posited seems to bring a flurry of new ones in its wake."[17]

On the basis of these axioms and their corollaries (which also might be applied retrospectively to his *Postmodernism* study), Jameson develops in the next two sections of the book a rich original analysis of the period of modernism. Jameson argues that modernism is now in fact to be understood as comprising two different periods, high modernism and what he calls "late modernism," the latter marked by both a retreat from the radical energies of an earlier modernism and the development of a depoliticized modernist aesthetic ideology. This is in fact the "liberal" resolution that arises in the postwar moment to the crisis situation articulated in Benjamin's late work (and a move repeated today in many of the antitheoretical, antihistoricist, and ultimately antipolitical calls for a return to aesthetics, ethics, and a "normative formalism").[18] Late modernism also serves as a transitional space, a kind of vanishing mediator in the ultimate emergence of postmodernism.

There are a number of significant implications that arise from these insights. First, the dialectical bifocality of periods and breaks, and the tendency of the latter to proliferate, hints at the ways in which another opening emerges between late modernism and postmodernism in Jameson's thought: this is, of course, the moment of the 1960s, at once a period in its own right and a transitional phase akin to Benjamin's nineteenth century and the 1920s.[19] Even more significant for my project, Jameson's analysis provides us with the ground to divide his period of postmodernism into "high" postmodernism, characteristic of the 1980s and the subject of Jameson's classic analyses, and what we might call a "late" postmodernism that only emerges in the 1990s. Crucially, however, the valences are in this case reversed, as it is the "late" moment that witnesses the revival of a radical political energy in abeyance in the earlier. It will be to the project of giving expression to the complex and dynamic energies of this last period that my book is dedicated.

There are a few issues concerning methodology and the choice of texts that I would like to address before offering a brief overview of the book's chapters. Two approaches tend to dominate contemporary studies of mass or popular culture. The first focuses on what I would call the pedagogical dimension of the text, looking at the content or the messages (including, of course, what Jameson calls the "content of the form") the work directs toward its audience—messages, it is understood, whose fundamental aim is to produce a certain kind of subjectivity. The second approach is the inverse of this first, taking the mass cultural audiences as its object of study, attending to the ways these audiences accept, reject, negotiate, or rework the messages of the text itself. While questions of pedagogical struggles will be central in the pages that follow, my approach to the material will be a different one. Following the lead of Gilles Deleuze's celebrated analysis of film and Jameson's discussion of postmodern architecture, I explore the ways in which mass cultural documents of the 1990s "think" in a particular and original fashion both the historical situation of their present and the very nature of historical movement.[20] The tools for such thinking are not the linguistic or ideational concepts of philosophy or theory, but rather the images, narratives, and other materials specific to these forms. Thus my readings will not be interpretations in the classical sense—hermeneutical minings that maintain a hierarchical relationship between theory and narrative—but shall be more akin to what Jameson calls "transcodings," translation operations that rewrite the specific codes of the examined texts into some of our theoretical ones, in the hopes of "determining what can and what cannot be said in each."[21] In this way, I hope also to bring to light some of the things these texts might teach our theories.

One of the most important tools for such thinking, and one I will touch on repeatedly in the following chapters, is that of allegory. "Allegory," Benjamin argues in his discussion of the practice, "is not a playful illustrative technique, but a form of expression, just as speech is expression, and, indeed, just as writing is."[22] Allegories enable complex or abstract historical processes to take on a concrete form. Indeed, allegories often offer figurations of these historical movements before the emergence of a more proper conceptual or theoretical language. Allegorical representations also have the capacity to condense different historical levels and conflicts into a single figure, enabling a kind of relational thinking that is not as readily available in other forms of expression. Allegories thus operate as a perfect vehicle for what Žižek calls a "political myth": "a political *myth* proper is not so much a narrative with some determinate political meaning but, rather, an empty container of a multitude of inconsistent, even mutually exclusive, meanings."[23] In their obvious artificiality and constructed nature, allegories are failures—"Allegories are, in the realm of thoughts, what ruins are in the realm of things"—and in this lies their power, Benjamin suggests, as they mark the explicit historicity of the problems and questions with which they are grappling: "For an appreciation of the transience of things, and the concern to rescue them for eternity, is one of the strongest impulses in allegory."[24]

Moreover, many of the historical events confronted in the mass cultural texts analyzed here—one especially prominent example in the pages that follow is the Vietnam War—are sites of collective trauma, and their allegorical representations have the additional virtue of indirection, allowing their audiences to deal with materials that might prove too disturbing if tackled head-on. Finally, allegories are fundamentally narrative in form, transforming antinomies into contradictions and enabling a working through, on the level of the imaginary at least, of the very historical crises and blockages that are the central problems addressed by these texts. And again, the lessons learned in the thinking of these narratives will have profound consequences in our "real world."

Similarly, the issue of genre plays a prominent role throughout my readings. Some of the genres I address explicitly include the historical novel, dystopia, Hollywood remake, "World Bank literature," and most extensively, science fiction and science fiction film. There is a deep kinship between generic and periodizing approaches to cultural study. The concept of genre, as Jameson argues of periodization, is also "intolerable and unacceptable in its very nature," for it presumes to inaugurate a process whose aim is nothing less that the unification of disparate textual performances into a coherent ensemble, a unity that will "remain inaccessible and unverifiable."[25] Also, as I will discuss in more detail in my first chapter in terms of periods, genres are inaugurated in repetition: the symbolic order or laws of a generic institution come into being not with the first effort (for example, Thomas More's *Utopia*), but with those subsequent works that look back to it as the template for a particular kind of labor (the writing of utopian fictions).[26] Generic texts are not masterpieces—"A major work will either establish the genre or abolish it; and the perfect work will do both"—and this is where their real value lies, for the thinking they engage in becomes, as Benjamin also stresses, "exemplary" of their historical contexts in ways that these other works may not.[27]

Moreover, genres, like periodizations, force us to think comparatively and historically. The identity of any particular generic text emerges primarily in a negative fashion, by way of its difference from those works that precede and follow it in the larger generic institution of which it is a member. And the generic institution itself only comes into focus when it is placed in a historical system of genres. Similarly, any periodizing model must posit a sequence of historical periods from within which various kinds of comparisons and contrasts are generated. In both cases, too, when the particular generic text or the particular period is located within this larger historical sequence, it appears as no more than a momentary crystallization of the energies of a fluid historical stream, not unlike the transient formations that pop up on the surface of the sentient "ocean" in Stanislaw Lem's *Solaris* (1961). I thus hope that my comments on genre in the following pages will not only shed productive light on individual texts and the historical contexts from which they emerge but also demonstrate the heuristic value of both periodizing and generic modes of thought.

My first chapter outlines some of the larger theoretical stakes in this project as it offers a way of thinking the 1990s as a particular historical period. The story that I subsequently tell in the rest of the book roughly parallels developments in the 1990s, as it moves from texts that respond to the end of the Cold War through a variety of attempts to imagine a new destiny for the United States before finally turning to texts that appear in the last part of the decade, just as the wave of the counterglobalization "movement of movements" begins to gather force, and in their own way try to think the utopian possibilities opened up by this situation. I begin with a discussion of the importance of repetition in history, using as my case study the work of the contemporary Scottish artist Ross Birrell, and in particular his late 1990s project, "Envoy." I then turn to an examination of the nature of the event that we have named 9/11. Drawing on the description of an Event offered by Badiou, I argue that no such Event in fact occurred on September 11, 2001. Rather than an encounter with the incalculable Real, September 11 was a repetition of an earlier such Event. The toppling of the World Trade Center buildings should be understood as a form of what Jacques Lacan theorizes as the "second death," an event that repeats an earlier "fall," that of the Berlin Wall in 1989. However, to describe 9/11 as a repetition rather than an Event is not to deny its significance: for endings are not in themselves beginnings, and it is only with the fall of the twin towers that the destruction of the symbolic universe of the Cold War is finally accomplished and a true new world order put into place. September 11 enabled the United States, in ways not possible in the immediate, uncertain aftermath of the Cold War, to assume a new global mantle and thus marked the opening of a new period in global history. Moreover, it is by making possible the constitution of this new symbolic order that the "sacrifice" of those who died on that September morning becomes so valuable, a logic made evident in the allegorical structure at work in the post-9/11 thriller *Phone Booth* (2002).

To mark these kinds of endings and beginnings and to think in terms of "before" and "after" necessitates as well that we rethink the 1990s — or more precisely, the span between November 9, 1989, and September 11, 2001 — as a coherent cultural period. I argue that the 1990s are the strange space between an ending (of the Cold War) and a beginning (of our post–September 11 world), one of those transitional phases that, once again following the leads of Lacan and Žižek, I call the "place between two deaths." This place, located as it is between the Real Event and its symbolic repetition, is strictly speaking "non-historical," and such an "empty place" is experienced in its lived reality, as Žižek suggests, in a Janus-faced fashion. On the one hand, it feels like a moment of "terrifying monsters," of hauntings by a living dead past. Yet it is also experienced as a moment of "sublime beauty," of openness and instability, of experimentation and opportunity, of conflict and insecurity — a place, in other words, wherein history might move in a number of very different directions. Three texts from the 1990s and its immediate aftermath — the films *Groundhog Day* (1993) and *Titanic* (1997) and the television series *Six Feet Under* (2001–5) — effectively stage what Žižek now calls the "parallax view" of what it means to live a life between two deaths. Thinking of the 1990s in this way enables us, as did Benjamin in the *Arcades* convolutes, potentially to draw connections between an immense range of phenomena, and in the following section of chapter 1, I offer a brief overview of some of these developments.

Finally, I conclude the opening chapter by looking at two other repetitious cultural texts that mark the historical shift I am talking about here: pre- and post-9/11 architectural projects by Daniel Libeskind and the Wachowski brothers' *Matrix* trilogy.

The first two chapters that follow the introduction examine in more depth narratives that help us better think about the nature of endings and beginnings of historical periods. Chapter 2 offers a reading of Don De-Lillo's novel *Underworld* (1997). In this ambitious work, DeLillo attempts to do two things: first, to write a cultural history of the Cold War in the United States, and second, to convey something of the unstable conditions in the years immediately following its conclusion. In undertaking this project, DeLillo revives and reworks one of the most significant of the modern realist narrative forms, the historical novel. However, DeLillo's historical novel differs from its nineteenth-century predecessors in that it attempts to map the emergence of a global rather than a national reality. The novel's efforts at historicizing its own present thus raise fundamental questions about the nature of any periodizing narrative. How do we know, the novel asks, when a period begins? And equally significant, when can it be said to have come to its conclusion? In the novel's celebrated first chapter, DeLillo bears out a point central for my argument: the Cold War itself begins with a repetition. However, given the years in which DeLillo was writing, the true end of the Cold War period is not yet available, and this absence haunts the narrative, preventing any satisfactory closure to it. Such closure, I argue, may in fact be located outside the narrative proper, in a cover image that uncannily seems to foreshadow the destruction of the World Trade Center.

Chapter 3 continues this analysis of endings and beginnings through a reading of the three *Terminator* films. This particular science fiction film series is especially interesting in that each film not only continues the narrative sequence begun earlier but also offers a repetition and revision of its predecessors. *The Terminator* (1984) plays on the Cold War fear of imminent nuclear annihilation that would be unleashed by powers that had long ago escaped the control of human agency. Arnold Schwarzenegger's first Terminator is the perfect embodiment of this vision of technological catastrophism, carrying out inexorably the single function for which it was devised. The conclusion of the film does not dispel these anxieties, as its time-loop–paradox narrative structure reinforces the sense of the inevitability of this event. However, the second *Terminator, Judgment Day* (1991), seems to reverse all this as it works to assure its viewers that such a disaster will never come to pass. Indeed, *T2* directly restages many of the events of the original film to "correct" the earlier vision, transforming the menace of the first film into the sequel's heroic center and arguing that the shape of the future can be manipulated. All this becomes disturbingly relevant when we realize that this same reductive vision of history was invoked in the first U.S. Persian Gulf war.

Terminator 3: Rise of the Machines (2003) is set a decade after the conclusion of *T2*. In this film, we witness a reworking of what had been the first film's nightmare of global war into a "dream" for the future. Here, John Connor is transformed into a figure of the United States, which, in the years following its ostensible victory over its greatest enemy, seemed to have lost its self-proclaimed messianic destiny as the leader of the so-called free world. However, in the terrible events that conclude this film, John again assumes his "proper" destiny. In this way, the film helps bring into focus the conservative fantasy of the true significance of the events of 9/11.

The following four chapters investigate different aspects of the unstable, fraught, and contested context of the 1990s itself. Chapters 4 and 5 look at the consequences of the ongoing neoliberal transformations of the economy and work for class identity in the United States. Chapter 4 uses changes in the three versions of the *Cape Fear* narrative as a way of bringing to the surface conflicts that occur in American life from the 1950s to the 1990s. Martin Scorsese's 1991 *Cape Fear* is a remake of J. Lee Thompson's 1962 noir classic of the same title. With its central figure of the hipster "white negro" Max Cady (Robert Mitchum), the earlier film unfolds as an allegory of racial conflict in the desegregating U.S. South. Scorsese's version distances itself from its predecessor, thematically locating the racial fears of the first film in a now apparently obsolete past. Robert De Niro's Max Cady thus becomes another popular icon of cultural difference, the poor white rural Southerner, thereby seeming to return to the imagery of John D. MacDonald's *The Executioners* (1957), the novel on which the films are based.

However, Scorsese's film undermines this iconography as well, opening up what then becomes a central thematic concern in the film: the necessity of learning to "read" Cady. In both the novel and the first film, the threat to the stability of the social order comes from the outside. In the most recent film, however, I show that the danger appears to be a distinctly internal one. Thus, in Scorsese's *Cape Fear*, we witness a veritable "return-of-the-repressed" of anxieties about class conflict, an explosive resurfacing in the 1990s popular cultural imagination of what had been long-submerged fears. The film acknowledges that the "throwaway populations" represented in it are "produced by and indispensable to present social organization," and the continued existence of this arrangement assures the increasing prevalence of these kinds of antagonisms.[28] This last fact is borne out a few months after the film's release in one of the most significant events of the early years of the period, the 1992 Los Angeles riots.

Chapter 5 continues the discussion of the transformations of work that occur in the decade through an examination of two dystopian films, *Fight Club* and *Ghost Dog*. What makes these two 1999 films so interesting is the way they adopt the formal strategies of the older genre of the naturalist dystopia to the new situation of an emergent global economy. Both films are deeply critical of modern corporate and consumer culture. However, when they attempt to move beyond this negative critical gesture and imagine history in the form of the collective political agencies that would lead us beyond the present impasse, they fall back into the same dilemmas of so many of their predecessors in the genre.

I begin my discussion of *Fight Club* with the image that concludes the film, that of collapsing skyscrapers. The image of the skyscraper coming down is also a figure that became a mainstay of cultural studies analysis, and I suggest that the film shares with much of the work in cultural studies a deeply populist orientation. Crucially, the film offers us a new kind of populist mass, one produced by the conditions of the U.S. postindustrial economy. However, as the film unfolds, the sympathetic image of a deeply alienated public becomes one of a secret underground fascist organization, one threatening to consume society in a maelstrom of violence. Here, I argue, we arrive at the political heart of this film. The general assault on social and cultural alienation that has been the focus of much of the conversation about this film actually serve as a pretense for investigating a far more troubling concern, one I take up in my following chapter as well: a fundamental sense of political alienation, the radical sense of otherness that too many feel when faced with the prospects of their own potential for action.

Ghost Dog makes its links to the historical context of naturalism explicit in a number of ways. This film, along with its companion, *Dead Man* (1996), offers devastating commentaries on the violence—environmental, racial, and cultural—both of capitalist modernization and of our dominant popular cultural forms. *Ghost Dog*'s connection to the traditions of literary naturalism is even more direct, as I suggest the film is also a remake of Jack London's classic of naturalist fiction, *The Call of the Wild* (1903). However, if London's novel is one of beginnings, narrating the emergence of a new masculine middle-class identity, *Ghost Dog* is concerned with endings. This points to the crucial link to *Fight Club*: both films, I suggest, give expression to middle-class men's anxieties about their own insecurity in an emergent post–Cold War global economy.

A similar set of dilemmas is evident in *Independence Day* (1996), the film that stands at the center of chapter 6. Although panned by many of its original reviewers, *Independence Day* went on to become one of the highest grossing films of all time. The reasons for the film's great success lie, I argue, in its effectiveness at tapping into some of the cultural anxieties of its moment and its prophetic vision of their resolution. I begin by investigating the resonance between the film's vision and that of its contemporary, Jacques Derrida's *Specters of Marx*. Derrida's central concepts in *Specters*, those of hauntology and a "messianic without messianism," serve as critical tools deployed against post–Cold War so-called end-of-history narratives and as a way of restoring to Marxism its revolutionary energies. A similar conjuration of the messianic occurs in *Independence Day*, now in the figure of the invading aliens. The appearance of the aliens also provides a solution to one of the other most pressing political questions of our present: How to forge and sustain a political bloc from the diverse interests and competing microgroups composing the political landscape? In this way, however, one of the great dangers Derrida's work guards against comes to pass in the film: the messianic desire becomes embodied in an "identifiable messiah," a figure that takes the form of a recentered U.S. leadership. What is a fantasy scenario in this mid-decade film—and one articulated shortly thereafter by the neoconservative Project for the New American Century—becomes, in the period after 9/11, a new global reality.

In my final two chapters, I shift directions and look at narratives that reject the visions offered in the works discussed earlier and that take the open situation of the 1990s as an opportunity for imagining new forms of collectivity. Michael Hardt and Antonio Negri maintain that one of the most pressing projects of our contemporary moment is that of the invention of new imaginaries of radical political agency, of figures that appear, from the perspective of ruling order, as monsters. It is precisely these kinds of monsters, I argue, that we find in science fiction and its various generic kin. Moreover, science fiction represents one of the most effective sites for the figuration of the project Jameson names cognitive mapping, a totalizing representation of the deep interconnection of the forces that constitute our present. Indeed, such cognitive mappings are crucial, Jameson maintains, before forms of agency appropriate to our global situation might develop.

Both the temporal and spatial aspects of such a mapping program are evident in Joe Haldeman's award-winning trilogy, *The Forever War* (1974), *Forever Peace* (1997), and *Forever Free* (1999). *The Forever War* provides a brilliant mapping of an earlier moment in the history of the present. One of the great science fiction allegories of the Vietnam War, *The Forever War* also offers, through its juxtaposition of vast temporal and spatial scales with the more local phenomenological ones, an early figuration of the disorienting and alienating experience of an emerging postmodernism. While not a true sequel, *Forever Peace* reworks in fundamental ways the issues and concerns of its predecessor. One of the most significant changes is the replacement of the "fighting suits" of *The Forever War* with war machines controlled by "jacked-in" military technicians. These "soldierboys" thus become allegorical figures of the new information technologies, also a prominent feature of an earlier, postmodern, cyberpunk science fiction. However, unlike in the classics of cyberpunk, these technologies serve in Haldeman's novel as a means of decentering the individual by a new form of collective life. This collective figured in Haldeman's novel resonates in some striking ways with the postnational democratic multitude first described by Baruch Spinoza in his *Ethics* (1677). Moreover, as with Spinoza's multitude, Haldeman's figure of the new collective signals the end of prehistory and an entrance into the realm of true freedom—an image developed even more explicitly in the trilogy's final novel.

In my final chapter I look at two recent popular fantasy and science fiction serial texts: the television series *Buffy the Vampire Slayer* (1997–2003) and Octavia Butler's *Parable* novels, *Parable of the Sower* (1993) and *Parable of the Talents* (1998). Both provide powerful critical allegories of our present cultural, economic, and political situation. However, what make both texts so interesting are the ways they move beyond this fundamentally negative gesture and offer us figurations of new monstrous forms of collectivity. Such an operation of radical figuration is made explicit in the *Buffy* episode titled "Family," where, as Judith Butler argues in her revisionary reading of *Antigone*, "the blood tie as the basis for kinship" is replaced "with consensual affiliation." [29] A similar form of monstrous collectivity is produced by the central protagonist in the *Parable* novels. I then show how both *Buffy* and Butler's fiction reject any kind of postmodern enclave politics that would attempt to found an alternative community outside the dominant global order: the only valid political project each maintains in its own way is one that would take as its aim nothing less than the transformation of our global totality. Even more significant, and rendered explicit both in the narrative trajectory of Butler's *Parable* novels and in the climax of the *Buffy* series, is the fact that the cement unifying these new collectivities takes the form of what Badiou names the "fidelity to an event," a shared commitment to a horizon of possibility that promises to transform everything. Indeed, in the magnificent final episode of *Buffy* we are offered a powerful figure of the true openness of the characters', as well as our, future.

fore in the work of the contemporary Scottish artist Ross Birrell. Birrell's project "Envoy" (1998–2002) takes as its central concerns the task of the work of art, the role of the artist, and the nature of utopian imaginings in the present. "Envoy" involves the undertaking of a journey, usually by Birrell himself, to a specific site to perform one or more of a number of different acts: throwing a sealed package or symbolic object into a body of water (a copy of Aldous Huxley's *Brave New World* into the river located on the former Cold War border between Norway and Russia); reading a text in a certain location (Henry David Thoreau's *Walden* in the forests of Lapland); or delivering a "gift" to a major international institution (a copy of Thomas More's *Utopia* to the International Court of Justice in The Hague). Each of these actions is recorded, the photographic or video images that result forming the basis of Birrell's exhibitions. In part taking its inspiration from Jacques Derrida's *The Postcard*, Birrell's project interrogates the double nature of the envoi both as the messenger (or the artist) and as the object dispatched, in this case, the work of art. In this way, "Envoy" stages Derrida's central insight about the nature of telecommunication: that there is no guarantee that the contents — the message, the meaning of the work — will arrive at their intended destination, or even that such a destination can be determined.

At the same time, the relationship between the detailed logistical planning involved in making the journey and the chance images produced (this is especially true in the case of the thrown objects, where there are no repetitions or rehearsals of the act, the captured image then highlighting its contingent nature) might also be understood as an allegory of the work of the utopian texts that make up many of the packages in Birrell's project. Whereas much intellectual energy is involved in detailing the various institutions, practices, norms, beliefs, and so forth of each utopian community — the pleasures of working in the form being those, Fredric Jameson suggests, "of construction . . . of the garage workshop, of the home-mechanics erector sets, of Lego, of bricolating and cobbling together things of all kinds" and of "miniaturization: replicating the great things in handicraft dimensions that you can put together by yourself and test" — there is no way to determine in advance the effects this or that particular vision will have when it enters into the world.[3] Innumerable utopian fictions have come and gone stirring very little interest, while a handful (Edward Bellamy's *Looking Backward*, George Orwell's *Nine-*

teen Eighty-Four, Sébastien Mercier's L'an 2440, Étienne Cabet's Voyage en Icarie, and, of course, Thomas More's founding work) transformed their worlds, often in unexpected ways.

Perhaps the most remarkable of Birrell's envoys took place on November 5, 2000. On this day, Birrell voyaged to New York City to do two things. First, as in the The Hague intervention, Birrell gifted a copy of More's Utopia, this time to the United Nations. In addition, Birrell took a trip on the Staten Island ferry and, at the moment the ferry was directly across from the Statue of Liberty, he tossed a U.S. flag into the harbor. All of this was recorded on videotape, and both the tape and a number of captured images were used in subsequent exhibitions. One of these images is especially striking: a black capped and jacketed Birrell has his arm extended straight out across the railing of the boat, a crumpled Stars and Stripes suspended in the middle of the frame, caught on the wind before it crashes into the water. Framing this image are, on the far left, the Statue of Liberty, and, on the far right, the skyline of downtown Manhattan. Soaring above the latter are the twin towers of the World Trade Center, the late fall sun setting their façades aglow (figure 1).

Of course, it would not be until the events of the following fall, with the September 11, 2001, terrorist attacks and the collapse of the World Trade Center buildings, that the real force and significance of this image became evident. I did not, in fact, view this image for the first time until the spring of 2004 and was immediately struck, as were most others in the audience, by the ways it seemed to both prefigure and speak so much about 9/11 and its aftermath. Even the luminescence of the building in Birrell's image has an uncanny prefigurative effect: in the opening panels of his In the Shadow of No Towers (2004), Art Spiegelman notes, "I still see the glowing tower, awesome as it collapses."[4] Spiegelman then uses throughout his subsequent work a visual image of the glowing tower, which fades to black only with the final panels of the work.

Moreover, that Birrell's original intervention took place on November 5, Guy Fawkes Day in Great Britain, adds additional resonance to it. Guy Fawkes Day marks the anniversary of the infamous 1605 Gunpowder Plot, a plan to blow up the English parliament with thirty-six kegs of gunpowder stashed under the House of Lords on the day King James I was to open sessions. (The notoriety of this event and the widespread anxieties it produced also left their mark on Shakespeare's Macbeth, first staged the

I Ross Birrell, *Envoy: New York, 2000*. The Stars & Stripes are thrown from the Staten Island Ferry in New York. Photo: Bryan Saner courtesy of Ellen de Bruijne Projects, Amsterdam. Reprinted by permission of the artist.

following year and referring to the events and actors of the plot in a number of ways.[5]) The conspirators were English Catholics outraged by the government's continued mistreatment of them, even after vague promises by James before his recent ascension to the throne to better their conditions. Yet doubt lingers to this day as to whether these men were actually responsible for, or even capable of, placing the explosives under the parliament buildings; indeed, some commentators maintain that the entire plot, as well as the late October letter to Lord Monteagle that first exposed it, were elements of a setup by the government, used to justify the elimination of leading Catholic dissidents (although the soldier Guido Fawkes was not the most important conspirator, he was the one first captured, and so the day is named after him). The surviving conspirators were rounded up, detained for extended periods, and tortured to provide evidence, some of it spurious, about the extent of the conspiracy's membership. Even more significantly, the plot was used as an excuse to launch a violent assault on the Jesuit leadership in hiding on the island—with the goal "to separate loyal and moderate Catholics from the mad extremists of the Plot"[6]—including the execution of its then head, Father Henry Garnet, even though he had no involvement in the plot and in fact worked to prevent its occurrence.

The parallels between these events and those following September 11, especially the subsequent U.S. invasion of Iraq, are striking. Antonia

Fraser in her 1996 popular history of the Gunpowder Plot writes of the conspirators, "They left, having decided on a course of action which would cause them, in the late twentieth century, to be described as terrorists."[7] The book's dust jacket further exclaims, "And in examining the lengths to which individuals will go for their faith, she finds in this long-ago event a reflection of the religion-inspired terrorism that has produced gunpowder plots of our own time." A more recent volume makes the link even more explicit: "In our time we are haunted by 11 September 2001. The equivalent date for the Jacobean English—a date still commemorated in England—was 5 November 1605."[8] Religious fundamentalist "terrorists," weapons of mass destruction, assaults on central institutions of power, failure to strike at the legislative seat itself, spurious conspiratorial links used to justify state violence, the effort to distinguish "good" from "evil" members of a religious faith, extended imprisonments, the use of torture to gather intelligence, suspicions about the state's real involvement: in short, 9/11 and subsequent U.S. actions seem to repeat crucial aspects of the Gunpowder Plot and its aftermath, albeit shifting its framework from a then only recently unified nation to our emerging global reality. (The resonances between Guy Fawkes and early seventeenth-century England and the post-9/11 world are explored further in the 2006 film adaptation of Alan Moore and David Lloyd's Thatcher-era graphic novel *V for Vendetta* [1982–88].)

Such interpretations are, of course, the products of retrospection, the owl of Minerva once more only taking flight at dusk. Or to put it another way, the true meaning of this image emerges only in repetition, in its viewings following 9/11, viewings that cannot after September 11, 2001, help but be repetitions, even if the spectator is seeing the image for the first time. The spectral or uncanny effects it generates are the by-products of what Derrida calls the "repeatable-iterable" dimension of any sign ("whether pictographical, hieroglyphic, ideographic, phonetic, alphabetic"), its capacity to be reproduced "in the absolute absence of the receiver" and "grafted" in a variety of contexts, "cut off from its putative 'production' or origin."[9] It is in these repetitions or iterations that the possibilities of meaning that I have been tracing out in Birrell's image arise.

Which brings me back to the central concerns of this book. All the works I examine here foreground in their very form and content issues of repetition, iterability, and doubling. They are examples of the Hollywood genre of the remake, as in the case of Martin Scorsese's *Cape Fear* (1991); or they play with or repeat the familiar conventions and expectations of popular genres, such as Roland Emmerich's *Independence Day* (1996) and Jim Jarmusch's diptych, *Dead Man* (1996) and *Ghost Dog* (1999); or they contain the classical figure of the doppelgänger and engage in the narrative operation Sigmund Freud calls "splitting," as in *Cape Fear*, David Fincher's *Fight Club* (1999), and the *Terminator* films (1984, 1991, 2003); or they refer explicitly to "repeated" events, as does the opening chapter of Don DeLillo's *Underworld* (1997); or they contain allegorical restagings of past events, such as the conflicts provoked by desegregation (*Cape Fear*) or the Vietnam War (*Independence Day* and Joe Haldeman's *Forever* trilogy [1975, 1997, 1999]); or, finally, they form extended serial texts that continuously revise their own narrative contents, as do the *Cape Fear* texts, the *Terminator* films, the *Forever* trilogy, Octavia Butler's two *Parable* novels (1993 and 1998); and Joss Whedon's *Buffy the Vampire Slayer* (1997–2003).

Moreover, a number of the later texts attempt to make sense of a specific history, namely, that of September 11 and its aftermath. This is very much the case in the allegorical codings of the two works that I discuss here that appear after the fall of 2001, the final *Terminator* film (2003) and the last two seasons of the *Buffy* series (2001–2 and 2002–3). Even more intriguing, however, are those works that, like Birrell's New York "Envoy," seem to prefigure, in essence repeating before the fact what occurs on September 11, 2001. We see this in the images of falling twin towers in the conclusion of *Fight Club* and in the smoldering ruins of the World Trade Center in *Independence Day*; in the unanticipated terrorist attacks on the United States in *Independence Day* and in *Forever Peace*; and in the haunting cover image of *Underworld* (this last becoming the topic of much Internet conversation in the weeks following September 11). Once again, as will become evident in the pages that follow, the true significance of these images emerges only through their repetition.

These various forms of repetition raise fundamental questions about our understanding of history, of the nature of events, of beginnings, and of endings. One of the concerns at the center of my project is how we might understand the event that we now refer to as simply 9/11. Should we take this date as signaling a historical break and the inauguration of a new epoch in global history, or as part of an unbroken historical continuum? Already infamous as the day in 1973 that the Augusto Pinochet–

led military overthrew the democratically elected socialist government of Chile, September 11 represented for some, like Chris Marker in his great film *A Grin without a Cat* (1977), an earlier such break, in this case with the radicalism and utopian possibilities of the 1960s. Derrida argues that September 11, 2001, "announced theatrically, or media-theatrically confirmed" the closure of the brief epoch of the "rogue state."[10] And for the members of the Retort collective, 9/11 marks a mutation in neoliberalism from "from an epoch of 'agreements' and austerity programs to one of outright war" (at the same time, they note that the subsequent "invasions and occupations are, for the most part, of a piece with an almost unbroken line of imperial American military interventions, stretching back almost two hundred years").[11] I, too, argue in this book that 9/11 marks both the ending of one historical situation and the opening of another; however, I do so in a somewhat different way.

To begin to unpack the real historical significance of 9/11 it is first necessary to make clear what I mean here by the term *Event*. In the pages that follow, I use the concept in the sense given by Alain Badiou: an Event is something that happens "that cannot be reduced to its ordinary inscription in 'what there is.'"[12] "It takes place in a situation but is not of that situation," and hence the Event is the "void of the situation, that aspect of the situation that has absolutely no interest in preserving the status quo as such."[13] Or as Slavoj Žižek formulates it—in a way that also recalls the related concepts of Derrida's hauntology and Ernst Bloch's utopian horizon—"the Event is *nothing but* its own inscription into the order of Being, a cut/rupture in the order of Being on account of which Being cannot ever form a consistent All."[14] In short, the Event is the very possibility of a radical new beginning, the inauguration of that which was unexpected, unknown, and uncounted. Since language itself is so deeply embedded within the known, an Event cannot, Badiou argues, "be communicated." Rather, it is *encountered*: "It is an Ethics of the Real, if it is true that—as Lacan suggests—all access to the Real is of the order of an encounter."[15] And yet, if it cannot be anticipated, it nevertheless must ultimately be recognized and named for the potentiality it opens on to be seized and realized.

In the sense given by Badiou, then, no Event occurs on September 11, 2001.[16] (Of course, this is not the same thing as denying that anything occurred that day, or as downplaying the incalculable suffering, agony, and human misery introduced into the world that grim morning, and not only for those in the towers.[17]) Rather than being an evental encounter with the incalculable Real, September 11 is itself a repetition of an earlier such encounter. This is because, as Žižek argues, every Event must in fact occur twice before it can become part of our world: "The crucial point here is the changed symbolic status of an event: when it erupts for the first time it is experienced as a contingent trauma, as an intrusion of a certain non-symbolized Real; only through repetition is this event recognized in its symbolic necessity—it finds its place in the symbolic network; it is realized in the symbolic order."[18] Similarly, every death, every ending point in history, must happen a second time before its import can be grasped. Indeed, until this "second death," the past will continue to live on in a twilight existence, not "knowing" that it is over. It is, Žižek suggests, like the cartoon Wile E. Coyote running over the end of a precipice and continuing out into space, not yet realizing that he no longer has ground under him: only when he recognizes this "fact," does the second death occur. This second death—a concept Žižek takes from Jacques Lacan's 1959–60 seminar on the ethics of psychoanalysis, and which Lacan in turn derived from the Marquis de Sade—is "absolute death," as opposed to the first, "natural" or Real death, precisely because it is "always the destruction of the *symbolic* universe."[19] And, as Lacan puts it, this sense of the death drive "is also a will to create from zero, a will to begin again."[20]

The toppling of the World Trade Center buildings can be understood as a form of second death, an incident that repeats an earlier "fall," that of the Berlin Wall in November 1989. This first fall was a true Event: unexpected and unplanned for, an encounter with a traumatic Real, it instigated a sequence of actions that would culminate two years later in the dramatic collapse of the Soviet Union and the subsequent end of the Cold War. What occurs in each case is, of course, very different. The fall of the Berlin Wall was the result of a peaceful and collective mobilization that emerged spontaneously within the Cold War situation; 9/11, on the other hand, was a violent, premeditated action, and the ultimate consequence of an emerging global order marked by the unprecedented concentration of "financial power in private hands, which allows individuals to become something like a state within a state, and endows them with a margin of political and even military autonomy. . . . bin Laden is one of these people . . . the poisoned fruit of a process that, unchecked, allows an unimaginable autonomy of action of all kinds."[21] However, from the perspective of the Cold War order itself, the two occurrences are the same: attacks on two of its most important symbols, the Berlin Wall and the World Trade Center (I discuss this symbolic dimension of the World Trade Center in more detail in my chapter on DeLillo's *Underworld*). Moreover, each fall involves its own meaning-generating repetition: for just as the real nature of the attack on the World Trade Center could not be understood until the *second* tower was struck—until that moment, it was assumed to be an "accident," an airliner off course—the true significance of the fall of the Berlin Wall would not become apparent until it, too, was "repeated" in the wide-scale popular resistance to the August 1991 coup attempt in the Soviet Union.

Thus to describe 9/11 as a repetition rather than an Event is not to deny its significance. Indeed, it is to make the opposite claim: for endings or Events are not in themselves beginnings, and it is only with the fall of the twin towers that the destruction of the "symbolic universe" of the Cold War, lingering on as it did in strange, twisted forms in the first Gulf War and through the subsequent decade, is finally and definitively accomplished and a true new world order put into place.[22] September 11 enabled the United States, in ways impossible in the immediate, uncertain aftermath of the Cold War, to assume a global mantle, giving rise to the so-called Bush doctrine of unilateralism and preemptive military violence—making all states in Derrida's sense rogue states—thereby marking the final closure of the world historical situation of the Cold War and the opening of a new period in global history. David Harvey also argues that this event marks the displacement of the neoliberalism of the previous decade by the form of neoconservatism championed by the Project for the New American Century; and "it was, of course, 9/11 that provided the impetus to break with the dissolute ways of the 1990s."[23]

Moreover, it is by making possible the constitution of this new symbolic order that the "sacrifice" of those who died on that terrible September morning becomes so valuable to this emergent global order. This logic is made evident in the allegorical structure at work in the post-9/11 thriller *Phone Booth* (dir. Joel Schumacher, 2002). The film tells the story of a slick Manhattan show business publicist, Stu Shepard (Colin Farrell), who is held hostage for an afternoon in one of the island's last phone booths by a gunman hidden in one of the nearby buildings (the film's release was delayed in light of the sniper shootings in Washington).[24] As the drama unfolds under the gaze of the assembled police and the mass-media apparatus, the gunman reveals to Stu, whom he keeps on the phone throughout the rest of the film, his knowledge of Stu's petty infidelities and betrayals and demands that he publicly confess them before he will be set free. Ultimately, Stu not only does so but also declares that this trauma has taught him what is of real value, and he vows to change his life. In this, we can hear echoes of the post–September 11 proclamations, not only in New York City but throughout the nation, that the events of that traumatic day convinced many of the need to reassess their lives, leading in part to a surge of virulent nationalism not previously seen in peacetime and an attack on so-called postmodern values. As the Republican Party activist and *Newsday* columnist James P. Pinkerton infamously declared, September 11 represented a "crushing defeat for irony, cynicism, and hipness" and taught us all "that there's more to life than nothing, that some things really matter." Of course, Pinkerton has a much more specific agenda in mind: "The victors now," he crows, "are sincerity, patriotism and earnestness."[25]

However, the conclusion of *Phone Booth* brilliantly unveils the necessary price of such a transformation. The police storm the apartment where the sniper is holed up, only to find that he slit his own throat moments before their arrival. When Stu is asked to identify the body, he realizes that the man is the same one who attempted to deliver a pizza to him at the phone booth shortly before his ordeal began. Stu is then put in an ambulance and sedated. In his hazy state another unknown figure appears before him (Kiefer Sutherland), whose words and voice lead Stu to realize that he is the person who had been on the phone all this time: he tells Stu he will be watching him in the future to make sure he does not return to his old ways.

It is the deliveryman who becomes the most significant figure in this tableau: while he is in fact only an innocent bystander, someone whose crime was that he happened to be in the wrong place at the wrong time, he is the one who enables Stu's fundamental transformation. In this way, the pizza delivery Everyman becomes a figure for those who died on September 11, necessary sacrifices for our redemption, mediators between an earlier state of decadent complacency and a new sense of global moral duty. Susan Willis calls this process of transformation the "federalization of 9/11": "Employees of private enterprise have become with their deaths America's war heroes."[26]

Moreover, it is this conservative identification of all of those killed in the towers as sacrifice, and hence as partaking in a economic logic of expenditure rather than accumulation, that makes sense of the hysteria that greeted the belated revelation of Ward Churchill's characterization of the "technocratic corps at the very heart of America's global financial empire" inhabiting the tower at the time of the attacks as "little Eichmanns." While such a vision challenges the characterization of those murdered on this day as innocent victims—and indeed, a 2005 Colorado State House of Representatives resolution condemning Churchill's essay repeatedly invokes this innocence[27]—it is a statement that Churchill makes later in the essay that proves even more damning: "The men who flew the missions against the WTC and Pentagon were not 'cowards.' . . . Whatever else can be said of them, the men who struck on September 11 manifested the courage of their convictions, willingly expending their own lives in attaining their objectives."[28] What is really at stake in this debate is the identity of the sacrifice itself: that is, who committed suicide, making the ultimate sacrifice of their lives for a higher cause (knowingly or not): those who crashed the planes into the towers or those killed therein? It is precisely the transformation of these people from victims to agents, from "falling men" to those who "fight back," that is at work in the two now canonical film representations of 9/11: Oliver Stone's *World Trade Center* and Paul Greengrass's *United 93* (both 2006). Of course, as Žižek points out, "This gesture of self-legitimization through the other is ideology in its purest: the dead are our redeemers, and by dedicating ourselves to continuing their work we redeem the redeemers."[29]

To mark these kinds of endings and beginnings and to think in terms of "before" and "after" necessitates as well that we think the 1990s—or more precisely, the span between November 9, 1989, 10:30 p.m. CET (the opening of the border crossing at Bornholmer Strasse in Berlin) and September 11, 2001, 9:02:54 a.m. EST (the moment Flight 175 struck the south tower of the World Trade Center)—as a coherent cultural *period*.[30] Periodization, Jameson argues, is an act that is "intolerable and unacceptable in its very nature, for it attempts to take a point of view on individual events which is well beyond the observational capacities of any individual, and to unify, both horizontally and vertically, hosts of realities whose interrelationships must remain inaccessible and unverifiable."[31] Nevertheless, he maintains, "We cannot not periodize:" these forms are as "inevitable" as they are unacceptable, a quintessential part of our deeper modernity, and to reject them often means no more than a return to such premodern forms as the chronicle. Moreover, periodization represents, in a moment fixated on the static, spatialized image, a "return of the repressed of narrative itself" and of the politically contestatory stances narrative always already involves.[32] Indeed, Jameson concludes, "periodization is not some optional narrative consideration one adds or subtracts according to one's tastes and inclinations, but rather an essential feature of the narrative process itself."[33]

If the 1990s constitute a period, then the question arises: how might we best characterize it? I have already described the counterintuitive asymmetry between the beginnings and endings of this period: its beginning is in fact an ending, the Event of the fall of the Berlin Wall, the eruption of the Real in history and a punctual break with the history of the Cold War; while its ending occurs with the 2001 repetition of this Event and the opening of a true post–Cold War global situation. The 1990s then are the strange space between this ending (of the Cold War) and beginning (of our post–September 11 world), one of those transitional phases that, once again following Žižek's inflection of Lacan's theorizations, we can call the "place 'between two deaths,' a place of sublime beauty as well as terrifying monsters."[34] (It is also this sense of the period of the 1990s as a moment "between" that is captured in Salman Rushdie's *Fury* [2001], a passage from which I used as one of the epigraphs for this book.) This place between two deaths, the location between the Real Event and its Symbolic repetition, is strictly speaking "non-historical," precisely because it is open to any number of possible "symbolizations/historicizations," all of which by their very nature are retroactive. Such an "empty place" is experienced in its lived reality, as the Žižek passage cited a moment ago suggests, in a Janus-faced fashion. On the one hand, it feels like a moment of "terrifying monsters," of hauntings by a living dead past, and of the "compulsion to repeat" that Mark Edmundson finds symptomatic of much of the culture of this moment.[35] Yet it is also experienced as a moment of "sublime beauty," of openness and instability, of experimentation and opportunity, of conflict and insecurity—a place, in other words, wherein history might move in a number of very different directions.

Lacan, too, suggests this doubleness when he identifies the place between two deaths with the "tradition of hell in different forms." Lacan notes, "After all, the human tradition has never ceased to keep this second death in mind by locating the end of sufferings there; in the same way it has never ceased to imagine a second form of suffering, a suffering beyond death that is indefinitely sustained by the impossibility of crossing the limit of the second death."[36] However, what is suffering from the normative position of order is also, as in William Blake's dramatic transvaluation of the concept of hell, the experience of radical freedom and true human creativity: "I now asked my companion which was my eternal lot? he said, between the black & white spiders. . . . I answerd. All that we saw was owing to your metaphysics; for when you ran away, I found myself on a bank by moonlight hearing a harper, But now we have seen my eternal lot, shall I shew you yours?"[37]

Three texts from the years I am focusing on in this book—the films *Groundhog Day* (1993) and *Titanic* (1997) and the television series *Six Feet Under* (2001–5)—effectively stage what Žižek now calls the "parallax view," a "constantly shifting perspective between two points between which no synthesis or mediation is possible" of what it means to live between two deaths.[38] *Titanic*—written and directed by James Cameron, who was also responsible for the first two *Terminator* films I discuss in chapter 3 and to which this later film bears some interesting connections—was one of the most significant film events of the period, ultimately becoming the highest grossing film of all time. Žižek argues for a parallel between the historical event on which *Titanic* was based and 9/11: "This, also, was a shock, but the space had already been prepared in ideological fantasizing, since the *Titanic* was the symbol of the might of nineteenth-century industrial civilization. Does not the same hold for these attacks? Not only were the media bombarding us all the time with talk about the terrorist threat; this threat was obviously libidinally invested."[39] Moreover, as we shall see later is the case with *Fight Club* and *Independence Day*, the film itself seems to offer what in retrospection can be understood as another prefiguration of 9/11 in a striking image of the sinking ship, its stern half towering skyward and diminutive human bodies plummeting from the doomed hulk (figure 2). (It is precisely the image of falling bodies that

2 The *Titanic* as a collapsing tower, from *Titanic* (1997).

have all but disappeared, as Jonathan Safran Foer's daring and controversial novel *Extremely Loud and Incredibly Close* [2005] reminds us, from the endless media representations of the day's events.)

One of those who perishes in the ocean that grim night is Jack Dawson (Leonardo DiCaprio), the short-lived love of the young socialite Rose De-Witt Bukater (Kate Winslet). Rose lives on for many decades after Jack's death, and only in the final moments of the film does the now aged woman pass away, on board a ship sailing above the wreck of the *Titanic*. The film ends with an image of the again youthful Rose reunited with Jack and the others who originally perished with the ship. In effect, all of Rose's life after 1917 is to be understood as unfolding in the space opened up between these two deaths. And yet, rather than a tragedy, the conclusion of the film suggests the utopian potential of precisely such a way of being in the world. For as the camera pans over a series of still photographs from Rose's long and active life, we realize that her "undead" existence has in fact been one of exhilarating freedom and experimentation, unshackled as she has been from the conventional social identity—be it that of the loveless spouse of her wealthy fiancé or even of the adored wife of the working-class Jack—to which she had seemed fated at the beginning and throughout the film. Indeed, her reunion with Jack appears in this light as the real tragic conclusion of the film, a closure not unlike 9/11 of this space between two deaths and the death of the possibilities of freedom and self-making that this made available.

The sense of what it means to live the life between two deaths offered in *Six Feet Under* is decidedly different and more along the lines of the figure of hell described by Lacan and figured by Blake's heavenly angel. The series is framed by two deaths: it begins with the sudden death of Nathaniel Fisher, the middle-aged director of a Los Angeles–area funeral home; and it comes to its climax with the equally unexpected death of his eldest son, who also happens to be named Nathaniel. On his father's death, Nate Jr. (Peter Krauss) reluctantly agrees to take charge of the family business: occupying his father's place, he thereby assures the continuation of the elder man's life in a grim zombielike fashion (and indeed, his father's ghost appears to him throughout the series' run). As the series develops over the course of the next five seasons, it becomes increasingly evident that this decision has trapped not only Nate but all the major characters in a kind of repetitious twilight existence, none of them seemingly able to break the hold of the past and move forward, like *Titanic*'s Rose, in a new way. It is only with Nate Jr.'s death and the selling of the heterotopia of the family business and residence, a funeral home — and all the locations Michel Foucault describes as heterotopias, psychiatric hospitals, prisons, cemeteries, gardens, libraries, fairgrounds, and ships (and this would include the *Titanic*), are in effect spatializations of the life between two deaths — that this spell is broken and the remaining characters reassume a historical (if not necessarily free) existence.[40] This transformation is borne out by a montage sequence in the concluding moments of the series' final episode, which highlights the future lives and inevitable deaths of each of the show's major characters.

Finally, the deeply utopian fantasy film *Groundhog Day* brings together both senses of what in means to live between the two deaths in a way that effectively captures the unique parallax experience of this period that will be the focus of this book. *Groundhog Day* is a contemporary example of the film genre Stanley Cavell names the "comedy of remarriage," a genre that turns on a sequence of repetitions. Cavell maintains that works in the genre bring home the lesson "the validity of marriage takes a willingness for repetition, the willingness for remarriage."[41] (Cavell's language also interestingly suggests the genre serves as a sustained reflection on the nature of fidelity in the condition or generic procedure Badiou names love.) This particular comedy of remarriage centers on a self-absorbed Pittsburgh television weatherman, Phil Connors (Bill Murray), who for some unexplained reason is doomed to awaken innumerable times on the same February 2 morning in what becomes for him the heterotopia of

Punxsutawney, Pennsylvania. Phil's initial response to his new situation is to plunge himself into a hedonistic existence with no care for future consequences (since there appear to be none). After a series of failed attempts to seduce his coworker Rita (Andie MacDowell), Phil sinks into a deep despair and attempts innumerable times to commit suicide. At this moment, Phil becomes the undead, suffering "the horrible fate of being caught in the endless repetitive cycle of wandering around in guilt and pain."[42] All this begins to change, however, when Phil shifts his perspective and comes to view his existence outside of history proper as a tremendous opportunity, both for self-remaking, developing new talents and becoming another kind of subject altogether, and to experiment in the creation of community and new truly human relationships, not only with Rita but with all those he encounters in his innumerable days in Punxsutawney. In Badiou's terms, it is only at this point that Phil ceases to be an animal and becomes a true Subject. The climax of the film, with the union of Phil and Rita and the beginning of a new day in what his labors have helped transform into a well-nigh utopian community, thus only renders concrete the new realities that have come into existence as a result of what we now understand to have been a precious open period of Phil's life.

Groundhog Day is valuable for another reason in this context, in that it helps us better understand that the identification, or naming, of the Event itself only occurs in an act of retrospection. Late in the film, Phil tells Rita that "the first time I saw you something happened to me. I never told you, but I knew that I wanted to hold you as hard as I could." And yet, when did this Event actually occur? After all, not only is it located, in Phil's own words, in some hazy indefinite moment in their shared past but this act of naming the Event also occurs only after an uncountable number of repetitions of this same February 2. Indeed, it is the naming rather than the Event itself, or more precisely, the repetition of the Event in its naming, that begins the process of escaping the closed temporal loop.

Thinking of the 1990s as a whole as a moment of life between two deaths—and, of course, the real power of any periodizing concept is heuristic, enabling us to see the familiar in new and productive ways—allows us to draw connections between "hosts of realities" that unfold in this period. Here I can only offer the briefest of outlines of some of these developments as a kind of prolegomena to a future fuller mapping of this moment, a collective *Arcades Project* of the 1990s perhaps, with each of these concepts, along with a host of others, serving as the basis of the various convolutes. First, the end of the Cold War sparks a wide-ranging debate of what has popularly been referred to as "globalization."[43] Although some more literal-minded critics rightly point out that capitalism has always been global in nature, the very ascendancy of this concept in this moment, as with the parallel case of postmodernism before it, signals at least the beginning of an awareness of changes in our world that render inadequate many older conceptualizations of it.[44] As Michael Denning puts it, "behind the powerful accounts of globalization as a process lies a recognition of a historical transition, of globalization as the name of the end, not of history, but of the historical moment of the age of three worlds," a period Denning locates as extending from 1945 to 1989—the period, of course, of the Cold War.[45]

Second, this period witnessed the unexpected and unplanned global expansion of the new communication and information technologies of the Internet and the World Wide Web. What began as a Cold War project designed to provide a functioning communications network in the case of a nuclear attack, exploded after the early 1990s development of Gopher, the first truly user-friendly interface to the Internet, and of the global hypertext space, the World Wide Web, and the Mosaic browser. In the five-year period from 1992 to 1997, for example, the number of Web sites in existence would leap from fifty to more than 1 million.[46] Such a quantitative growth would lead to a wealth of speculations on the ways such technologies would enable us to reinvent our concepts and practices of communication, information, literacy, community, property, space, and even the subject itself. Such visions served, as Benjamin wrote on the experiments with new technologies in the analogous moment of the early nineteenth century, as "the most authentic proof that technological production, at the beginning, was in the grip of dreams. (Not architecture alone but all technology is, at certain stages, evidence of a collective dream.)"[47] Benjamin's conclusion about the ultimate fate of such imaginings is also relevant here: this earlier moment, he writes, proved "incapable of responding to the new technological possibilities with a new social order."[48]

Third, and perhaps most significant, the 1990s witnessed the explosive emergence of a new kind of counterglobalization political movement—a movement whose global spread was in part fueled by the communicational possibilities of the Internet—whose moments of crystallization bear the names, among others, of Chiapas, Seattle, Genoa, Quebec City, and Porto Alegre. A collection of discussions from the World Social Forum in this last site bears the title *Another World Is Possible*, and in their foreword to this volume, Michael Hardt and Antonio Negri—the authors of *Empire* (2000) and *Multitude* (2004), two of the most widely read, discussed, and debated figurations of this nascent movement—bear out its deep utopian aspirations: "The World Social Forum at Porto Alegre has already become a myth, one of those positive myths that define our political compass. It is the representation of a new democratic cosmopolitanism, a new anti-capitalist transnationalism, a new intellectual nomadism, a great movement of the multitude."[49]

Fourth, the 1990s gave rise to a series of original and influential "universalizing" theoretical projects. Hardt and Negri's is perhaps the most well known, but similar trajectories also arise in the recent work of Žižek, Judith Butler, Derrida, Jameson, Giorgio Agamben, Gayatri Spivak, Kojin Karatani, and Badiou, to name only a few of the other most prominent examples (and the resurgence of interest in the universal and, as Jonathan Israel argues, non-national thought of Baruch Spinoza is also an important index of this context).[50] All these projects mark an authentic "negation of the negation," a post-postmodernism, or movement beyond the paralyses of the postmodern in the theoretical domain at least and a resurgence of the radical transformative energies of the modern itself.[51] A similar turn occurs in cultural studies work, as the 1990s witnessed a turn from the classical cultural studies focus on subcultural forms of resistant consumption to a growing interest in the way these communities concretely actualize alternative forms of collective being in the world: this turn is at work in projects by such diverse figures as Butler, Jameson, Meaghan Morris, Bruce Robbins, Kristin Ross, and Allan Feldman. I will discuss the work of many of these thinkers in more detail in the following chapters.

There are also a number of equally symptomatic transformations that occur within a number of different areas in the arts and within cultural production more generally. For example, the 1990s witnessed an efflorescence of a number of new kinds of architectural and urbanistic experiments whose kinship is more to that of the great modernists than to their immediate postmodern predecessors. Rem Koolhaas and his interest in figures such as Ludwig Mies van der Rohe and in his reappraisal of the modernist "typical plan" is emblematic in this regard. Indeed, Koolhaas describes the situation of the 1990s in this way: "In a landscape of disarray, disassembly, dissociation, disclamation, the attraction of Bigness is its potential to reconstruct the Whole, resurrect the Real, reinvent the collective, reclaim maximum possibility."[52] Moreover, one of the central loci for new work and unbridled experimentation in this moment turns out to be, appropriately enough, the city of Berlin, the void in the heart of the city represented by the Wall zone serving as a spatial emblem of the open nature of the historical continuum at this historical point.[53]

Similarly, Don Letts's documentary film history, *Punk: Attitude* (2005), suggests that after the initial anarchic explosion of punk music in the mid-1970s, in New York City, London, Los Angeles, Washington, D.C., and other sites, there was a waning of this energy in the 1980s as the more marketable New Wave pop came to predominate and the punk scene was largely driven underground. However, in the early 1990s, centered in the Seattle "grunge" movement, punk witnessed a dramatic resurgence in the public imagination. This, too, was coupled with a new politically progressive spirit that was less evident in its earlier moment. Indeed, the argument could be advanced that grunge punk helped set the context for Seattle's place later in the period in the emergence of the counterglobalization movement. As Jello Biafra puts it late in the film, "Punk definitely had a major influence on the eruption of militant anticorporate activism that first came to light over here in the Seattle protests."

This period also witnessed a number of significant transformations in the area of literary narrative. First, there appear in the 1990s a number of major new utopian fictions. These would include most prominently, in addition to those I will discuss directly in my later chapters, Leslie Marmon Silko's *Almanac of the Dead* (1991), Toni Morrison's *Paradise* (1997), Kim Stanley Robinson's *Pacific Edge* (1990), *Mars* trilogy (1992–96), and the alternate history *The Years of Rice and Salt* (2002), Ken MacLeod's Fall Revolution quartet (1995–99), and Philip Pullman's *His Dark Materials* trilogy (1995–2000). These works also differ from many of their predecessors in the genre in that they focus less on the utopian worlds and more on the processes, the political actions, and the moments of decision, or what Georg Lukács characterized as the *Augenblicken* by which these new worlds come into being.[54]

Second, Daniel Grassian claims that the 1990s represent the third great moment in the twentieth century of a collective efflorescence of new African American writing. The first two "literary African American Renaissances" are the 1920s, "composed primarily of poets such as Langston Hughes, Countee Cullen, and Jean Toomer," and the 1960s, "when a centralized but diverse group of African American writing emerged," including, among others, Samuel Delany, Toni Morrison, Maya Angelou, Rita Dove, and Alice Walker. The third group, then, "born in the 1960s or early 1970s, includes, but is not limited to, writers such as Jake Lamar, Colson Whitehead, Paul Beatty, and . . . Danzy Senna."[55] Not coincidentally, Grassian's three periods are also those during which we see a deep intensification of what Badiou names the "passion for the real." I would also add that there appear in the 1990s a number of other young novelists writing in English—among others, Foer, Arundhati Roy, Gary Shteyngart, and Zadie Smith—who deal explicitly with the cultural and social consequences of the end of the Cold War and of globalization and whose ambitions are akin to that of earlier generations of "modernist" writers.

Finally, the 1990s witnessed significant transformations in the work of some important established writers. To take one well-known example, Thomas Pynchon's *Mason & Dixon* (1997) both breaks with the postmodernism of his previous novel *Vineland* (1990) and "repeats" the formal and political energies of his earlier masterpiece *Gravity's Rainbow* (1973). At the same time, the novel crafts a powerful vision of an earlier moment of globalization and spatial mapping. In this way, *Mason & Dixon* can be said to be about the 1990s in the way that *Vineland* is about the "period" of the 1980s and *Gravity's Rainbow* about the 1960s (and now, *Against the Day* [2006] is about the post-9/11 world).

All these developments indicate the degree to which the 1990s represent a unique moment of struggle, one enabled by the Event of the collapse of the Soviet bloc and waged *over* the significance of this Event. For the Event of the first death, the end of the Cold War, in effect ended for the global cultural and political left the legacy of the twentieth century and opened up the space for new kinds of political and cultural experimentation. And crucially in this decade, no outcome was determined outside this struggle: that is, there was no way a priori to know what the repetition of the Event might be. Indeed, it will be the identification of the second death that becomes during the 1990s the very prize struggled over by a number of competing forces. This, too, accounts for the proliferation in this moment of catastrophic images that, as I will argue in this book, serve as prefigurations of 9/11: they all signal the depths of the collective desire for the repetition of the original cataclysmic Event, this time within the other half of the Cold War dyad, that would signal a new Symbolic Order being set into place. And while—as my discussions of *Terminator 2: Judgment Day*, *Fight Club*, and *Independence Day* make evident—we do see more conservative visions of what such a reinscription might look like (indeed, the first Gulf War itself was a failed attempt to impose such a vision on the world), we need to always keep in mind the fact that in their moment they are no more than positions staked out in a highly contested field and that radically other possibilities were available.

The *passage à l'acte* that was September 11, so effectively hegemonized by the U.S. neoconservatives, marked the closure of this space.[56] Not only did the "self-sacrifice" of those who perished that day effectively deliver us from being "condemned to wander in the domain 'between the two deaths'" but 9/11 also interrupted the consolidation and maturation of the emergent oppositional movements and enabled the installation of a new hegemonic logic (one, needless to say, that is still contested on a number of fronts).[57] Indeed, Jameson points out, "The opponents of an antiglobalization politics will certainly be quick to identify bin Laden's politics with the antiglobalization movement generally and to posit 'terrorism' as the horrible outcome of that misguided antagonism to the logic of late capitalism and its world market. In this sense, bin Laden's most substantial political achievement has been to cripple a nascent left opposition in the West."[58] Regardless of the subsequent failures of the U.S. neoconservative movement, then, this crippling is one of the most undeniable legacies and "triumphs" of 9/11.

One of my real hopes in writing this book is to fight this last trend and to keep faith with the original counterglobalization movement of movements and other forms of cultural and political experimentation that emerged in this decade, movements whose radicality in the moment following September 11 have come under question, not only as we would expect from a ferocious chorus on the right but even from some on the left.[59] If the changed global field of the post-9/11 situation will require a rethinking of specific tactics and strategies, the forms that came into being in this decade are still extremely valuable, and we would do well to do all we can to sustain their energies and potentialities into the future.

Such an act of fidelity to the unrealized potential, the accumulating dead of the now-time (*Jetztzeit*) of not only this historical situation but of our own as well (for we, too, are the dead, as Orwell reminds us), is also, I believe, what lies at the heart of Benjamin's historical materialist periodizing "law of dialectics at a standstill." "This standstill," Benjamin goes on to write, "is utopia and the dialectical image, therefore, dream image." On the other hand, "The history that showed things 'as they really were' was the strongest narcotic of the century."[60] And it is precisely the purveyors of this particular drug that have not ceased to be victorious.

Two final indicators of the historical shift I am talking about here can be found in two of the most well-known architectural projects of Daniel Libeskind, the first located in Berlin and the second intended for New York City, as well as in the Wachowski brothers' celebrated *Matrix* trilogy (1999, 2003, 2003). Both Libeskind's Jewish Museum (1992–99) and his "Memory Foundations" designs for the World Trade Center site are projects that center on the figure of voids. However, each deploys these voids in a significantly different manner and thereby becomes a symptom of the specific historical situations out of which it arises. The voids in the Jewish Museum, on the one hand, disrupt the very mimetic and repetitive logics of commemoration: "Inside the building you repeatedly encounter empty rooms which do not serve a purpose and are divided among different floors. Initially, these so-called 'voids' should have been inscribed with the names of murdered Jews similar to a burial chamber. However, this would have been all too obvious and would have given the voids a clear function of commemoration. That would have damaged the abundance of associations linked to the architecture."[61] In this way, the space of the museum, one that Julian Wolfreys describes as "participatory and performative (and therefore transformative, auto-transformative)," becomes, among its abundance of other associations, an expression of the very experience of open historical possibilities, of a future to come, that I am arguing is characteristic of the 1990s.[62] Indeed, Libeskind himself marks the open utopian horizons of his experimental spatial form: "The work is conceived as a museum for all Berliners, for all citizens. Not only those of the present, but those of the future who might find their heritage and hope in this particular place."[63]

However, this abundance of associations is short-circuited in the World Trade Center site plan, as the project, designed to retain the sunken footprint of the two towers as its central feature (aspects of the plan were subsequently modified), clearly takes on the function of commemorating the dead of the attack, dead whose names will be listed in the void of the memorial site. Thus, keeping the trauma of that day open, the project would in fact "repeat" infinitely the inaugural event of our particular post-9/11 global reality, raising it to the level of the symbolic order itself. Christopher Hawthorne notes, "The ruling above-ground gesture of Libeskind's plan, seen especially in the towers that would ring the site, is that of the shard, the sharp fragment unleashed by shattering or explosion. Combined with the idea of keeping the pit as open as a fresh wound, the shards seem to aestheticize the violence of Sept. 11."[64] Hawthorne's words uncannily recall those of Benjamin in his famed essay, "The Work of Art in the Age of Its Technological Reproducibility." To paraphrase Benjamin, we might say that whereas the Jewish Museum "politicizes art," this memorial would "aestheticize politics." And, Benjamin writes, "All efforts to aestheticize politics culminate in one point. That one point is war"—in this case, the terrible infinity of the new war on terror.[65]

The sequence of *Matrix* films, whose first and second-third entries (the second and third films were shot simultaneously and released within months of each other and thus can be thought of as a single narrative), similarly bridge the historical break of September 11, 2001, and thereby offer a vision of the different status of radical oppositional politics before and after this moment. Not only was the first film a global box-office phenomenon—celebrated, like one of the works I will discuss below, *Independence Day*, for its innovative computer special effects—but it generated an interest in the scholarly community in popular science fiction film not seen since the early 1980s with the release of Ridley Scott's *Alien* (1979) and *Blade Runner* (1982), and *The Terminator*. Much of the interest in *The Matrix* lies, I would suggest, in the figuration it provides of the emerging oppositional energies of the late 1990s. In its presentation of the central protagonist, Neo (Keanu Reeves), this film is haunted by a fundamental structural ambivalence: Do we take him as the Messiah whom we, like the character of Morpheus (Laurence Fishburne), await for redemption? Or is he the spectral embodiment of a more general and collective "messianic without messianism," the promise of "the coming of the other, the absolute and unpredictable singularity of the *arrivant as justice*"? Or finally, is he to be understood as a figure for the status quo resisting the radically other posthuman future represented by the machines?[66] In all three cases, Neo's story in this first film is one of increasing radicalization and action. First, with the help of Morpheus, Neo comes to a newfound consciousness of his condition of unfreedom within an all-encompassing global order, the massive computer-simulational world that is the Matrix itself (human beings have literally been reduced to nothing more than biopower, serving as living batteries for the machines). He confronts and overcomes what G. W. F. Hegel famously calls the slave's fear of death; and in the end, he announces what Badiou names a fidelity to the Truth-Event of a new radical project. Entering into a very different phone booth dialogue than that of Stu, Neo declares, "I know you're out there. I can feel you now. I know that you're afraid. You're afraid of us. You're afraid of change. I don't know the future. I didn't come here to tell you how this is going to end. I came here to tell you how it's going to begin. . . . I'm going to show these people what you don't want them to see. I'm going to show them a world without you. A world without rules and controls, without borders or boundaries. A world where anything is possible." The "world" announced here is a figure of that being struggled for by the contemporary counterglobalization movements, a struggle for the collective rather than the corporate control of the global commons. The film's commitment to the politics of these movements is then reconfirmed by the soundtrack, the left-wing rock band Rage against the Machine's "Wake Up" (a band stricken from many radio station's playlists after September 11) accompanying the final images of Neo looking at the people moving by him on the city streets before launching himself into the sky—a wish image more from fantasy than from science fiction, "a figure for the enlargement of human powers and their passage to the limit, their actualization of everything latent and virtual in the stunted human organism of the present."[67]

An immense anticipation built up in the four years between the first and the second film's release. However, both the popular and critical responses to the next two films, *The Matrix Reloaded* and *The Matrix Revolutions*, were largely ones of disappointment. Indeed, many critics seemed to gloat in the film's failure to fulfill its initial promise (as they did, for different reasons, in their scathing dismissals of the effective post-9/11 allegory of Ang Lee's *Hulk* [2003]). The retreat from the radical vision of the first film is already evident in the new titles, suggesting not the revolutionary break promised at the end of the first film, but rather cyclical repetitions, something that will indeed prove very much to be the case in *The Matrix Reloaded*. Appropriately enough, too, the sumptuous visual portrait in the early parts of *The Matrix Reloaded* of the revolutionary community of Zion is replete with references to one of the milestones of twentieth-century science fiction film, Fritz Lang's *Metropolis* (1926), for like *Metropolis*, the *Matrix* trilogy brings to the surface emergent radical desires, only in the end to recontain them.[68] At the climax of the film, Neo encounters the architect of the Matrix's simulational reality, an embodiment of the central operating system itself, and learns that his current "rebellion" is only the latest of a long sequence of such actions, each representing a consolidation of anomalies that are expunged as the system resets or reloads itself.

In this manner, the radical revolutionary vision of history expressed in the first film is replaced by a despairing notion of alternating cycles of social ferment and stasis that is the hallmark of many far more conservative visions of twentieth-century U.S. history, in which the radicalism of the 1920s and 1930s or 1960s is understood to be followed inevitably by periods of conservative retrenchment in the 1950s and the 1980s. Not only does such a vision of historical movement close off any possibility of real change—what Badiou terms the evental break—it effectively takes human agency out of the historical picture, portraying such pendulum swings as an irrevocable law. As Žižek puts it in his review essay, "By the end of *The Matrix Reloaded*, everything is cast in doubt: The question is not only whether any revolutions against the Matrix can accomplish what they claim or whether they have to end in an orgy of destruction, but whether they are not taken into account, planned even, by the Matrix itself. . . . This is where *The Matrix Reloaded* ends: in a failure of 'cognitive mapping' that perfectly mirrors the sad predicament of today's left and its struggle against the System." He then concludes on a prophetic note: "If the forthcoming part three, *The Matrix Revolutions*, is to succeed with anything like a happy ending, it will have to produce nothing less than the appropriate answer to the dilemmas of revolutionary politics today, a blueprint for the political act the left is desperately looking for."[69] While the final film does at least hold open the possibility that the struggle between the rebels and the Matrix will continue into the future, the conflicts it imagines now are confined to strictly local ones, the structure of the system remaining in place for any conceivable future.[70] Indeed, we learn

Two

OCTOBER 3, 1951, TO SEPTEMBER 11, 2001

Periodizing the Cold War in Don DeLillo's *Underworld*

What good's a story without an ending?
DON DELILLO, *Underworld*

All plots tend to move deathward.
DON DELILLO, *White Noise*

It's gone!

Sportscaster **ERNIE HARWELL,** October 3, 1951

THE NARRATIVE ACT OF PERIODIZATION — what Fredric Jameson describes as the attempt "to unify both horizontally and vertically hosts of realities whose interrelationships must remain inaccessible and unverifiable" — is at the very heart of Don DeLillo's monumental historical overview of U.S. Cold War culture and its immediate aftermath in his novel, *Underworld* (1997).¹ The concern for making connections that forms an essential component of any periodizing narrative emerges as an explicit theme at a number of places in DeLillo's long and ambitious work. As one character asserts, "everything connects in the end, or only seems to, or seems to only because it does."² Such connections do not, DeLillo suggests, lie on the surface of the everyday: "And how can you tell the difference between orange juice and agent orange if the same massive system connects them at levels outside your comprehension?" (*U*, 465). Instead, they must be recovered through a careful hermeneutic investigation, if not an explicitly paranoid one, akin to the similar narrative process that Jameson names "cognitive mapping."[3]

Both the spatial process of cognitive mapping and the temporal one of periodization possess what one character in the novel will later describe as "lyrical" truth: "Unprovably true, remotely and inadmissibly true but not completely unhistorical, not without some nuance of authentic inner narrative" (*U*, 172). Indeed, such practices, the novel suggests, may grasp a truth inaccessible to any merely empirical investigation; and in this DeLillo's novel hints at its kinship with the earlier masterpieces of Joseph Conrad: "They wanted facts. Facts! They demanded facts from him, as if facts could explain anything!"[4] Finally, the practice of periodization expresses a deep desire for narrative itself, narrative being one of those human experiences expelled, as DeLillo so carefully diagnoses in his earlier masterpiece, *White Noise*, from the posthistorical present, the postmodern "landscape of silence and ice."[5] Thus, to paraphrase Jameson again, an "insistence" on narrative "in a situation in which the narratives themselves henceforth seem impossible" is a "declaration of intent to remain political and contestatory"—precisely the stance, I want to argue, taken up by DeLillo's novel.[6]

In order to engage in this kind of intervention, DeLillo revives and reworks one of the most significant of the modern realist narrative forms, the historical novel. This is not DeLillo's first effort at the historical novel: *Libra,* his controversial fictionalization of the life of Lee Harvey Oswald and the events surrounding the 1963 assassination of John F. Kennedy, was published nine years earlier. Nor, interestingly enough, is DeLillo alone in reviving this important narrative form. Indeed, many of the most significant contemporary U.S. authors published during the 1990s major historical novels, including Toni Morrison's monumental trilogy of *Beloved* (1987), *Jazz* (1992), and *Paradise* (1997) (loosely based on Dante's *Divine Comedy*); Thomas Pynchon's *Mason & Dixon* (1997); Barbara Kingsolver's *The Poisonwood Bible* (1998); and Russell Banks' *Cloudsplitter* (1998). Moreover, one of the most significant contemporary American science fiction writers, Kim Stanley Robinson, has given us in his *The Years of Rice and Salt* (2002) a marvelous specimen of that formal fusion of the historical novel and science fiction, the "what if?" or alternate history. (In this work,

Robinson poses the question, what if the "Black Death" of the fourteenth century had in fact killed most of Europe's population?[7] Such an efflorescence of the genre in this moment again highlights the degree to which the period of the 1990s witnesses, after the slumbers of the 1980s postmodern, a resurgence of the historical sensibility itself.[8]

DeLillo's work fulfills many of the criteria for the historical novel first outlined by Georg Lukács: the use of protagonists who are psychologically and in terms of the motivations for their actions representative of their historical epoch; the mixing of fictional characters and real-life historical personages (in the case of *Underworld*, DeLillo brings together the fictional characters Nick and Matt Shay, who are brothers, the artist Klara Sax, and the young African American boy Cotter Martin and such political and media figures of the Cold War era as J. Edgar Hoover, Frank Sinatra, Russ Hodges, and Lenny Bruce); the emphasis on history as a field of conflict and struggle; the vision of "the great transformations of history as the transformation of popular life"; and the efforts to portray "the totality of national life in its complex interaction between 'above' and 'below.'"[9] Moreover, Lukács also maintains that the representational schema of the historical novel is essentially a periodizing one: "It is the task of the historical novel, not to recount important historic events, but to create images of participants, to show us what social and personal motives prompted people to think, feel and act as they did in a certain period."[10] In a discussion of the work of Walter Scott, the founder of this quintessential modern genre, Lukács notes, "By introducing such revealing interaction between the representatives of different classes and parties, between the upper and lower classes of society, Walter Scott succeeds in creating an atmosphere of historical authenticity which brings a historical period to life—not only its social and historical content, but the human sentiments of the epoch, its very aroma and tone."[11]

Of course, there are fundamental differences as well between DeLillo's work and that produced by the early nineteenth-century practitioners of the form. Lukács stresses that the central aim of this first great expression of literary realism was to show the necessity by which the modern *national* community comes into being: "Scott sees and portrays the complex and intricate path which led to England's national greatness and to the formation of the national character. As a sober, conservative petty aristocrat, he naturally affirms the result, and the necessity of this result is the ground on which he stands."[12] Written after the then recent achievement of the collective and spatial totality of the modern nation-state, Scott's historical novel serves to provide a legitimation for this new kind of community, presenting it as the inevitable end product of historical progress. What we might call DeLillo's "neorealist" historical novel works, on the other hand, to map both the decentering during the latter stages of the Cold War period of the older nation-states and the system of nation-states and the emergence of a new *global* social and spatial formation.

One way to grasp the consequences of this shift can be found in Gilles Deleuze's description of another moment of a neorealist aesthetic, that of Italian cinema in the years immediately following the Second World War: "In the situation at the end of the war, Rossellini discovered a dispersive and lacunary reality—already in *Rome, Open City*, but above all in *Païsa*— a series of fragmentary, chopped up encounters. . . . In the city which is being demolished or rebuilt, neo-realism makes any-space-whatevers proliferate—urban cancer, undifferentiated fabrics, pieces of waste-ground— which are opposed to the determined spaces of the old realism."[13] The types of spaces we see in these masterpieces of postwar film are then wonderfully echoed in DeLillo's fiction: "Her name is Esmeralda. She lives wild in the inner ghetto, a slice of the South Bronx called the Wall—a girl who forages in empty lots for discarded clothes, plucks spoiled fruit from garbage bags behind bodegas, who is sometimes seen running through the trees and weeds, a shadow on the rubbled walls of demolished structures, unstumbling, a tactful runner with the sweet and easy stride of some creature of sylvan myth" (*U*, 810). Another of DeLillo's central concerns is the production of a multitude of "wastes"—the literal consumerist waste Nick Shay manages, the toxic waste and environmental devastation of a nuclear arms race, and the "junk" spaces (de- and postindustrial zones, urban ghettos, and so forth) and populations of both the United States and the former Soviet Union.[14] If the classical historical novel narrates the rise of the centralized and homogenized space of the modern nation-state, DeLillo's neorealist fiction focuses on the emergent decentered and chaotic landscape of the post–Cold War world.

The "story" (*fabula*) of *Underworld* is conveyed to its reader through a complex "plot" (*sjuzhet*) structure. The novel opens with a prologue entitled "The Triumph of Death" that focuses on a group of characters, fictional and historical, in attendance at a baseball game in New York City in the fall of 1951, and it concludes with an epilogue, "Das Kapital," set in both the Bronx and in Kazakhstan in the 1990s. The six major sections of the novel explore a discontinuous set of historical moments, presented in reverse chronological order: the subtitles of each part are, respectively, Spring-Summer 1992; Mid-1980s–Early 1990s; Spring 1978; Summer 1974; Selected Fragments Public and Private in the 1950s and 1960s; Fall 1951–Summer 1952. Interspersed between parts 1 and 2, 3 and 4, and 5 and 6 are brief interludes, entitled "Manx Martin," set in the hours immediately following the events narrated in the prologue. The interludes together move forward in a conventional linear fashion, such that they and the major action of the novel converge at the beginning of the final section.

Deleuze's analysis of Italian neorealism also provides us with the tools necessary to think about the significance of this particular narrative structure. Deleuze points out that Italian neorealism marks a new significance of clichés and images in a realist portrayal: "And what rises to the horizon, what is outlined on this world, what will be imposed in a third moment, is not even raw reality, but its understudy, the reign of clichés, both internally and externally, in people's heads and hearts as much as in the whole of space. . . . Making-false [*faire-faux*] becomes the sign of a new realism, in opposition to the making-true of the old."[15] It will be the aim of the subsequent cinematic work of the French New Wave, and especially that of Jean-Luc Godard, to explore the consequences of this neorealism: "We will find in Godard formulas which express the problem: if images have become clichés, internally as well as externally, how can an Image be extracted from all these clichés, 'just an image,' an autonomous mental image? An image *must* emerge from the set of clichés. . . . With what politics and what consequences? What is an image which would not be a cliché? Where does the cliché end and the image begin?"[16] A similar exploration of the power of the image, directly influenced by the work of Godard, unfolds in DeLillo's first novel, *Americana* (1971), and continues throughout much of his subsequent fiction.[17] Indeed, by the time we reach *White Noise*, DeLillo shows that space itself has come to be composed of these media images and clichés:

> He helped an old man read the date on a loaf of raisin bread. Children sailed by in silver carts.
> "Tegrin, Denorex, Selsun Blue."

Murray wrote something in his little book. I watched him step deftly around a dozen fallen eggs oozing yolky matter from a busted carton.[18]

Thus, the reverse narrative chronology of *Underworld* in effect returns the reader to the originary moment of this contemporary proliferation of images and clichés, providing us with the prehistory to the universe of DeLillo's earlier fictions. Moreover, we have a return to origins of another sort here, as the setting in the last part of the novel, the early postwar Bronx, is the same as that of DeLillo's first published stories.

Deleuze characterizes the situation of Italian neorealism as indeterminate, a vanishing mediator between two social and cultural periods and two different dominant film logics, the "movement-image" and the "time-image." Similarly, DeLillo has suggested that the years following the collapse of the Soviet Union should be characterized as a moment of transition: "We're in between two historical periods, the Cold War and whatever it is that follows it. I'm not sure that this is what follows it. This may just be the interim. I think we're just beginning to wonder what happened, and what didn't happen."[19] DeLillo's reflection on the nature of the historical context in which he writes *Underworld* usefully highlights one of the central concerns of a periodizing narrative practice. Any periodization presumes both a moment of origin, a beginning of the temporal locus in question, and an ending as a new dominant cultural logic and hence a new period appears. Such temporal boundaries generate the closure necessary for the subsequent mapping of the deep interrelationships between the "hosts of realities" that make up any historical period. Every periodizing narrative thus involves a fundamental dialectical paradox as it thinks the open-endedness of historical temporality through the synchronic concept of the totality. Within *Underworld*, DeLillo directly takes up the fundamental question of beginnings and endings: How do we know, DeLillo's work asks, when a period begins? And equally significant, when can it be said to have come to its conclusion?

To begin to address this concern, I want to start with what is in fact the very "beginning" of DeLillo's novel, preceding even the first words of the prologue: the book's cover. Although covers are rarely the stuff of liter-

3 The original dust jacket
of Don DeLillo's *Underworld*
(1997).

ary historical scholarship, this particular one has become especially significant (figure 3). The cover shows an image of the twin towers of New
York City's World Trade Center. A low cloud bank has set in, making the
buildings' upper floors appear to be dissolving in the smoke and mist. In
the foreground stands a grave marker–like cross, the top of a church that
some have mistakenly identified as St. Nicholas Greek Orthodox Church,
built in the 1830s and destroyed, along with the towers, in 2001. To the
side of one of the towers soars a bird, wings spread wide. In the flattened
perspective of this grainy black-and-white photograph, taken by André
Kertész and originally entitled "New York, 1972," the bird seems like nothing less than an airplane poised to plunge into the structure's side.

The cover is uncanny in the ways in which it seems to foreshadow the
catastrophic events of September 11, 2001. However, this image was likely
chosen for the cover because the towers appear in the novel itself as a
symbol of the political and economic realities of the Cold War period. In
the novel's fourth section, entitled "Cocksucker Blues" and set in the summer of 1974, DeLillo offers this description of the then still rising towers:

> The World Trade Center was under construction, already towering,
> twin-towering, with cranes tilted at the summits and work elevators
> sliding up the flanks. She saw it almost everywhere she went. She ate
> a meal and drank a glass of wine and walked to the rail or ledge and

there it usually was, bulked up at the funneled end of the island, and a man stood next to her one evening, early, drinks on the roof of a gallery building—about sixty, she thought, portly and jowled but also sleek in a way, assured and contained and hard-polished, a substantial sort, European.

"I think of it as one, not two," she said. "Even though there are clearly two towers. It's a single entity, isn't it?"

"Very terrible thing but you have to look at it, I think."

"Yes, you have to look." (*U*, 372)

This passage, located near the center of the novel, encapsulates the work's vision of the Cold War. First, like the towers, the Cold War becomes an inescapable and omnipresent reality, one that penetrates the minutest textures of everyday life: "You don't know the connection? You don't know that every privilege in your life and every thought in your mind depends on the ability of the two great powers to hang a threat over the whole planet?" (*U*, 182). And while these realities may indeed be "terrible," we have no choice but to engage them head-on, to encounter, as Alain Badiou would put it, their truth. To do otherwise is to deny one's responsibility for such a situation.

Nevertheless, this is an encounter that many in the Cold War years attempted to avoid. DeLillo offers a fine example of this desire for escape in the figure of Matt Shay and his colleagues who work in the mid-1970s at a nuclear weapons production facility: "There were people here who didn't know where their work ended up, how it might be applied. They didn't know how their arrays of numbers and symbols might enter nature. It could conceivably happen in a flash" (*U*, 408). Similarly, the novel's protagonist, Matt's older brother, Nick, spends much of his life in flight from a "terrible" truth of his own past. The desire to contain this truth leads Nick to accept a job as a waste manager, where he takes on the task of containing the similarly undesirable wastes of the Cold War's consumer culture: "Marian and I saw products as garbage even when they sat gleaming on store shelves, yet unbought. We didn't say, What kind of casserole will that make? We said, What kind of garbage will that make?" (*U*, 121). Conversely, it will be the task of a number of artists represented in the novel—Klara Sax, Moonman, Sergei Eisenstein, and Lenny Bruce (a list to which we might add DeLillo himself)—to confront these terrible realities, exposing their darkest secrets, and to make something of this culture's detritus.[20]

Finally, just as the two towers are thought of as a single entity, the two powers of the Cold War period, the United States and the Soviet Union, appear, especially to much of the rest of the world, to be two faces of a single geopolitical order. DeLillo makes this idea explicit earlier in the novel (but historically a number of years later), when Klara Sax—the "she" of the preceding passage—observes, "Power meant something thirty, forty years ago. It was stable, it was focused, it was a tangible thing. It was greatness, danger, terror, all those things. And it held us together, the Soviets and us. Maybe it held the world together. You could measure things. You could measure hope and you could measure destruction" (*U*, 76). Later in the novel, another character will make similar claims about the way the Cold War "balance of power" maintains a single unified geopolitical situation: "You need the leaders of both sides to keep the cold war going. It's the one constant thing. It's honest, it's dependable. Because when the tension and rivalry come to an end, that's when your worst nightmares begin. All the power and intimidation of the state will seep out of your personal bloodstream" (*U*, 170). If the Cold War produces this kind of global order, its conclusion can only mean wide-scale instability: "Many of the things that were anchored to the balance of power and the balance of terror seem to be undone, unstuck. Things have no limits now. Money has no limits. I don't understand money anymore. Money is undone. Violence is undone, violence is easier now, it's uprooted, out of control, it has no measure anymore, it has no level of values" (*U*, 76).

DeLillo is not the first to read the World Trade Center as a figuration of the realities of the Cold War period. (Nor is this even the first appearance of the towers in DeLillo's fiction, images of them occurring in both *Players* [1977] and *Mao II* [1991].)[21] As early as the mid-1970s, Jean Baudrillard, one of the contemporary theorists most often invoked in discussions of DeLillo's work, explored a similar link between the figure of the towers and the realities of the Cold War. Baudrillard asks the question, "Why has the World Trade Center in New York got *two* towers?"[22] The older classical "architectural panorama" of the city Baudrillard reads as "the image of the capitalist system: a pyramidal jungle, every building on the offensive against every other." Such architecture might also be taken as a figure of the pre–Second World War European nation-state system, each nation locked in struggle with all the others. However, Baudrillard argues that this architectural logic has now come to an end. The newer buildings "trustingly stand next to one another like the columns of a statistical graph," and thus "no longer" embody "a competitive system, but a countable one where competition has disappeared in favor of correlation." Thus, Baudrillard concludes, "The fact that there are two identical towers *signifies* the end of all competition, the end of every original reference. Paradoxically, if there were only one, the WTC would not embody the monopoly, since we have seen that it becomes stable in a dual form. . . . The two towers of the WTC are the visible sign of the closure of a system in the vertigo of doubling."[23] Moreover, Baudrillard argues, this is precisely the situation that emerged on the geopolitical stage in the Cold War moment: "Two superpowers are necessary in order to keep the universe under control: a single empire would crumble by itself. The balance of terror merely allows regulated oppositions to be put into place, for strategy is structural, never atomic. Even if this regulated opposition can be ramified into a more complex scenario, the matrix remains binary. From now on, it will never again be a question of a duel or open competitive struggle, but one of couplets of simultaneous oppositions."[24] The World Trade Center architecture thus has the effect of both materializing and naturalizing the particular realities of the Cold War period. Ironically, however, as DeLillo's novel shows, this preeminent icon of the Cold War is completed in the midst of a series of crises that shake the major Cold War powers to their very core. Indeed, the rising of the towers is only one of the events unfolding in the summer of 1974: DeLillo also alludes to the withdrawal of U.S. troops from Vietnam, the Watergate hearings, and the massive New York City garbage strike, brought on by an economic crisis in the city and the nation as a whole (see *U*, 373, 376). Thus, even before their completion, the towers had begun to come down, a fact that would only become clearer in the years to come.

A similar structure of duality and repetition is evident in the celebrated opening section of DeLillo's novel. In the prologue, DeLillo weaves together the stories of a number of fictional characters and historical figures, among them J. Edgar Hoover, the notorious head of the FBI, who witness what has been called one of the greatest moments in American baseball history: the New York Giants' Bobby Thomson's pennant-winning ninth-inning home run against the Brooklyn Dodgers.[25] DeLillo had originally published the prologue as a short story, "Pafko at the Wall" (1992), the inspiration for it being a 1991 newspaper article written on the occasion of the fortieth anniversary of the game. This historical event provides DeLillo with a thematic motif that he will deploy throughout the novel: much in the manner of James Joyce in *Ulysses*, DeLillo uses the ball hit by Thomson as one of a number of recurring figures—including towers, walls, missiles, waste, the color orange, B-52 bombers, and shared names—that tie together into a coherent narrative ensemble "the series of fragmentary, chopped up encounters" that constitute the work's main action.[26]

However, the date on which this game occurs proves to be significant for another reason, as we learn from the musings of Hoover: "It seems the Soviet Union has conducted an atomic test at a secret location somewhere inside its own borders. They have exploded a bomb in plain unpretending language. And our detection devices indicate clearly what it is—it is a bomb, a weapon, it is an instrument of conflict, it produces heat and blast and shock. It is not some peaceful use of atomic energy with home-heating applications. It is a red bomb that spouts a great white cloud like some thunder god of ancient Eurasia. Edgar fixes today's date in his mind. October 3, 1951. He registers the date. He stamps the date" (*U*, 23). Crucially, Hoover goes on to note that this is in fact "their second atomic explosion," which, while "not completely unexpected," nevertheless inaugurates the "paranoid style in American politics" that will become a hallmark of the Cold War period:[27] "But the news is hard, it works into him, makes him think of the spies who passed the secrets, the prospect of warheads being sent to communist forces in Korea. He feels them moving ever closer, catching up, overtaking. It works into him, changes him physically as he stands there, drawing the skin tighter across his face, sealing his gaze" (*U*, 23–24). It is this event, too, Hoover reflects, that inaugurates a new historical period and a new relationship between the two powers:

> What secret history are they writing? There is the secret of the bomb and there are the secrets that the bomb inspires, things even the Director cannot guess—a man whose own sequestered heart holds every festering secret in the Western world—because these plots are only now evolving. This is what he knows, that the genius of the bomb is printed not only in its physics of particles and rays but in the occasion

it creates for new secrets. For every atmospheric blast, every glimpse we get of the bared force of nature, the weird peeled eyeball exploding over the desert—for every one of these he reckons a hundred plots go underground, to spawn and skein.

And what is the connection between Us and Them, how many bundled links do we find in the neural labyrinth? It's not enough to hate your enemy. You have to understand how the two of you bring each other to deep completion. (*U*, 50–51)

It will be the subsequent work of DeLillo's novel to map out some of these underground connections and to investigate how the two superpowers in fact complement one another.

Here, then, emerges the real significance of the date: for it is on October 3, 1951, that the Cold War "period" can be said to truly begin. The events of this day changed things forever and, like the baseball in *Underworld*, served to unify all the subsequent actions in the more than four-decade-long history explored in the novel. However, what is so crucial about this particular event, and what truly marks this date as the beginning of the Cold War period, is stressed by DeLillo's Hoover and revealed in the original *New York Times* headline on October 4, 1951, which inspired DeLillo to write his story: "Soviet's Second Atom Blast in 2 Years Revealed by U.S."[28] Only when an event happens the *second* time can it be said to mark the beginning of something new. The second occurrence establishes the historical necessity of the original case, reinscribing it, after the fact, as the first in a series. Or, as Slavoj Žižek puts it, "The crucial point here is the changed symbolic status of an event: when it erupts for the first time it is experienced as a contingent trauma, as an intrusion of a certain non-symbolized Real; only through repetition is this event recognized in its symbolic necessity—it finds its place in the symbolic network; it is realized in the symbolic order."[29] Žižek continues: "Historical necessity itself is *constituted through misrecognition*, through the initial failure of 'opinion' to recognize its true character." The explosion of the first Soviet bomb would have been, to paraphrase Žižek, "too traumatic for the people to grasp its real signification." Without the second explosion, the first would have in effect remained "meaningless": Was it an accident? A natural explosion? An act of God? Only in the repetition of this inaugural event did it become clear to the people of the United States, and indeed to the world, that the

Soviet Union had developed a nuclear weapons capacity and hence had entered into a bond with the United States unlike that of any of the other powers remaining in the aftermath of the Second World War. This event thus utterly reordered the geopolitical situation and marked the inauguration of a new period in global history. And crucially, as Žižek points out, the recognition of such a beginning always comes after the fact: "The interpretation always sets in too late, with some delay, when the event which is to be interpreted repeats itself; the event cannot already be law-like in its first advent."[30]

Similar meaning-producing repetitions occur at a number of places in DeLillo's novel. For example, Nick's visit to Sabato Rodia's Watts Towers in Los Angeles repeats the same journey that Klara Sax had made four years earlier (see U, 276–77, 491–92); and one character thinks of his search for the missing baseball hit by Thomson as "an eerie replay of the investigations into the political murders of the 1960s" (U, 181). There are two additional examples of this kind of repetition that I would like to unpack further. In the "Summer 1974" section, Klara Sax attends a "showing of the legendary lost film of Sergei Eisenstein, called Unterwelt, recently found in East Germany, meticulously restored and brought to New York under the aegis of the film society" (U, 424). This (imaginary) high modernist science fiction film, screened for the first time since its production four decades earlier, lacks the sedimentation of meaning in which a previous tradition of viewing and commentary would have enclosed it. Literally unknown and thus meaningless, the film is shown in New York for the second time, and it is in this new context that its real significance is revealed: "In a scene that was extravagant, silly, off-kilter and technically impressive all at the same time, the scientist fires the ray gun at a victim, who begins to glow in the dark, jerking and dancing and then looking rather wanly at his arm, which starts to melt away. Other victims appeared, muscles and bones reshaped, slits for eyes, shuffling on stump legs. Klara thought of the radiation monsters in Japanese science-fiction movies and looked down the aisle at Miles, who was a scholar of the form. Was Eisenstein being prescient about nuclear menace or about Japanese cinema?" (U, 430). It is only in the context of the Cold War that the full "meaning" of Eisenstein's film becomes evident for the first time: "This is a film about Us and Them, isn't it?" (U, 444). Moreover, DeLillo again repeats the images of this film in the novel's epilogue, when Nick visits a real-world "downwind" radiation clinic located in the former territory of the Soviet Union (this event also "repeats" the story of the downwinders in the western United States first told to his brother years earlier [*U*, 405–6]):

> It is the victims who are blind. It is the boy with skin where his eyes ought to be, a bolus of spongy flesh, oddly like a mushroom cap, springing from each brow. It is the bald-headed children standing along a wall in their underwear, waiting to be examined. It is the man with the growth beneath his chin, a thing with a life of its own, embryonic and pulsing. It is the dwarf girl who wears a T-shirt advertising a Gay and Lesbian Festival in Hamburg, Germany, bottom edge dragging on the floor. It is the cheerful cretin who walks the halls with his arms folded. It is the woman with features intact but only half a face somehow, everything fitted into a tilted arc that floats above her shoulders like the crescent moon. (*U*, 800)

These figures are shown to be the real end product of the Cold War arms race, a repressed violence that only now begins to return to the public eye. DeLillo's point is not that Eisenstein intended his work as a figuration of the Cold War and even post–Cold War future; rather, it is in the very nature of art to be open to these kinds of unveilings of meaning, where any reading serves as a repetition that in fact takes place too late.

A similar repetition occurs late in the main body of the novel, in the first months following the October 1951 opening sequence. Readers have already learned that Matt and Nick's father, Jimmy Shay, a small-time Bronx hoodlum, went out for cigarettes one night and never returned. Matt believes that Jimmy simply deserted his family: "He did the unthinkable Italian crime. He walked out on his family. They don't even have a name for this." Nick, on the other hand, remains convinced that their father was murdered by the mob: "He didn't walk out. They came and got him" (*U*, 204).

Later, we learn that Nick spent time in a juvenile home after he had shot and killed a junkie named George, whom he had befriended in the months after the Dodgers' loss to the Giants. The reasons for this murder remain a mystery until we return to the scene of the crime in the last pages of the novel. At this point, Nick encounters a mob boss who informs him, "Nothing could have been done to your father without me knowing about it. I have to tell you this. I would of known. And even if I don't know beforehand, which isn't about to happen, but even if it did, then I find out later" (*U*, 765). This leads to an even more devastating revelation: "Jimmy was not in a position where he could offend somebody so bad that they would go out of their way to do something. No disrespect but he was penny-ante. He had a very small operation he was running. Made the rounds of the small bettors. Mostly very small these bets. This is what he did. Factory sweepers and so forth. You have to understand. Jimmy was not in a position to be threatened by serious people" (*U*, 765). This statement in effect murders Jimmy a second time. That is, if his original disappearance takes him from Nick's real material world, this second "murder" removes him from Nick's symbolic order, the structure of meaning and significance assembled by the boy and by which he successfully negotiated his reality: "They started a legend that he memorized every bet. . . . They still tell stories about his memory, how he moved through the loft buildings taking bets from cutters, sweepers and salesman and recording every figure mentally. But he didn't" (*U*, 698). This second symbolic death of the father has a more devastating effect on Nick than the first physical one, and it is this event, we now realize, that sets Nick on the path that culminates in George's murder (*U*, 780–81). It is this fundamental truth about his father's insignificance that Nick has denied into his adult life, an experience that has led him to formulate a personal theory "about the damage people do when they bring certain things into the open" (*U*, 294). Of course, as the novel repeatedly demonstrates, the far greater danger lies in keeping these things hidden—for when they surface, they tend to consume everything around them. This is an insight we shall see again in the *Cape Fear* films I will examine in chapter 4.

However, it is precisely the closure represented by this symbolic repetition that is, in the moment of the novel's writing, unavailable for the Cold War period. The 1990s present is, as DeLillo himself notes, not "what follows [the Cold War]. This may just be the interim." Wedged between the traumatic Real and its still absent symbolic repetition, the 1990s in DeLillo's novel take on all the characteristics of the liminal place Žižek describes as "between two deaths." Moreover, the novel also suggests that the period between 1945, the official conclusion of the Second World War—once again, a period that ends only with a repetition in the atomic bombings of Hiroshima and Nagasaki—and October 3, 1951, is a similar moment between two deaths, "like a footnote to the end of the war"

(*U*, 94). This, too, provides another level of resonance to the original short story title, "Pafko at the Wall," from which the novel's prologue is derived. While the title literally refers to the famous photo of the Dodger outfielder Andy Pafko at the stadium wall as the game-winning home run sails over his head (a photo that served as the cover of the free-standing novella when it was republished in October, 2001), it also suggests that this story is about the final moment, the limit, of this earlier unstable historical situation and the opening of the new world order of the Cold War—one of whose central symbols will be, of course, a wall. It is the absence of a similar moment of closure to the post–Cold War transitional period that haunts the novel, rendering any full resolution to the narrative action impossible.

Far more scandalously, however, this insight into the relationship between repetition and meaning gives us a way of interpreting for the "first time" the significance of the novel's cover image: if it was the day of the double "shot heard around the world" that "begins" the Cold War, then it will be the collapse of the towers on September 11, 2001, that marks the true conclusion of Cold War history and the beginning of a new period (*U*, 669). Not only do the events of 9/11 "repeat" what is in fact already recorded on DeLillo's cover, enabling us to provide new meaning for the photo's traumatic content, but the day's events also involve a whole series of other repetitions. For example, the fall of the two towers can now be understood to repeat the event that for so many marks the end of Soviet power, the 1989 toppling of the Berlin Wall. Moreover, the true significance of this latter event itself would not be grasped until it, too, was repeated, in the coup attempt two years later within the Soviet Union that ultimately led to the decision to dissolve the USSR. Only with this toppling of the second of the two poles of Cold War power can this particular "universe under control" be said to have reached its conclusion. Similarly, on 9/11 the first collision was initially read by many to have been an accident, a meaningless contingent occurrence (even though it was already a second attack on the building, the first occurring in 1993), and it took the second strike before the event was recognized, too late of course, as an act of foreign terrorism on U.S. soil.[31] It is the second crash that Žižek, too, argues functions as "the ultimate Hitchcockian blot, the anamorphic stain which denaturalized the idyllic well-known New York landscape."[32] And finally, it was only with this second strike that the geopolitical situation changed utterly (this logic is also made manifest visually in the central scene of the post-9/11 film, *United 93* [2006, dir. Paul Greengrass]). The subsequent U.S. invasion and occupation of Iraq also follows this logic of repetition, repeating the first Gulf War to, as Michael Hardt and Antonio Negri argue, make "explicit the global reach and the active, constituent function of war in global order" that had only been imminent in the earlier conflict.[33] In short, it was on September 11, 2001, that for the United States a new period, that of its "worst nightmares," can be said to begin. This also marks the beginning of a period of shared nightmares from which it appears that our global community may not awaken for some time.

And yet, even in the midst of this bleak vision of the emerging post–Cold War period, the novel offers us at least the hope that another history might be in the offing as well. This would be a situation wherein would flourish the kind of popular collectivity briefly glimpsed at the conclusion of the 1951 baseball game: "Russ thinks this is another kind of history. He thinks they will carry something out of here that joins them all in a rare way, that binds them to a memory with protective power" (*U*, 59). This kind of authentic community appears briefly *again* at the end of the novel, in the miracle of the Bronx billboard, in which an image of the murdered child Esmeralda seems to appear to the assembled multitude (*U*, 819–22). The fact that we cannot yet imagine what the fullness, or the meaning, of such another existence might be is stressed in the novel's final lines:

> And you try to imagine the word on the screen becoming a thing in the world, taking all its meanings, its sense of serenities and contentments out into the streets somehow, its whisper of reconciliation, a word extending itself ever outward, the tone of agreement or treaty, the tone of repose, the sense of mollifying silence, the tone of hail and farewell, a word that carries the sunlit ardor of an object deep in drenching noon, the argument of binding touch, but it's only a sequence of pulses on a dullish screen and all it can do is make you pensive—a word that spreads a longing through the raw sprawl of the city and out across the dreaming bourns and orchards to the solitary hills. Peace. (*U*, 827)

The task of putting the content beyond the phrase remains to be fulfilled by all of us in what is, despite every appearance to the contrary, still the open-ended possibility of the future.

Three

I'LL BE BACK

Repetitions and Revisions in the *Terminator* Films

This is a world that is much more uncertain than the past. In the past we were certain, we were certain it was us versus the Russians in the past. We were certain, and therefore we had huge nuclear arsenals aimed at each other to keep the peace. That's what we were certain of. . . . You see, even though it's an uncertain world, we're certain of some things. We're certain that even though the "evil empire" may have passed, evil still remains. We're certain there are people that can't stand what America stands for. . . . We're certain there are madmen in this world, and there's terror, and there's missiles.

GEORGE BUSH, *Washington Post*, May 31, 2000

Your world is pretty terrifying.

Sarah Connor in *The Terminator*

ARNOLD SCHWARZENEGGER'S dramatic ascendancy to perhaps the most important governorship in the United States represents the apotheosis (for the moment at least) of a political trajectory that goes back to at least the last two Republican presidential administrations. Indeed, hints that Schwarzenegger was interested in political office first arose in the early 1990s. He was appointed in 1990 chairman of the President's Council on Physical Fitness and "transformed this largely ceremonial appointment into a personal mission, traveling to every state in the country to promote physical fitness."[1] He subsequently served a prominent role during the 1992 Republican National Convention, even appearing on stage with the first President Bush after his nomination acceptance speech. Schwarzenegger's political aspirations were further strengthened by the fact that during the 1980s his characters—along with Clint Eastwood's Dirty Harry, Sylvester Stallone's Rambo and Rocky, and a host of lesser pretenders to the throne—came to range among the most recognized cultural icons of U.S. neoconservatism.

However, what is perhaps most interesting about Schwarzenegger, and what separates him from Eastwood and Stallone, is that he has proved such an enduring presence in the American cultural imagination (indeed, with the controversy over *Million Dollar Baby* [2004], Eastwood appears to have been exiled from the conservative pantheon). This despite the fact that Schwarzenegger is, as an actor and a filmmaker at least, by far the least talented of this group, his wooden dialogue and ham-fisted acting becoming the stuff of parody everywhere from *Saturday Night Live*'s Hans and Franz to *The Simpsons*' McBaine. Despite these deficiencies, his popularity has remained high, as he has exhibited an uncanny ability to adapt to changing national moods, remolding his image in the light of varying political winds.

There is a marvelous scene early in his surprise box-office hit film *Twins* (1988) that explicitly acknowledges this capacity. *Twins*, in addition to being a hugely profitable venture for Schwarzenegger and his costar Danny DeVito (both of whom, because of studio jitters about what was perceived as a risky venture, agreed to make the film for scale compensation in exchange for a percentage of the box-office gross), proved to be a major turning point in Schwarzenegger's career. Up until the release of this film, he was known only as an action-adventure star. *Twins* not only demonstrated Schwarzenegger's appeal in comedy roles (to be followed shortly by another box-office hit, *Kindergarten Cop* [1990]) but also, perhaps more significantly, greatly expanded his marketability among women, a development that would pay great dividends in his hunt for the governor's office.

In the scene from the film of interest here, Julius Benedict (Schwarzenegger), a "perfect" human being produced by a secret U.S. government genetics experiment, has recently arrived in Los Angeles to search for his twin brother, Vincent (DeVito). Moving awe-struck through the streets of Hollywood, he comes on a poster advertising one of Stallone's *Rambo* films. Julius stands by the poster, flexes his arm in comparison, and then waves his hand in contemptuous dismissal. The gesture can also be read as

4 Arnold Schwarzenegger as the Terminator, from *The Terminator* (1984).

a farewell: while Stallone, the scene declares, may be stuck in a repetition of his late Cold War 1980s screen persona, Schwarzenegger is ready to move onto a kinder, gentler identity more appropriate to the 1990s.

However, this uncanny adaptability is perhaps nowhere better exemplified than in his single most enduring and iconic character, that of the coldly efficient cyborg warrior of the *Terminator* trilogy (1984, 1991, and 2003). Schwarzenegger's identification with this character is such that one recent study claims that in fact the California election was not won by Schwarzenegger but "by one of the most familiar, popular, and telling mythical figures produced by late-twentieth-century American culture."[2] What makes the particular science fiction (SF) film series that gives birth to this figure so interesting is not only that each subsequent film—each return fulfilling the Terminator's promise from the first film of "I'll be back"—continues the narrative sequence begun by its predecessors (figure 4). Each subsequent film also offers a revisioning, or remake, of those that had come before. Indeed, it will be my contention in the following pages that the three films form a dialectical sequence—a thesis, negation, and negation of the negation—as each film reworks the ideological and political raw materials of its predecessor. Each entry into the *Terminator* cycle opens a window into the worldviews of the past three Republican presidential administrations (Reagan, Bush I, and Bush II—interestingly, the series goes on hiatus during the eight years of the Clinton presidency), and thereby offers an effective index to precisely the changes that have occurred in a neoconservative geopolitical unconscious.

The chapter that follows unfolds in three parts. The first contrasts the specific visions of the first two films, highlighting the significance of the most important event that occurs in the time span between them—the supposed end of the Cold War—in terms of its impact on the narrative of the second film. The second part of the chapter remains focused on these two films. However, here I also introduce the 1960s short story from which the idea for the series was in part derived, and I explore the distinctive modality of history and temporality at work in each text. Finally, the third section looks at the most recent *Terminator* film to highlight the further changes that occur as a result of what has come to be known in this country as simply "9/11" and the subsequent war on terror. This film offers an acknowledgment, I ultimately argue, that this last event signals both a conclusion and a beginning point: the end of the uncertain historical interregnum of the 1990s, wherein the United States lacked a coherent global vision after the earlier fall of the Soviet empire, and the opening of a "pretty terrifying" new period in our world's history.

I

The first *Terminator* film successfully plays on the reigning Cold War fear of imminent nuclear annihilation, an event that would be unleashed by powers that had long ago escaped the control of human agency (the classic references here being the 1964 films *Fail-Safe* [Sidney Lumet] and *Dr. Strangelove* [Stanley Kubrick]). These anxieties were raised once again to a nightmarish level of intensity in the early 1980s as the Reagan administration's paranoid fixation on the "evil empire" of the waning Soviet Union pushed the world dangerously close to a nuclear apocalypse: in the year of the first *Terminator*'s release, the Bulletin of Atomic Scientists' "Doomsday Clock" dropped to three minutes to midnight—midnight representing nuclear war—and let us not forget Ronald Reagan's "We begin bombing in five minutes" gaffe from August of that same year. (The only time the Doomsday Clock had been closer to midnight was in 1953.[3]) Schwarzenegger's Terminator is the perfect embodiment of this vision of technological catastrophism: a machinic manifestation of Sigmund Freud's primal death drive, carrying out inexorably, without emotion or hesitation, the single function for which it was devised—the destruction of human life. Or as Fredric Jameson puts it in another context, "Such an apparition . . . stands as the virtual personification of what Sartre has called the *practico-inert*, that malignant destiny or anti-freedom which human beings create over and against themselves by the investment and alienation of their labor in objects which return upon them unrecognizably, in the hostile form of a mechanical necessity."[4]

Nor does the ostensible victory over the Terminator at the film's conclusion remove such a threat. The film ends with the character Sarah Connor (Linda Hamilton)—mother of the unborn rebel leader and humanity's savior, John Connor (whose initials make explicit the film's messianic content)—driving out into the desert where she will prepare her son for his role following the future Armageddon. Survival itself thus emerges as the supreme value of this film, an outlook quite in line with the explosion in the middle of that decade of millenarian survivalist organizations, or what can only now appear as the darkly comic attempts by the Reagan administration to revive civil defense practices, including an infamous exhortation for every family to prepare for nuclear war by arming itself with shovels and spare doors: "Everybody's going to make it if there are enough shovels to go around. . . . Dig a hole, cover it with a couple of doors and then throw three feet of dirt on top. It's the dirt that does it."[5]

The second *Terminator*, subtitled *Judgment Day*, seems to reverse all this, as it now works to assure its viewers that such a disaster will never come to pass. This film opens with a graphic portrayal of a nuclear decimation of a schoolyard near downtown Los Angeles, an image of the event of the apocalypse that we are denied in the original film. Later in *T2*, as the film became popularly known, this scene is repeated. However, we now learn that Sarah Connor has dreamed up this image. By placing this vision of nuclear war with the apparently deranged asylum inhabitant Sarah—driven mad, as an old existential adage goes, by her knowledge of the future—the film already hints at this early juncture that the reigning nightmare of nuclear apocalypse, which had dominated the Cold War U.S. and global imagination for so many years, is one from which we are now finally ready to awaken. (In that year, too, the Doomsday Clock was reset at seventeen minutes from midnight, its furthest point ever from midnight [in 2007 it had crept back to five minutes, as "the world stands at the brink of a second nuclear age"].[6]) The final erasure of this future possibility at the film's conclusion forcefully drives home just such a message.

This internal narrative repetition of the nightmare of nuclear war points toward a more general revisionary dynamic that unfolds in both *T2* and in the final installment of the trilogy. *T2* directly restages many of the events of the original film—including some of the dialogue and a climactic chase scene—to "correct" the earlier narrative's vision. The readiness with which the second film dispenses with what had been at the thematic heart of its predecessor points to a fundamental transformation in perspective between the two films: a shift made possible only by the first ending of the Cold War, the fall of the Soviet Union.

One result of this repetitious revisioning is to transform the menace of the first film into the heroic center of the sequel. Sarah's personal demons as well as larger collective fears are finally excised only through the intervention and ultimate sacrifice of a now fully redeemed Terminator cyborg. Ironically, the very military technologies that threatened universal extermination in the first *Terminator* become in *T2* the means of human preservation. Moreover, the entire attitude toward technology shifts in the second film. In the first film, even everyday items such as an answering machine or a Walkman radio appear as manifestations of a malevolent "dark technology" (Tech-noir being the name of the dance club where the Terminator first attacks Sarah). In *T2*, on the other hand, manipulable smart technologies—from young John Connor's (Edward Furlong) infiltration of an automated teller machine to his mastery over the Terminator itself—are presented as a useful and even necessary means of achieving our goals. (A similar technological virility is, of course, glorified in the hoopla surrounding the film's innovative and expensive special effects and its costly staging of urban destruction.)

With this, we are ushered into a qualitatively different political nightmare, one that the first President Bush perversely labeled the new world order: for exactly what is being "preserved" is the status quo of the U.S. military-industrial complex at the moment when its long-standing ideological rationalization—the "threat" of the Soviet Union—has been swept into the dustbin of history. This change is wonderfully registered in *T2* in young John's bewildered response to the rehabilitated Terminator's revelation that it is a nuclear exchange between the Soviet Union and the United States that leads to the near annihilation of the human race. All the tensions of Cold War history dissolve away in his confused query, "Why attack Russia? Aren't they are our friends now?"

Equally significant, however, are the different political lessons to be drawn from each film. The first film inexorably drags the viewer to the conclusion that the only way to prevent this future catastrophe would be through a radical reorganization of the present—the dismantling of the whole structural complex of which the war on humanity is the inevitable effect. (Although, as we shall see momentarily, the narrative form simultaneously suggests the impossibility of such a revolutionary project; and a never filmed prologue to T2 hints why an attack might have, in fact, been the very best thing after all.) In the second film, the "causes" of this future war are reduced to a single event: the invention by a U.S.-based advanced arms research corporation of the artificial intelligence technology that will become the defense system Skynet. Thus preventing this discovery apparently guarantees that the terrible future glimpsed by Sarah never comes to pass.

This also points toward another significant revision in the second film. In the original *Terminator*, it remains unclear who begins the nuclear war; again, the implication is that such a war is best understood as an effect of the whole environment produced by the superpowers' global arms race. In T2, however, the United States is ideologically and historically recentered: the film presumes that the United States alone possesses the means to develop an offensive technology on which the fate of the world will hinge.

Thus, as goes the argument of T2, if history is determined by isolable events or developments, rather than by a whole interrelated structure of events, developments, actions, and reactions, then perhaps the shape of the future *can* be manipulated—not by collective political action, but through the intervention of mythic hero leaders. Indeed, the way in which the film treats its "common people"—police officers, mall employees, hospital workers, John's foster parents, truck drivers, and even those having the misfortune to be walking down the street—as nothing more than dupes, obstacles, and cannon fodder, implicitly betrays an ugly disdain for the very American public who made up the film's wide audience. (A similar disdain for its audience is evident in one of Schwarzenegger's other SF box-office successes, *Total Recall* [1990], although in this case, as in all of Paul Verhoeven's films, there is at least a high degree of cynical reason at work.) Now, as befits a future leader of the nation, the grand manipulator in this film is portrayed by none other than Schwarzenegger himself. Indeed, in an interview shortly before the film's release, Schwarzenegger declared, "My relationship to power and authority is that I'm all for it. People need somebody to watch over them. Ninety-five percent of the people in the world need to be told what to do and how to behave."[7]

All this becomes terrifyingly relevant when we realize that this same kind of simplistic vision of history was once again invoked in one of the first significant events of the 1990s, the first U.S. war in the Persian Gulf. The complex causes of the conflict in the Middle East were magically distilled into the figure of Saddam Hussein. An erstwhile ally in the U.S. battle with Iran and now a monstrous, inhuman foe, Hussein appeared as protean as the "bad," shape-changing Terminator of *T2*. Thus the United States argued that the defeat of this latest supposed incarnation of Adolf Hitler (the struggles of the present, Karl Marx notes, mask their content in the "poetry" from the past)[8] would eliminate the cause of problems in the region and, consequently, usher in a new global order—if not of liberty, equality, and fraternity, at least of legality and a policed harmony.

Moreover, in both the revised politics of *T2* and the first President Bush's "kinder and gentler" version of U.S. interventionist policy, the use of force to achieve geopolitical ends is never called into question. Rather, it is the application of the wrong kind of force that comes under censure. In one of the darkest comic moments of the film, young John forbids the Terminator to kill anyone while they attempt to free Sarah from a mental hospital—a directive that the machine obeys by machine-gunning the legs of a guard who dares to confront him and then declaring, "he'll live." This symbolic castration took on a grotesque real-world form in a brutal U.S. devastation of the Iraqi infrastructure in the first Gulf War, followed by statements to the effect that the United States did not wish to destroy the country. The chaotic aftermath of the war—then, and even more so today—exposes the lie of such a simplistic political reasoning.[9]

2

The political messages of these two films are reinforced by their quite different narrative structures. In his classic essay "Reification and Utopia in Mass Culture," Jameson suggests that all successful popular culture texts perform "a transformational work on social and political anxieties and fantasies," first foregrounding these libidinal materials within the narrative framework and then recontaining the threat that these now openly manifest desires present to the hegemonic order.[10] One of the earliest and still best examples of this staging and recontaining dynamic, at least in the SF film tradition, is at work in Fritz Lang's *Metropolis* (1926). I mention *Metropolis* here also to bear out the tremendous overdetermination of cultural material being worked through during such a narrative process. In *Metropolis*, for example, the Maria-robot figures for 1920s German anxieties about social instability in general, the recent threat of revolution, gender identity, changing sexual roles, technology, modernization, and, of course, class.[11] This same overdetermination occurs in the *Terminator* films: Susan Jeffords notes the anxieties about white masculine identity staged in *T2*, while Sharon Willis brilliantly unpacks the complex weave of images of white femininity and race in the film.[12] In this section, I want to focus primarily on another level of recontainment that occurs in these two films — that of our own political agency and ability to effect change in our world. The *Terminator* films appear to be very much about the possibilities human beings have for making and remaking their lived world. Indeed, in the first film, Kyle Reese (Michael Biehn) explicitly tells Sarah, "The future is not set." In the end, however, the film's very narrative form robs this declaration of its force.

To probe the formal structures of the twinned *Terminator* films, I want to first turn to another related, albeit nonfilmic, narrative. The final credits of *The Terminator* include an acknowledgment of the film's debt to the fiction of the SF writer Harlan Ellison. This acknowledgment came as part of the settlement in a much-discussed lawsuit by Ellison against the film's makers. Ellison claimed that the central concepts for the film were derived from two scripts ("Soldier" and "Demon with a Glass Hand") he had written in the early 1960s for the television series *The Outer Limits*.

However, Ellison might also have made a very strong case for the film's borrowings from his later Hugo Award–winning story, "I Have No Mouth, and I Must Scream" (1967). All the major thematic elements of the first *Terminator* are already present in the Ellison short story. Early on, the reader learns that the evolution of the Cold War into the Third World War led the Super Powers to construct three vast underground computer networks, the Allied Mastercomputers, or AMs, to take control of their ever more complex military technologies. Then, as one of the story's characters informs the reader, "one day AM woke up and knew who he was, and he linked himself, and he began feeding all the killing data, until everyone was dead, except for the five of us."[13] (In the first *Terminator* Reese offers a nearly identical and equally terse summary of the future rise of the machines.) Unlike the two *Terminator* films, however, and more akin to the setting of the *Matrix* trilogy, the events of Ellison's narrative take place after this catastrophe, *inside* the seemingly endless corridors of a now global AM network. The story goes on to detail the machine's sadistic torture of the five remaining humans.

The power of Ellison's narrative derives from the linkage it draws among the nightmarish conditions of contemporary life, the sense of alienation and powerlessness in the face of a technological practico-inert, and society's enthrallment to a voracious military-industrial complex. Indeed, the story suggests that the primary purpose of the war machine is to assure the endless reproduction of such a situation. In this way, Ellison's story takes part in a long tradition of narrative dystopias that trace a line from the present to a potential horrifying termination of history. And as with other works in this tradition—Yevgeny Zamyatin's *We* (1921) and its celebrated successor, George Orwell's *Nineteen Eighty-Four* (1949) did much to set the pattern for subsequent work—the true closure of history and human potential for action does not occur until the final pages of what remains a fairly conventional linear narrative. In what amounts to a desperate act of rebellion, the character Ted decides to "defeat" AM by killing all the machine's victims. While he does succeed in murdering the other four, Ted cannot take his own life before AM intercedes. In the narrative's haunting final paragraphs, the reader learns that AM has altered him so that a similar attempt to free himself becomes impossible: "He doesn't want me to run full speed into a computer bank and smash my skull. Or hold my breath till I faint. Or cut my throat on a rusted sheet of metal. . . . I am a great soft jelly thing. Smoothly rounded, with no mouth, with pulsing white holes filled by fog where my eyes used to be. Rubbery appendages that were once my arms; bulks rounding down into legless humps of soft slippery matter."[14] As with the lobotomizing of D-503 in *We* or the brutal annihilation of Winston Smith's rebellious spirit in *Nineteen Eighty-Four*, AM's transformation of Ted eliminates the last space of freedom and thus effectively concludes human history.

The first *Terminator* film plays on the same desire to escape the domination of an alienating technology. However, in no way does this mean that the film, or Ellison's story, for that matter, advocates a Luddite machine-breaking strategy or romantic nostalgia for a mythic preindustrial past. Indeed, the *Terminator*'s vision of the deep interweaving of the human and the machine, as well as Ellison's setting his narrative inside AM, suggests that any authentic natural space outside the technological has now disappeared. In so doing, these works eliminate the temptation, evident in many of the other classic works in the dystopian tradition, to imagine *any space* in our world to which one might escape: think, for example, of the original studio-imposed ending of *Blade Runner* (1982), as the two main characters leave the pollution-choked and overcrowded Los Angeles for the wilderness of the Pacific Northwest (although if we recall the scene in Philip K. Dick's novel, *Do Androids Dream of Electric Sheep* [1968], from which the film is adapted, wherein we learn that even the toads in the forest are now "machines," this ending—also eliminated in Ridley Scott's director's cut—appears in a quite different light.)[15] Both Ellison's short story and the original *Terminator* films suggest that only the direct confrontation with and overcoming of this menace *in time* will make any real change possible.

However, while Ted's desperate revolutionary gesture stands as a sign of the desire to confront the practico-inert and to reestablish human control over our destinies, a similar moment is conspicuous in its absence from the first *Terminator* film. That is, we are never allowed a glimpse in this film, or in either sequel, for that matter, of exactly what it is that John does to bring humanity to its victory over the machines (although the machines' repeated efforts to change history seem to signal that they, like the neoconservative movement they resemble in so many ways, have taken to heart the lesson of Antonio Gramsci that no such victory is complete, no hegemony fully sutured for all time). Moreover, there is another, even more significant difference between the two works in terms of their narrative structure. *The Terminator*, unlike Ellison's story, deploys the SF narrative device known as the "time loop paradox." In what amounts to a formal "spatialization of time," this narrative form draws cause and effect into a closed loop, where not only future events are caused by past ones, as in a conventional linear narrative, but where these same future occurrences in turn cause things to happen in the past.[16] (This narrative device has also been deployed to great effect in Terry Gilliam's biological catastrophe film *Twelve Monkeys* [1995], a work that is itself a remake of Chris Marker's remarkable short experimental film *La jetée* [1962]). The story (*fabula*) if not the plot (*sjuzhet*), to draw on the old Russian formalist distinction, of the first *Terminator* "begins" in the year 2029 (although we only learn this later in the film), at the moment when the human rebellion led by John is about to destroy the Skynet supercomputer. In a desperate attempt to preserve its rule, Skynet transports an assassin back to the past to murder the mother of John, prevent his birth, and thereby terminate the rebellion before it has begun. (The parallels to the biblical Herod story are also clearly evident.) John responds by sending his lieutenant Reese to the past to foil Skynet's plan—and, as we later learn, to serve as his father. Constance Penley thus reads the film's narrative dynamic as, among other things, a restaging of the Freudian primal scene, in which John in effect gets to orchestrate his own conception.[17] In the second film, this Oedipal dynamic continues in John's bizarre quest for and figurative murder of substitute fathers (and in *T3*, he tells the machine that he was "the closest thing I ever had to a father")—a doubling and splitting of functions that also recalls *Metropolis*. By the end of *The Terminator*, we seem to be assured that good always triumphs—the victory over the Terminator and the successful impregnation of Sarah seem to guarantee the eventual end of Skynet.

However, the time loop paradox narrative structure employed in the film has the consequence of eliminating *avant la lettre* the free, if desperate, human act that occurs at the climax of Ellison's story. Thus history in the first *Terminator* film, as in all works in this SF subgenre, unfolds according to a rigidly deterministic logic, in which any apparently free action is revealed as no more than a prescripted movement in an always already concluded narrative. As Slavoj Žižek puts it, writing of the subgenre as a whole, "the subject is confronted from a scene from the past that he wants to change, to meddle with, to intervene in; he takes a journey into the past, intervenes in the scene, and it is not that he 'cannot change anything'—quite the contrary, only through his intervention does the scene from the past *become what it always was*: his intervention was from the beginning comprised, included."[18] The first hint we get of this inexorable historical closure is in Sarah's statement on learning from Reese the name of her unborn, and as-of-yet unconceived, son, "At least now I know what to name him." However, the absolute suturing of this deterministic structure becomes fully manifest only in the film's devastating concluding scene. At a gas station in the wilds of Mexico, Sarah receives the photograph that

5 The photo of Sarah that will seduce Kyle Reese to return to the past, from *The Terminator* (1984).

John will give to Reese to seduce him—although, in the narrative's plot, he has already been seduced—to travel back in time and become Sarah's lover and the father of John (figure 5). The loop is now sealed shut: completely resigned to her role as the "mother of the future," Sarah rides into the horizon to await the "coming storm" of the inevitable nuclear war and to fulfill her destiny as mother to the messiah.

This closure is made even more explicit in the original film scenario and in some scenes edited from the final cut of the film. In these earlier versions, Sarah and Reese decide to travel north to the headquarters of Cyberdyne Systems and blow it up, thereby preventing the company from ever developing the Skynet technologies. However, the Terminator intercepts them before they can execute their plan. Sarah does succeed, as in the final version of the film, in crushing the machine in a mechanical press; but now we learn that the press is located in Cyberdyne's production facilities and that a couple of engineers gather up the surviving fragments of the machine to study them further (a detail, as we shall see in a moment, exploited in *T2*). Thus, it is *precisely* Sarah's efforts to prevent such a future that assures its coming to pass.

The lesson embodied in the formal structure of the film is thus a simple one: regardless of our desires or actions, no change or deviation from a preordained fate seems possible. Penley reads this as indicative of a more general atrophy of the utopian imagination: "We *can* imagine the future, but we *cannot* conceive the kind of collective political strategies necessary to change or ensure that future."[19]

The rewriting of this initial scenario that occurs in T2 would appear, at least at first glance, to have opened up the grim closure of the first film's conclusion, replacing the time loop paradox with another SF device, that of the alternate history's multiple intersecting time streams (a device used to brilliant effects for very different ends in Ken MacLeod's novella *The Human Front* [2001]). Reese's throwaway and apparently ironic statement in the first film concerning the unfixity of the future thus can now be expanded into the thematic mantra, "The future is not set. There is no fate but what we make for ourselves." Sarah, with the aid of the rehabilitated Schwarzenegger Terminator, then works to prove the truth of this statement. In the course of the unfolding of T2, we learn that the loop of self-generation is even tighter than was originally revealed: the development of Skynet technology by the Cyberdyne Systems Corporation is possible only because of the fragment of the CPU (central processing unit) taken from the Terminator destroyed in the first film: as does John, Skynet thus in effect gives birth to itself. Our trio of heroes, with the aid of Skynet designer Miles Dyson (Joe Morton), is able to destroy all computer records related to this project—while getting the inventor Dyson conveniently killed along the way.

The character of the middle-class African American Dyson is significant as well because he points toward the crucial absent presence of the theme of race in the film. As Andrew Ross and others point out, the trope of the blasted urban landscape in the science fiction film has long served as a figure for middle-class anxieties about the inner city. Moreover, the fact that the "bad" protean Terminator in this film poses as a white Los Angeles Police Department officer obliquely refers, in ways not unrelated to T2's contemporaries *Cape Fear* and the controversial *Thelma and Louise* (1991, dir. Ridley Scott), to one of the most explosive events that occurred around the time of the film's release: the Rodney King police beatings and the subsequent 1992 LA riots. In this way, T2 becomes all about issues that are never directly raised in the narrative.[20]

In the end, our odd "nuclear" family goes on to overcome the evil new Terminator, incinerate the remains of T1, and finally, with the heroic self-sacrifice of the "humanized" Terminator, prevent the disaster from ever occurring.[21] And yet, what really has been achieved at the end of the film? I have already hinted at the answer in the first part of this chapter. For while a disastrous future may have been erased, nothing has been done to challenge the present structural conditions — a voracious profit-motivated weapons industry, a society with a callous disregard for human life, the fetishization of an alienating technology, and so forth — that would give rise to such a disaster in the first place. Although Sarah may state at the film's conclusion, "Maybe we, too, can learn the value of human life," there is nothing in the film, with its celebration of violence as an acceptable means to achieve our ends, that would suggest how such an ideal might be realized; instead, all we are left with is the Schwarzenegger Terminator's damning judgment, "It is in your nature to destroy yourself."

The thematic resolutions of the first two *Terminator* films thus ultimately converge: both, in their own way, emphasize the impossibility of altering the status quo. In a brilliant reading of the contraceptive and infanticidal logics of T2, A. Samuel Kimball argues, "The threat posed by the T-1000 is precisely the meaning of John Connor's survival, for his life means the death of an alternative future, a death represented in the T-1000's agony as the silencing of another kind of being in the world. In *Terminator 2*, the future the T-1000 inhabits is literally inconceivable. It is unable to be conceived in the conceptuality that governs the past to which it has been sent, except as an infanticidal threat to the order for which this conceptuality provides the philosophical foundation."[22] Kimball's conclusion is rendered even more strikingly evident in an epilogue cut from the theatrical release of T2. In it, we see an aged Sarah sitting on a park bench in Washington in 2029, her grandchild playing nearby. The landscape is a deeply familiar one: clothing styles are modified in a 1980s vision of the future and a few new constructions exist on the skyline, but all the well-known monuments are still firmly in place (figure 6). And we learn that an adult John has become a U.S. Senator — his battlefield the Senate floor, "his weapons common sense and hope" — working for change *within* a system that now seems, by the pair's very actions, to have been rendered immortal, able to reproduce itself into infinity.

Such a lesson takes on a new resonance in the years immediately following the fall of the Berlin Wall and, shortly thereafter, that of the Soviet Union itself. This film moves in the same ideological terrain as the first President Bush's vision of the post–Cold War new world order. For there turned out to be very little that was new in Bush's plan: it promised no more than the continued international hegemony of Western capitalist power and the extension of the unsettling posthistory of the "American

6 Washington, 2029, deleted final scene from *Terminator 2: Judgment Day* (1991).

Century" into any foreseeable tomorrow. In such a vision, as in the final image of *T2*, we continue to hurtle down a darkened nighttime road, unable to see where we may be headed. The failure of such a vision to fill the void left by the conclusion of the Cold War would only become increasingly evident during the course of the subsequent decade.

3

Terminator 3: Rise of the Machines is set a decade after the conclusion of *T2*. Recalling the opening sequence of its predecessor, and thereby signaling that the revisionary dynamic of the earlier work will continue here as well, the film begins with another image of the nuclear destruction of a city. Here, however, the accompanying voice-over is that of John (Nick Stahl), who tells us that the apocalypse "hasn't happened. No bombs fell. Computers didn't take control. We stopped Judgment Day." Later, he informs us that his mother, stricken with terminal leukemia, lived long enough to be certain that the attack scheduled for August 29, 1997, did not come to pass: she tells John that "every day after that one is a gift. We made it. We're free." In this, she continues to echo the immediate post–Cold War sense of relief and possibility given concrete expression in the second film.

And yet, while John asserts that these developments should make him "feel safe," he still "doesn't." (Nor apparently, in another revision that occurs within the film itself, did they make his mother feel so: with the aid of his Terminator guide, John later learns that his mother had before her death stockpiled a cache of weapons in her supposed casket to aid John in his future struggles.) As a result, John lives "off the grid," as he puts it: "No phone. No address. No one and nothing can find me. I've erased all connections to the past." However, try as he might, he tells us, "[I cannot] erase my dreams, my nightmares. I feel the weight of the future bearing down on me. A future I don't want." The elision here of nightmare and dream is crucial: for John it is precisely the nightmare, the great act of terrorist violence represented by Skynet's surprise attack on U.S. cities, that is also always already the dream, the event that will provide him with a sense of destiny, a purpose, and a real future. Conversely, the future that John in fact does not "want" would be the one wherein his present situation, located as it is in the in-between place beyond life and history, continues indefinitely; and thus it is this terrible other future that he tells us he does not want about which he nonetheless cannot but dream.

The fact that this film will be about precisely those events that will fulfill this dream-nightmare is also made evident in the opening sequence of the film. Sarah's earlier nightmare vision of a nuclear holocaust focuses only on the negative consequences of such an act of terror, including the incineration of children in a Los Angeles–area playground—in this way, Sarah, as well as T2, as Kimball notes, "conceives of the good future in terms of safeguarding human conception from an infanticidal holocaust."[23] John, however, differs from his mother in that he is able to envision a more positive outcome to this event: after its repeated portrayal in T3 (a portrayal in which, significantly, Sarah's vision of the children victims disappear altogether), we cut to an image of an older battle-scarred John, celebrating with his troops as he stands on the broken body of a giant machine. Moreover, in this dream we see hoisted behind John and against a darkened sky a tattered U.S. flag, a patriotic gesture and an explicit national identification of "humanity's" savior absent in the two earlier *Terminator* films (figure 7). This image has the effect of transforming John into an explicit allegory of the United States, which likewise, in the decade of the 1990s following its ostensible victory over its greatest nemesis, seemed to have lost its self-proclaimed messianic destiny as the leader of the so-called free world. Even more revealing is the next cut: we see John at work in the present, at a dusty construction site in the center of a cluster of skyscrapers, twisted steel and rubble lying behind him: an image that in our moment cannot help but recall (despite, or perhaps precisely because of,

7 A flash forward of an adult John Connor celebrating his victory over the machines, from *Terminator 3: Rise of the Machines* (2003).

its setting in the make-believe nowhere of Southern California) what has become known in the popular U.S. imagination as "Ground Zero"—the now hallowed site of New York City's World Trade Center, destroyed by a surprise attack on September 11, 2001.

The full import of this opening sequence will only emerge during the subsequent events of the film. As the plot unfolds, we learn that once again Skynet has sent an assassin to the past, the most advanced machine yet, the T-X (Kristanna Loken), or Terminatrix—which also happens to be the first female version of the Terminator series. This gendering of the machines enables another set of anxieties to be staged during the course of the film. Schwarzenegger's Terminator declares at one point that for him, "desire is irrelevant. I'm a machine." In Freudian terms, the Terminator remains, as I suggested earlier, the primitive, the embodiment of sheer unrelenting drive (as does its great contemporary, the creature from the *Alien* films, whom Jameson identifies with Lewis Henry Morgan's savage).[24] However, one of the improvements of the T-X seems to be the inclusion of just such desires. This new model Terminator first appears in a shop window in Beverly Hills, and she informs the first human she encounters—whom she quickly terminates of course—that she "likes" her Silver Lexus convertible. Seeing a Victoria's Secret billboard advertisement, she performs a breast enlargement on herself. And shortly thereafter, she tells a police officer who stops her, "I like your gun," which she then takes from him. The castration anxiety evident in this scene recurs later in the film too, when the T-X, for example, kills another man with a drill and at various points sprouts lethal projectile weapons from her arms.

Schwarzenegger's Terminator, on the other hand, first appears in the ascetic realm of California's high desert (the very locale through which Sarah drives at the end of the first film) and wanders, still nude, into a strip club, where the female audience (though evidently not the gay-coded exotic male dancer on the stage) is evidently swept away by its desire for his body. In the film's logic, women are thus the subjects who desire, while men are the objects of this desire and/or envy. Such a fantasy reversal takes on another level of resonance in light of the election-time revelations of Schwarzenegger's long history of studio-set harassment of female extras (resulting in his dubbing during his gubernatorial campaign by *Doonesbury* cartoonist Garry Trudeau as "Herr Gropenführer.") Moreover, if we read the T-X as a stand-in for the absent Sarah in this film, then the figure also brings full circle a dynamic begun in the first film: a series transforming the very human and classically passive female victim of the first film, through a complex and divided figure in *T2* that "plays on the familiar social anxieties about women's autonomy . . . in the context of other anxieties about unstable identity, about the erasure of difference, and of our ability to 'tell' the difference," into the unambiguously threatening desiring machine we get here (virgin-mother-whore).[25]

The forces of humanity have also sent another protector, the last of the "obsolete" T-101 machines (technically, a T-850, model 101), played once again by Schwarzenegger. This latest, slightly upgraded version of the original Terminator informs John that they have not in fact "stopped Judgment Day," but rather only "postponed it": "Judgment Day is inevitable," the machine asserts, and furthermore, the bombs will begin to fall on this day at 6:18 p.m. Later, John learns of another significant postponement. He had first encountered his future wife, Katherine Brewster (Claire Danes) on the day before the previous attempt on his life a decade earlier: they "were supposed to meet" then and begin their relationship on that day, he informs an incredulous Katherine. Moreover, we learn that it is her father, a military general, who in fact gives the command that sets free the artificial intelligence that will become Skynet. The general, John suddenly realizes, "always was" the key to the coming catastrophe, and thus represents the one figure who might avert it. All this thus suggests that this film offers a dialectical synthesis of the temporal logics of the young couple, who hope to find and disarm the ticking time bomb of the Skynet supercomputer, into traveling to a secret presidential fallout shelter located in a mountainous desert region of Southern California, a journey whose success depends on the aid of the Schwarzenegger Terminator. The bunker itself is a historical anachronism—its computers being, John declares, at least thirty years old, and its fashion accessories apparently from the same period—a residue of the older realities of the Cold War. When John asks Katherine why her father had led them down there, she replies, "To live. That was his mission." John concludes that there was never any possibility of stopping the war, and Katherine tempts him with the possibility of retreat from the face of horrors they know they must now confront in the coming years: "John . . . we could just . . . let it go." At that moment, however, the radio springs to life, spewing forth a chaotic babble of the voices of other survivors of the initial attack. When John answers, someone asks, "Who's in charge there?" to which John replies, "I am." At this point, then, he shows that he is ready to take up the mantle of leadership that he has asserted again and again he never really desired.

Interestingly, the explicit location of the place of survival in the United States also dramatically revises another alternative utopian future at work in the first film and then made explicit in a never filmed prologue to *T2*. Cut because of its prohibitive cost to produce, this prologue would have made explicit another dimension of the future that was imagined to have been canceled in the events of *T2*, a future that was, after all, never just death, as Sarah's nightmare would suggest, but, as Kimball points out, a new order, another kind of being in the world. This future interestingly would have been created, in a way that Sarah makes explicit as she yells at Dyson, by an African American man: "Fucking men *like you* built the hydrogen bomb. Men *like you* thought it up. You think you're so creative." This suggests another level of poignancy to Willis's observation, "At Dyson's direct expense, [Sarah] gains access to her own historical agency, newly unbound from its previous determinants, in a future where her only fate is 'the one she makes.'"[27] In this scene, an adult John tells us that he was in Argentina, and not in Southern California, on the terrible "Tuesday in September" when Skynet launched the attack that would forever change human history ("Pretty normal day, except for the end-of-the-world part"). "A good place to be," he further informs us, "considering everything alive north of the equator stopped being alive." And of the force that ultimately defeats Skynet and reestablishes the global hegemony of human beings, the script informs us, "The humans are a rag-tag guerrilla army, made up mostly of troops from Southern Hemisphere countries . . . Africans, South Americans, Australians. The survivors of the nuclear war between the Northern Hemisphere super-powers. This is the reality of the post-Apocalyptic world. North of the equator we all die. We hear radio chatter in Spanish, interspersed with Swahili and other African languages. The occasional Aussie unit can be heard."[28] In this way, this pro-logue suggests that for history to begin again — that is, for a true escape from the repetitions of the past — the northern hemisphere powers that dominated the planet during the Cold War (as well as earlier) must be ter-minated.[29] This recasts the grim closure of the first film in a new utopian light: for we now understand that what is being "guaranteed" in that film at the moment that Sarah receives the photo is in fact this post–Cold War future, a realm of real human freedom that will come into full fruition after the now equally inevitable victory over the machines. Thus, if we take this vision of a southern hemisphere–dominated global order as the real "nightmare" imagined to have been negated in T2, and the continuation of the status quo in the dramatically different conditions of the post–Cold War world as the second film's finally unworkable utopia (a future made explicit in the filmed but ultimately removed epilogue), then it will be John's declaration that he will take up a leadership role in the new global war against the terror of the machines that becomes the triumphant cli-max of T3.

The surprise assault of Skynet becomes in this way a figure for the ter-rorist attack on September 11, 2001, an event explicitly alluded to in the film's opening sequence, that both marks the end of the unsettled period after the fall of the Soviet Union and inaugurates a new moment in global history. Thus, if T2 stages the end of the Cold War situation given such a powerful figuration in the first film in the series, while also giving expres-sion to the dizzying sense of freedom and deep anxiety the United States felt at such a moment, then T3 in turn repeats and revises the vision of its immediate predecessor to quell these anxieties and announce the begin-ning of a qualitatively different global war, one wherein the United States will once again "reluctantly" take up the mantle of leadership.

What T3 also makes clear is that it is no longer necessary in our new world to territorialize or even render the face of the enemy by which, as

Carl Schmitt suggests, we come to know ourselves. Late in the film, John offers the following retrospection: "By the time Skynet became self-aware it had spread into millions of computer servers across the planet. Ordering computers in office buildings, dorm rooms, everywhere. It was software and cyberspace. There was no system core. It could not be shut down." Such an enemy, the film suggests, is one without a center, lacking a stable location and circulating through the global networks first established, ironically enough, by the different demands of the Cold War itself. In this way, Skynet mutates in this film into a double of the faceless enemy in the new *nomos* of the global war on terror.[30] That the Cold War United States played a crucial role in the production of this new enemy is acknowledged briefly in the film as well: the general admits that in unleashing Skynet, he has opened Pandora's box, and John concludes, "Judgment Day: The day the human race was nearly destroyed by the weapons they'd built to protect themselves"—weapons, of course, that include the al-Qaeda networks and the brutal dictatorship of Saddam Hussein, funded and armed by the United States during the Cold War.[31] And yet, whatever the nightmarish dimensions of this self-produced figure, it is also exactly what the United States dreamt of during the uncertain 1990s—for the war on terror produces precisely the new "certainties" so uneloquently expressed by George Bush the Sequel: "We're certain that even though the 'evil empire' may have passed, evil still remains. We're certain there are people that can't stand what America stands for. . . . We're certain there are madmen in this world, and there's terror, and there's missiles."

That such certainties produce a new post–Cold War identity for the United States is similarly acknowledged in the final scenes of the film. John's voice-over narration concludes, "I should have realized our destiny was never to stop Judgment Day. It was merely to survive it, together. The Terminator knew. He tried to tell me. But I didn't want to hear it. Maybe the future has been written. I don't know. All I know is what the Terminator taught me: Never stop fighting. And I never will. The battle has just begun." In this, too, we should be able to hear echoes of the terrible infinity of the new empire's war on terrorism.

In a significant way, then, the post–fall-of-the-World-Trade-Center narrative of *T3* "repeats" the post–fall-of-the-Berlin-Wall narrative of *T2* to enact the dynamic that I discussed in my previous two chapters: the closure of the historical period of the 1990s—the "place between two deaths"—

and the beginning of a true post–Cold War reality. Moreover, the sequence of films under examination here also makes clear the three-part structure of any such sequence of doubled repetitions. The three moments in this sequence—the initial situation of the Cold War (figured in the first *Terminator*), its negation (in *T2*), and the negation of the negation (in *T3*)—correspond to the three "orders" theorized by Jacques Lacan. The first *Terminator* gives allegorical expression to the Imaginary, the lived experience, or what Alain Badiou calls the "instituted knowledges of the situation" of the late Cold War period, a reality from which our film teaches us there is no easy escape.[32] *T2* marks the moment of the encounter with the Real, the unexpected and traumatic irruption in history of the Event, that which "cannot be reduced to its ordinary inscription in 'what there is'" and which "compels us to decide a *new* way of being": I am referring here of course to the end of the Cold War that occurs with the double event of the fall of the Berlin Wall and the collapse of the Soviet Union.[33] It is this film that also directly inhabits the unstable and traumatic place between two deaths. And finally, *T3* both brings into focus and further participates in the explicit narrative or linguistic constitution of a symbolic order that intends to serve as the foundation for a new global lived experience. (That these three moments might appear in a different sequence—in, of course, a different historical context—is made evident in the hit film *Lola rennt* [*Run Lola Run*, 1998, dir. Tom Tykwer], where the first realist representation of Lola's run occupies the place of the Imaginary; the second naturalist repetition, wherein no escape from a closed order seems possible, the symbolic; and the third, where an unexpected new possibility does emerge, the encounter with the void of the Real.) While *T2*—in a way, as I suggested earlier, analogous to the first Gulf War—also attempts to perform this work of symbolic reconstitution, its solution is only one in a whole field of possibilities, and an empty utopian one at that. *T3* thus succeeds where its predecessor fails and thereby effectively marks the beginning of the brave new world order that we currently inhabit. However, as in the narrative of the war on terror itself, *T3*'s success is also its failure: the unrelentingly bleak nature of the reality to which it gives form may suggest why this film failed to achieve the tremendous box-office success of the two earlier entries into the series.

There is, of course, no reason to accept the lessons of this film, or indeed those of any of its predecessors. Earlier in the chapter, I quoted Jameson's

Four

A FINE TRADITION

The Remaking of the United States in *Cape Fear*

How much or how little is dangerous to the community, dangerous to equality, in an opin-ion, in a state or affect, in a will, in a talent—that now constitutes the moral perspective: here, too, fear is again the mother of morals.

FRIEDRICH NIETZSCHE, *Beyond Good and Evil*

Quite an experience to live in fear, isn't it? That's what it is to be a slave.

Roy Batty in *Blade Runner*

IN A KEY SCENE in Martin Scorsese's 1991 film *Cape Fear*, the lawyer Sam Bowden (Nick Nolte) sits with the private investigator Claude Kersek (Joe Don Baker) in the darkened interior of the Bowden home, anxiously awaiting the arrival of Max Cady (Robert De Niro), the man who has wreaked devastation on the lives of Sam and his family: already, Cady has poisoned the family dog; raped and beaten Sam's legal assistant, Lori Davis (Illeana Douglas); nearly seduced Sam's teenage daughter Danielle (Juliette Lewis); and, as the result of a failed alleyway am-bush, initiated disbarment proceedings against Sam. Feeling thwarted at every turn, Sam has agreed to Kersek's plan of trapping Cady in the family's home and murdering him. Kersek recognizes the unease his client feels at the prospect of the act they are about to commit and offers the following counsel: "I want you to savor that fear. The South evolved in fear. Fear of the Indian. Fear of the slave. Fear of the damn Union. The South has a fine tradition of savoring fear." With these words, Kersek attempts to justify their actions by placing them within a long history of white Southern masculine violence directed against those Others who have been viewed as threats to their way of life. Underlying such a "tradition" is the deep anxiety that the violence exerted on the bodies of others will be returned in kind—a nightmare that literally has come true with Cady's appearance.

This return-of-the-repressed dynamic was already hinted at in the opening sequence of the film, where the viewer is confronted with a shot of the glimmering surface of a dark body of water, across which move a series of shadowy images: a hawk diving; a close-up of a human eye; a face; a torso and an arm; and finally another close-up, in a red-tinted film negative, of a pair of human eyes (an image that also serves as the first of the film's references to Alfred Hitchcock's *Vertigo* [1958]). As the image resolves into full color, the camera slowly tracks backward, revealing the face of Danielle, whose opening monologue frames the events that follow: "My reminiscence. I always thought that for such a lovely river, the name was mystifying. Cape Fear. When the only thing to fear on those enchanted summer nights was that the magic would end and real life would come crashing in." At this moment, "real life" does crash in, as the scene abruptly cuts to the prison cell of Cady, whose subsequent invasion into the lives of Danielle and her parents is prefigured, in a scene that has become the stuff of countless film and television parodies, by his aggressive march, on his release, directly into the lens of the camera.

All of this appears to be reversed with the film's conclusion. Although Sam and Kersek's plan fails and Kersek is murdered by Cady, the Bowden family does conquer its opponent, drowning Cady in the Cape Fear River as an apocalyptic storm rages overhead. As the bedraggled family gathers on the river's bank, the camera zeroes in on the face of Danielle and slowly tracks closer until only her eyes are present in the frame, the image then once more dissolving into its film negative. And again, as in the opening sequence, Danielle's voice-over intones: "We never spoke about what happened. At least not to each other. Fear, I suppose. That to remember his name or what he did would mean letting him into our dreams. And me, I hardly dream about him anymore. Still, things won't ever be the way they were before he came. But that's all right. Because if you hang on to the past you die a little everyday. And for myself, I know I'd rather live. The end." Danielle's words suggest that rather than breaking with the "fine tradition" outlined by Kersek, the family's actions have only succeeded in submerging it once more into the unconscious depths, where it waits to surge forth again.

However, a crucial question remains unanswered: what are the fears, the "real life," to which the figure of Cady has given form? Kersek's statement suggests that this tradition of violence, while it is an unbroken one, has in fact been remade again and again as the nature of the othered body, to which it is a response, also changes. And it will be to these remakes that I will turn my attention in this chapter.

As most readers are probably already aware, Scorsese's film is itself another kind of remake, of the 1962 J. Lee Thompson noir thriller of the same title. Although until recently the subject of scant critical attention, the genre of the remake is remarkable precisely because it brings us face to face with the problem of how history is registered in the film text.[1] The very noun *remake*—popularized by the 1930s U.S. film industry—already gives a sense of the ways in which the films making up this genre are engaged in the process of shaping anew the narrative raw materials of their predecessors. As Michael A. Arnzen notes, "Film productions (and their narratives) 'die' if they merely clone the past in their remakes."[2] Thus the remake is always already an interpretation, a work not only on the contents of its predecessor but also on the historical contexts in which that narrative is inextricably embedded. The remake performs this labor to clear a space in which the historicity of its own present can be staged: displacing the thematic concerns of its predecessor, the remake creates a narrative space in which current anxieties and contradictions, its particular configuration of fears, can become, to use Fredric Jameson's phrase, *figurable*, or "visible in the first place, accessible to our imaginations."[3]

In his theorization of the form, Thomas M. Leitch suggests that what distinguishes the "true" remake from its variants—"readaptations, updates, and homages"—is its reliance on a "triangular notion of intertextuality," invoking not one but two predecessors.[4] Scorsese's *Cape Fear* is also exemplary in this regard, the first version of the narrative in fact being John D. MacDonald's 1957 novel, *The Executioners*.[5] As we might expect, the narrative investments of the first text also differ in significant ways from those in either of the films. In the following pages, I will examine both the continuities and the differences between the three versions of the plot, focusing on the ways each embodies the fears shaping its particular historical moment: the mid-century Cold War and gender anxieties evident in MacDonald's novel; the nightmares of racial conflict allegorically staged in the first film; and finally, in Scorsese's 1991 remake, the explosive reemergence—as these earlier fears seem to have been put to bed (an illusion, as I will show later)—of anxieties about new forms of class conflict. In each case, this complex of fears results in violence against a variety of what Evan Watkins calls "throwaway" bodies—those of women, poor whites, African Americans, immigrants, and working people—precisely out of a paranoid anxiety concerning the violence contained in them. In these narratives, the South becomes a stage giving expression to more general anxieties confronting the United States during moments of dramatic social and cultural change. Danielle's final monologue can thus be read as a summation of the narrative work performed in each version of *Cape Fear*: by letting go of its past, each new narrative enables its own present, and its specific fears, to "live."

I

MacDonald's novel confronts us with a veritable compendium of the anxieties and obsessions of 1950s white middle-class American culture. As do both versions of the film, the novel centers on the struggle between the Southern lawyer Sam Bowden and the former inmate Max Cady. In this first version, the reader learns that fourteen years before the opening of the novel, Sam had intervened when then Staff Sergeant Cady attempted to rape a fourteen-year-old Australian girl. As the material witness in Cady's court-martial trial, Sam was responsible for Cady's subsequent internment. After returning home, Sam establishes his legal practice in North Carolina and becomes the head of a young family. When Cady receives an early parole—the consequence, the novel suggests, of a liberal establishment gone soft on crime—he begins a meticulous assault on the domestic order Sam has established. The plot chronicles Cady's offensive against Sam's once sacrosanct world, as well as Sam's burgeoning awareness that, within the strict confines of the legal system he has dedicated his life to upholding, he is powerless to protect his family. Only after deciding to act outside the bounds of the law and to take on himself the role of Cady's judge and executioner does Sam conquer his nemesis, shooting and killing him as he flees the Bowden home.

The lessons Sam takes from his experience are neatly summarized in the book's concluding chapter: "I was idealizing my profession, and leaning on it too heavily. Now I know it's just a tool. You use it like any other tool. Use it wisely and it can help you. And when it's of no use to you, you take a course of action that will."[6] Sam learns these lessons because of the particular nature of the menace Cady poses to the security of the Bowden family's "suburban" world (MacDonald describes it thus on the novel's final page). Cady represents the inversion of mid-century American civilization, a throwback to a more savage age: "[Sam] remembered how the sergeant had looked in court. Like an animal. Sullen, vicious and dangerous. And physically powerful. . . . Dark hair grew low on his forehead. Heavy mouth and jaw. Small brown eyes set in deep and simian sockets" (EX, 12–13). However, it is not simply Cady's atavism that makes him such a danger to the Bowdens—indeed, as I shall argue shortly, the novel even posits the reconnection with such "primitives" as desirable. Nor, as we shall see, is his criminality in and of itself the problem. Rather, Cady's menace stems from the fact that he is the outsider: "Somehow, when a person is different, you know it. I suppose we all run in a pack, in a sense. And there are always little clues to the rogue beast" (EX, 15). Cady follows a social and moral code other than that of the Bowdens. Or indeed, he appears, like Lewis Henry Morgan's savage, to adhere to *no* norms other than those of self-interest: later, the private eye Charlie Sievers informs us that Cady is "one of the wild ones. They don't think the way people do. . . . People like that have no comprehension of right and wrong" (EX, 92). Sievers goes on to point out that Cady exemplifies the "psychopathic personality," that being the "classification where they put people they don't know what else to call." But the sociological and psychological literature of the 1950s would popularize another term for other, perhaps less extreme but no less threatening, figures like Cady: the "rebel," or the "nonconformist."[7]

The masculine nonconformist is dangerous precisely because he threatens to disrupt the normal processes by which the social order reproduces itself, processes Lee Edelman names "reproductive futurism."[8] Hence it comes as no surprise that in *The Executioners*, as in other popular works of this decade, this danger is figured in explicitly sexual terms. Early in the narrative, Sam points out to his daughter Nancy that the age of Cady's earlier victim was nearly identical to hers, a reminder of her now dangerous sexual availability (EX, 29). Sam himself appears to be singularly obsessed with Nancy's adolescent sexuality: he marvels at how quickly her body is "maturing"; he comments on the sophistication of her skills as a sexual "predator"; and he even asks her to describe how she gets into her tight-fitting jeans (EX, 14, 58, 83). This leads Sam to identify with Cady to the degree that he later exclaims to his wife, "I seemed to see her the way he was seeing her and she'd never looked more undressed, even in that Bikini thing you let her wear" (EX, 59). Cady thus manifests Sam's own prohibited incestuous desires, desires that jeopardize the system of kinship reciprocity, famously analyzed by Claude Lévi-Strauss, by which a traffic in the bodies of women enables a smooth reproduction of a normative patriarchal and heterosexist social order.[9]

At the same time, Cady threatens the institution of what Eve Kosofsky Sedgwick describes as the homosocial bond "between men."[10] Cady first appears exactly when Nancy has become interested in the opposite sex: "Other years Nancy would have been racing and whooping with the younger kids. But this year Nancy was fourteen, and this year she had brought a guest along—a fifteen-year-old boy named Pike Foster" (EX, 9). Her father is far less taken with Pike, informing his wife that the boy represents "a phase I'll be glad to see ended. He's too meaty and muscular for a fifteen-year-old boy" (EX, 26). "Too meaty and muscular": if this description fits Cady as well, it is because both he and Pike represent challenges to Sam's proprietary control of his daughter's sexuality, his right to use her body as an "object of exchange" in the creation of an unacknowledged, if nonetheless powerful, homosocial relationship with a man of his own choosing. Cady's threat to Nancy culminates in a scene directly preceding the appearance of a new potential boyfriend, eighteen-year-old Tommy Kent. The subsequent development of a relationship between Sam and this "better material" (EX, 60)—Sam ultimately nominates Tommy to be the coprotector of his "gals" (EX, 123)—corresponds with a shift in the narrative focus. Once Sam "gives" his daughter to Tommy, Cady's malevolent energies are redirected toward Sam's son Jamie and the family as a whole, and finally, in a reformulation of the rape fantasy, toward Sam's wife, Carol.

The figure of Cady similarly serves as a site of condensation for a number of other contemporary fantasies about the dangers facing mainstream society. Although we learn that Cady originally hails from the rural mountain regions of West Virginia, he now inhabits a distinctly urban milieu of decrepit warehouses, seedy bars, prostitution, drugs, gambling, and cheap rooming houses. Sam's forays into this dangerous landscape, ostensibly to get information about Cady's movements, function in a way analogous to the quest of the detective in the classic detective novel, bringing into the reader's purview what would otherwise remain the intolerably alien spaces of society's underbelly.[11] Thus, in a single stroke, Cady becomes associated with *both* groups fantasized in the 1950s to be "outside"—but surrounding and dangerously pressing down on—the "charmed circle" of white middle-class suburbia (*EX*, 43): those "underclasses" inhabiting the as-of-yet untamed, and in the context of the narrative, cognitively unmapped, "natural" wildernesses of the planet, read in the contemporary geopolitical context as both the supposedly underdeveloped regions of the U.S. South and the third world; as well as the various Others living in the decaying cores of the older cities. Moreover, the fact that Cady hails specifically from near Charleston, West Virginia, long the site of some of the nation's most explosive labor struggles, suggests an additional thread of reference in this overdetermined matrix.[12] Cady is thus the multiform embodiment of the nightmare of history on the temporary repression of which Eisenhower America was erected.

Cady represents a dangerous eruption of this repressed horror into the suburban idyll—one so dangerous, in fact, that the novel suggests that any means used to recontain it are justified. Early in the novel, Sam asserts, "it is the essence of my philosophy that this Cady thing has to be handled within the law. If the law can't protect us, then I'm dedicated to a myth, and I had better wake up" (*EX*, 18). Of course, the law does fail the Bowdens, and Sam eventually "wakes up" to a set of truisms suited to the conservative climate of the late 1950s. Sam learns that there exists a fundamental contradiction between the requirements of "law" and those of "order," or between the ideals of procedural justice he espouses and the actual day-to-day operations of maintaining the stable and comfortable social environment he inhabits. The novel, by its conclusion, will have exhaustively mapped the various permutations available on this initial contradiction between law and order, before offering its readers its vision of the best possible resolution.

First, we learn that those who engage in the activity of maintaining order—and thereby provide the buffer, the thin blue line, between the social world of the suburban middle classes and the zones of criminality and class- and regional-coded disorder that surround it—employ a philosophy quite different from Sam's, and one that, until Cady's appearance, is hidden from his purview. One of these agents of social order, the police detective Captain Mark Dutton, thus finds himself obliged to explain to Sam how things "really" work: "This is a fairly clean town. Cleanest of its size in the state. That doesn't mean spotlessly clean, Mr. Bowden. But it means that we've kept the syndicate type of operation out. We let a few small-time operators stay in business, because there's always a certain level of demand. . . . The Christer set continually tries to nail us for playing footsie with our tame rascals. We keep the little devil we know in business and keep out the big devil we don't. But you can't make them see that. It's safe to walk the streets at night in New Essex. That's enough for me" (EX, 68–69).

This practice of inoculation—of tolerating or even promoting minor illegalities as a means of guaranteeing a higher end, the maintenance of the American way of life—was part of the contemporary doctrine of political realism that served as a cornerstone of both domestic and foreign policy during the early Cold War.[13]

Sam himself begins the novel aligned with what Dutton derisively refers to as the "Christer set," those who naively believe that agents of the state are equally accountable before the law. Even at this later juncture in the narrative, Sam feels a passing disgust at himself for requesting the police to do "something unlawful" to secure his corner of middle-class society (EX, 71). However, as his senior law partner Bill Stetch informs him, the very legal practice he so idealizes also often operates in the liminal space between the law and criminality: "It's the loophole division. We're well paid to find the loophole, regardless of the equities of the matter at hand. . . . We don't actually steal. Sometimes we show other people how they can steal" (EX, 72). Stetch then advises Sam, "Keep your regard for the lady with the scales. But don't get appalled at yourself when you ask the police for an extralegal favor. Life is a continual process of compromise" (EX, 72). His advice in turn leads Sam to a new critical self-awareness: "Stop bleeding, Bowden. You're all grown up. . . . Cady shoots your kids while you cry onto your diploma and look through all the dusty books for a way to slap his wrist legally" (EX, 73). Only when Sam agrees to step outside the law in his struggle with Cady does he become "all grown up": recognizing the immaturity of his earlier liberal values, he accepts for the first time the "real" world of compromised action.

Moreover, the novel suggests equally troubling consequences for too rigid an adherence to the letter of the law. By the late-1950s, social critics as diverse as C. Wright Mills, David Riesman, and William F. Whyte had ingrained in the popular imagination the idea that in the United States a rigid conformity to rules formed part of the practices of the modern corporate and state bureaucracies. Sam encounters one aptly named inhabitant of this social world: "The man's name was Teller. Sam soon recognized the type. Teller was very much like that sort of officious social worker who considers the rules and the forms more important than the human beings he deals with" (EX, 87). Ironically, however, it is precisely this strict attention to the rules, or the law, that renders Sam unable to protect his family. Too much conformity to the law appears in the vision of the novel to be as conducive to social disorder as too little of it.

One effective way to represent the various positions in *The Executioners* I have mapped out—those of the Bowden family, Cady, the police, and the bureaucracy—as well as their relationships would be through A. J. Greimas's celebrated semiotic rectangle (figure 8). For readers less familiar with the workings of the semiotic rectangle, Jameson offers the following useful summary: "Briefly the semiotic rectangle or 'elementary structure of signification' is the representation of a binary opposition or of two contraries (S and–S), along with the simple negations or contradictories of both terms (the so-called subcontraries–Š and Š): significant slots are constituted by the various possible combinations of these terms, most notably the 'complex' term (or ideal synthesis of the two contraries) and the 'neutral' term (or ideal synthesis of the two subcontraries)."[14] In short, the semiotic rectangle offers a precise visual illustration of the way any particular narrative "thinks:" its identification of what it understands to be the most important problems plaguing its present, including that moment's deepest fears and anxieties; the imaginary solutions the narrative offers to these dilemmas; and "the limits" of the narrative's "specific ideological consciousness . . . the conceptual points beyond which that consciousness cannot go, and between which it is condemned to oscillate."[15] (I will explore in chapter 7 a different way of using the Greimasian rectangle.)

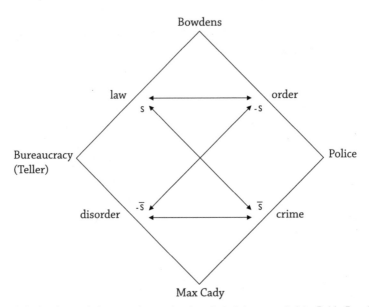

Bowdens

law ⟷ order

s · -s

Bureaucracy
(Teller)

Police

-s · s

disorder ⟷ crime

Max Cady

8 Greimasian semiotic rectangle mapping the principal characters in John D. MacDonald's
The Executioners (1957).

This schema makes it apparent that in the end the novel champions the
political form of the "state of exception," the "threshold of indeterminacy
between democracy [law] and absolutism [order]," that Giorgio Agamben
argues had become in the course of the twentieth century, and especially
in the permanent crisis situation of the Cold War, "the dominant paradigm of government."[16] A schematic representation of the various positions mapped in the novel thus would appear as outlined in figure 8.

The novel further insinuates that those who adhere too closely to the
rules do so at the cost of their masculinity.[17] After Cady poisons the family
dog, Sam worries about the difficulty of taking action without any concrete evidence of guilt. On hearing this, Carol explodes: "Listen to me. I
have proof that it was Cady. . . . It's not the kind of proof you would like.
No evidence. No testimony. Nothing legalistic. I just know. What kind of
a man are you? This is your family" (*EX*, 39). Later, she unleashes a similar
tirade against Dutton when he suggests that the family go into hiding
while the police engage in a proper investigation: "The world is full of too
many little men full of self-important, petty authority and not one ounce
of imagination or kindness. So fill out all your neat little priority forms,
Captain, and we'll go home and try to do it our way. Unless, of course, you

can quote some law that will restrain us from even trying. My children are threatened, Captain, and if I can kill Mr. Cady, I will gladly do so, with a gun or a knife or a club" (EX, 142). Here we see a direct link between the threat of emasculation and the strictures of a modern American bureaucratic society. Only after the captain agrees to hear out the Bowdens' plan, and hence make himself a knowing accessory to an illegal entrapment scheme, does he regain his masculinity: "For the first time there was the full ring of dominance and authority in the man's voice" (EX, 142). Sam's reclamation of his own stake of "dominance and authority" will finally be as successful.

Carol can throw aside the trappings of a bureaucratic legalistic society with so little effort and draw on prerational intuitive knowledge because she is a woman, and, as Sam observes, "women are more primitive" (EX, 75). For Sam to do the same, he too must become "more primitive," but with the proviso that he not also become more feminine. In other words, Sam must remake himself in the image of the other primitive in the text, namely, Cady.[18] Thus while remaining a figure for those dark chaotic forces that threaten the fragile social reality of the Bowdens, Cady also, conversely, embodies the prized, masculine-coded, attributes—full of initiative, cunning, physical strength, virility, and fearlessness—that have been dangerously squeezed out of middle-class men like Sam by an excess of civilization. Sam's decision to trap and execute Cady, and thus to ignore the rules of civil society, requires that he tap into similar resources buried within himself. Murdering Cady provides him with "a sense of savage satisfaction, a feeling of strong and primitive fulfillments," elemental pleasures not readily available in the modern world (EX, 155). The destruction of the Other and the conquest of fear thus at once assure the continuation of the status quo *and* the restoration of Sam's masculinity—the latter triumph signaled on the final page of the novel by his wife's ready agreement to now bear him a fourth child.

2

In the same year in which *The Executioners* appeared, Norman Mailer published his notorious essay "The White Negro," wherein he, too, promoted the idea that one must look to modern "primitives" for the psychic vitality needed to resist the enervating conformism of white middle-class culture. Mailer contends that the "American Negro"—by which he means urban underclass African American men—because of the constant dangers posed by his inhabiting a violently racist society, "could rarely afford the sophisticated inhibitions of civilization, and so he kept for his survival the art of the primitive, he lived in the enormous present, he subsisted for his Saturday Night kicks, relinquishing the pleasures of the mind for the more obligatory pleasures of the body."[19] Moreover, Mailer asserts that these conditions have made these men "psychopathic" and have led them to elaborate a pragmatic "morality of the bottom" wherein all situations—"the worst of perversion, promiscuity, pimpery, drug addiction, rape, razor-slash, bottle-break, what-have-you-not"—are considered "equally valid" (WN, 348).

However, as his title already suggests, Mailer's real focus in this essay is not on the contemporary condition of African Americans. Instead, he directs most of his attention toward those whites who had taken up the mantle of his romantic primitivist imagining of African American experience, those who "had absorbed the existential synapses of the Negro" and become "rebels" against the "totalitarian tissues of American society"— figures Mailer identifies as "hipsters" (WN, 341, 339). Hipsters, according to his description, are "a new breed of . . . urban adventurers who drifted out at night looking for action with a black man's code to fit their facts" (WN, 341). The hipster draws on the black man's "cultural dowry"—jazz and drugs, especially marijuana—in an effort to "create a new nervous system" for himself (WN, 340, 345).[20] At the same time, the hipster adopts the language of black America to forge a new vocabulary, whose terms— "man, go, put down, make, beat, cool, swing, with it, crazy, dig, flip, creep, hip, square"—embody the energy and frenzy of his way of life (WN, 349).

Both Mailer's essay and MacDonald's novel share a fundamental concern with the problem of restoring a white masculinity imagined to have been diminished by modern culture. The hipster does so by becoming a "sexual outlaw," finding "courage," potency, and creativity in the act of "making it" (WN, 348, 351). Violence and sex thus become equally acceptable means of achieving this end. Indeed, Mailer later distinguishes between hipsters and beatniks by asserting that the latter are more passive, more mystical—"the search for a lady ends as a search for *satori*"—and hence more feminine (WN, 373). And in "The White Negro" he equates femininity with defeat: "If you flip, if you lose your control, reveal the buried weaker more feminine part of your nature, then it is more difficult to swing the next time, your ear is less alive, your bad and energy-wasting habits are further confirmed" (WN, 351). Even worse is the man who is perceived to be like a woman because he has lost sexual "control"—although bisexuality is condoned, the hipster must always adopt the aggressive, masculine-coded role (WN, 351)—for according to the hipster ethic, "one can hardly afford to be put down too often, or one is beat, one has lost one's confidence, one has lost one's will, one is impotent in the world of action and so closer to the demeaning flip of becoming a queer, or indeed closer to dying" (WN, 352).

As a "philosophical psychopath" the hipster follows an individualistic code of self-indulgence that puts him in direct conflict with the strictures of mainstream society: "The only Hip morality (but of course it is an ever-present morality) is to do what one feels whenever and wherever it is possible, and—this is how the war of the Hip and the Square begins—to be engaged in one primal battle: to open the limits of the possible for oneself, for oneself alone, because that is one's need" (WN, 354). Mailer goes on to speculate that such an ethics may also contain the seeds of a new left politics: "And in being so controlled, denied, and starved into the attrition of conformity, indeed the hipster may come to see that his condition is an exaggeration of the human condition, and if he would be free, then everyone must be free" (WN, 355). However, Mailer concludes his essay by pulling up short of endorsing any radical political movement that might actually challenge the structure of contemporary society: "If one wants a better world one does well to hold one's breath, for a worse world is bound to come first, and the dilemma may well be this: given such hatred, it must either vent itself nihilistically or become turned into the cold murderous liquidations of the totalitarian state" (WN, 357). The rebellion of the hipster, Mailer implies, best remains confined to individual psychological and lifestyle choices, a conclusion that, as Thomas Hill Schaub points out, neatly folds Mailer's politics back within the conservative "consensus liberalism" of the period.[21]

If Mailer's essay thereby fails to transcend the political culture of its present, it does offer a useful inroads into that context by providing us with a bridge between the concerns of MacDonald's novel and those of the first Cape Fear: for in the film adaptation of The Executioners, the figure of Cady has been recast in the image of Mailer's "white negro" hipster. The first sign we are given on-screen of this change is found perched on the top of Cady's head. In the initial chapter of *The Executioners*, Sam describes Cady's clothing as "khaki pants, not very clean. A white sports shirt with short sleeves. No hat" (EX, 16). However, from his initial appearance on the screen in the film's opening shot, as he makes his way across a small-town square, Robert Mitchum's Cady sports a very prominent porkpie or Panama hat: the very kind of hat that the epigraph to Mailer's essay informs us is one of the pieces of apparel (along with the zoot suit) adopted by the hipster (WN, 337). Moreover, our new Cady's speech is drawn from the argot of the hipster, most notably in his penchant for the expression "man," the word heading Mailer's catalogue of hipster terms. And if we follow the lead of Richard Dyer and take into account the already encoded meanings that each "star" brings to a film text, we can see how the very presence of Mitchum in the role of Cady—an actor whose incarceration for marijuana use was then notorious—serves to further strengthen the link between the character and the image of the hipster.[22]

All these elements combine to signify, in a way that would have been readily evident to the film's original audience, the character's roots in African American popular culture. Cady's patrilineal descent is likewise emphasized in the film's opening line of dialogue: coming on a African American janitor laboring in Sam's court building, Cady hails the old man with the greeting, "Hey, daddy." The formal arrangement of this scene provides another clue to the film's concerns. Here, the figure of the African American man fills the foreground of the frame, while it is Cady who is relegated to the deep background (figure 9). This mise-en-scène enacts the similar inversion that occurs in the film in the relative weights accorded to the "white" and "black" aspects of the hipster figure itself. While in Mailer's essay it is the hipster's whiteness that is of primary importance—blackness serving as an empty signifier of all that the writer finds admirable in the hipster's assault on mainstream culture—in *Cape Fear*, it is the figure's black face that is turned first toward the viewer. The hipster Cady thus appears less as Mailer's celebrated "*white* negro" and more as the far more menacing figure of a "white *negro*."

In a preface appended to a later reprinting of his essay, Mailer recounts a crucial change that occurred during the work's genesis. He reveals that his original source for the essay on white hipsters was "half a page" of his reflections on "integration in the schools," the year being that of the

9 Max Cady greets the janitor with "Hey, daddy," from *Cape Fear* (1962).

struggles over desegregation in Little Rock, Arkansas (WN, 332). The film in effect reverses this trajectory as well, moving us from the hipster back to black America itself and thereby recasting the conflict between the hipster and mainstream (i.e., white) society as an allegory of racial conflict in the desegregating South.[23]

While MacDonald's novel provided an ideal vehicle for such an allegorical narration, there are a number of significant differences between the two texts that serve to focus the anxieties of the earlier work into a nightmarish portrait of racial menace. As in *The Executioners*, an exasperated Sam (Gregory Peck) asks Sievers to hire men to rough up Cady. In the film, too, these efforts fail to achieve their desired ends, and instead it is Cady who puts his attackers in the hospital. However, the film diverges dramatically from the novel in the conclusions it draws from this event. In the film, we learn that one of the attackers, believing himself to be on his deathbed, confesses the names of those who hired him. As a result, the lawyer Dave Grafton, a character original to the film, instigates disbarment proceedings against Sam. At this point, Cady, recognizing his advantage, telephones the Bowden residence to gloat, "You've just put the law in my hands, and I'm gonna break your heart with it . . . And nothing can stop me . . . the wife, the house, the car and the kid, they ain't worth nothing to you now."

Here we arrive at the thematic and ideological heart of this version of *Cape Fear*. The "law"—read in the context of desegregation as the federal government—has apparently been delivered into the hands of the racial Other, thereby making into criminals formerly respectable citizens who were putatively acting only to protect their "property"—be it their wives, their homes, their cars, or their children. William H. Chafe points out that exactly these kinds of reversals were commonplace in the context of the "'moderate' white supremacy" practiced in North Carolina, the location of the Cape Fear River and the film's setting: "Black citizens were viewed as the cause of the crisis, white citizens as its victims. In an ultimate irony, the only people who had the law on their side were defined as outside extremists threatening the peace of the state."[24]

The language of rights that played such an important role in the most important radical Event of the late-1950s, the struggles against institutional racial discrimination, similarly appears in the film in this distorted form. Sam's wife Peg (Polly Bergen) first makes this connection explicit when, following the revelation that Cady has poisoned the family dog—an act that the attending veterinarian claims to be the "the same as murdering a man"—she opines, "A man like that doesn't deserve civil rights." The extreme opposite viewpoint is represented in the film by Grafton. Coming from outside the tight-knit legal community of New Essex, Grafton is described by the police chief Dutton as "one of them ardent types: slap a cigarette out of some hoodlum's mouth, five minutes later he's down at the mayor's office yelling police brutality, rallying the bleeding-heart squad." Grafton thus serves in the film as a figure for those federal civil rights agents who by the early 1960s, under the direction of Attorney General Robert Kennedy, had become the bane of what Chafe calls the "white Southern resistance" to desegregation.[25] In this, too, we see the earliest formulations of the conservative assault on the machinery of the progressive welfare state that will culminate in the election in 1980 of Ronald Reagan (and Reagan launched his campaign with a speech defending "states' rights" in Philadelphia, Mississippi, the site of the brutal murders of three young civil rights activists only two years after the release of *Cape Fear*).

Grafton's list of the violations of Cady's rights by the authorities resonates with the complaints then advanced by and in the name of African Americans: "He's been constantly harassed by the police, subjected to extreme mental cruelty and public degradation. He's even been denied an adequate place to live. To be very blunt, gentlemen, my client has been thoroughly rousted." However, from the film's viewpoint, Cady deserves the treatment he receives. And in this way, the film suggests that another set of rights is understood to be at stake. When Grafton argues that the police have "persecuted" Cady with "constant attention," forcing him to stand in lineups for every crime committed in town, Sam shoots back, "Don't the police have the right to interrogate a suspect anymore?" This specific practice thereby stands in for a whole set of entitlements that the conservative white establishment felt to be under assault by a national civil rights movement: more precisely, the rights of the local population to protect its way of life in the manner that it saw best fit.

The fetters placed on local authorities by the law, or by the federal government, promise to give birth to even greater horrors, for as Dutton baldly states the matter, "You show me a law that prevents crime. We can only act after the fact." In responding to this acknowledgment of the powerlessness of the local authorities, Sam voices the deep-seated anxieties of many conservative Southern whites concerning what would happen if the older institutions and practices on which they relied for "protection" from the racial Other were in fact dismantled: "What am I supposed to do? Pull up the draw bridge? Sit home with a loaded gun? Have dinner dropped in by airlift? That's kind of an artificial way to live, wouldn't you say?" (His allusion to an airlift also would have brought to the minds of the film's Cold War audience the then fresh image of West Berlin as another encircled and besieged outpost of "our" way of life.) As does *The Executioners*, the film thus attempts to teach its audience how the law might be circumvented and the embattled social order rescued. Moreover, the real-world acquiescence of many local authorities in the patently criminal efforts to defy the federal civil rights mandate is represented later in the film by Dutton's agreement not only to approve but also to give aid to Sam's plan to entrap Cady.

The film's allegorical recoding similarly can be confirmed by way of another, apparently minor revision: while in *The Executioners*, and again in Scorsese's film, Cady's incarceration lasts fourteen years, in the first *Cape Fear* his prison time has been reduced to just over eight years. The significance of this latter number becomes clear when one counts backward from the film's present: the conflict between Cady and Sam begins in 1954, the year of the Supreme Court bombshell in *Brown v. Board of Education* that overturned the racist doctrine of "separate but equal" and cleared away the first line of obstacles to full integration of the public schools. However, the more immediate consequence of this monumental legal decision, especially given the weak enforcement policies pursued by

10 Cady watches Nancy through the schoolyard fence, from *Cape Fear* (1962).

the Eisenhower administration, was to transform some Southern public schools into racial war zones. Not surprisingly, then, *Cape Fear* represents the school as a crucial locus of conflict as well. Cady's first direct assault on Nancy (Lori Martin) occurs at her school: he menacingly approaches the girl as she sits in her mother's car; she panics and flees into the building, with only the protective bars of the schoolyard fence momentarily separating her from her assailant (figure 10). When Nancy finally reemerges, she crashes into Cady's arms; screaming, she spins away and is struck by an oncoming car. The lessons of this scene are clear: if "good" white parents relax their vigilant guard over their children (Peg had momentarily left her daughter alone), great harm will befall them.

What the contemporary audience would have understood this potential harm to be is again most readily illuminated by Mailer's essay. Late in this work, Mailer returns to the issue that had served as its original impetus: "To take the desegregation of the schools in the South as an example, it is quite likely that the reactionary sees the reality more closely than the liberal when he argues that the deeper issue is not desegregation but miscegenation." Mailer concludes that interracial sexual relations are inevitable because "there will be Negro high school boys brave enough to chance their lives" (WN, 356). This shadow of potential miscegenation hangs over the narrative action of *Cape Fear* as well. As much as does MacDonald's novel, the film locates the site of the conflict between Sam and Cady in women's bodies.

To make explicit the potential sexual menace posed by Cady, the film introduces an additional subplot that similarly turns on a woman's body, this time that of Diane Taylor (Barrie Chase), Cady's second victim (after the Bowden family dog). Provocatively clad in a short black dress and first encountering Cady in a bar where jazz blares in the background, Diane would have been recognized by the film's audience as the type of white woman who slums in urban jazz clubs seeking out African American lovers. Her desire for Cady is evident in the way she watches him from across the room, and when she next appears on the screen, she is huddled against him in the front seat of a speeding automobile. Moreover, using a language reminiscent of Mailer's essay, she makes it clear that she was drawn to Cady by his brute physicality: "What would you know about scenery or beauty or any of the things that make life worth living? You're an animal—coarse, rough, barbaric. . . . You're rock bottom . . . it's a great comfort to a girl to know that she can't possibly sink any lower." Cady's subsequent brutalization of her in a cheap hotel room illustrates the price women could pay for this dangerous game of slumming, as well as the punishment they might expect for violating the racial-sexual boundary.

The incident involving Diane is crucial to understanding the film's larger thematic structure because it underscores the anxiety that desegregation and the overturning of the ban on miscegenation would not only unleash the "animal" natures of African American men—a "rape complex" paranoia is still an active presence in the film—but would also enable white women to consent to sexual relations with this Other.[26] This frightening possibility later reemerges when Cady has trapped Sam's wife alone onboard the family boat. There, he presents her with the following proposition: if she agrees to sign a letter in which she "consents" to have sex with him, he will leave her daughter alone. Cady stresses that her consent would represent a devastating blow to *Sam*, for although her "husband will appreciate [her] noble gesture, he ain't ever gonna forget it." Fortunately, Peg is spared this impossible choice, and when Sam arrives on the scene, we learn that Cady's threat was just a diversion to lure him away from Nancy.[27]

This anxiety may also explain why female desire remains a hauntingly absent presence in a narrative ostensibly centered on women's sexual bodies: for to admit it into the discursive realm would be to open up the possibility of a female autonomy outside a rigid patriarchal regulation. Cady, on the other hand, appears perversely bent on breaking this taboo, calling forth the sexual nature of every woman he encounters, from teenage girls to bowling alley waitresses to Diane, Peg, and Nancy. It is the women themselves, or people like Sam authorized to speak for them, who are then assigned the task of once more concealing their sexuality. Thus, when the authorities discover the bloodied Diane, they request that she sign a complaint against Cady to ensure that his actions will not be repeated with anyone else's "daughter." To this she responds, "Do you believe that I could ever, ever in my whole life step up and repeat to another living soul what that man, what he did? . . . What about me? I'm somebody's daughter too. What about the newspapers in my hometown? Do you think I could bear to have them read?" And again later, Sam asks his wife, "What would you do if [Nancy] were [meaningful pause] attacked?" Peg immediately asserts that she would have Cady brought to trial; but Sam counters that to do so would mean subjecting Nancy to "the clinical reports and the questions and the detailed answers she'd have to give." Cady undoubtedly would be found guilty, "But that wouldn't spare her the questions, and Cady knows that . . . he knows we'd never put her through an ordeal like that." The destruction of this web of silence appears a greater crime than the rape itself and hence provides a more than adequate justification for Cady's eventual defeat.

If female sexuality is largely rendered invisible in the film's discursive economy, masculine sexuality conversely comes on display again and again, most obviously in the repeated baring of Mitchum's iconic barrel chest. During one of the earliest encounters between the film's primary male characters, the police attempt to humiliate Cady by demanding he submit to a strip search. Their efforts fail miserably, and it becomes increasingly evident that it is Sam and his allies who are humbled before the exposure of Cady's masculinity (figure 11). In the original letter that had inspired the composition of "The White Negro," Mailer scandalously suggests that the "comedy" of desegregation lay in the fact that "the white loathes the idea of the Negro attaining equality in the classroom because the white feels the Negro already enjoys sensual superiority. So the white unconsciously feels that the balance has been kept, that the old arrangement was fair" (WN, 332). Cady, as the allegorical representative of the African American male, also appears to possess this kind of "sensual superiority," and hence the figurative restoration of order in the film must unfold by way of Sam's wresting from Cady symbols of phallic power.

In the climactic narrative sequence, Sam decides to use Nancy as bait

11 The police strip search Cady, from *Cape Fear* (1962).

to draw Cady out to a secluded dock on the Cape Fear River. Cady attacks Sam with a large wooden club, a thick metal bolt embedded in its end. Sam in turn pulls from the mud an even more potent phallus—the gun of police officer Kersek, earlier murdered by Cady—and shoots his foe. The rearmed Sam's decision to let the "wounded" Cady live out his life in prison makes this victory even more complete. With this gesture, the film rewrites the novel's conclusion as a version of G. W. F. Hegel's dialectic of the "lordship and bondage"—or in terms that have a deeper resonance in our context, the dialectic of "master and slave"—which requires that both subjects remain alive at the conclusion of their "life-and-death struggle": "If one of the adversaries remains alive but kills the other, he can no longer be recognized by the other; the man who has been defeated and killed does not recognize the victory of the conqueror. . . . Therefore, it does the man of the Fight no good to kill his adversary. He must overcome him 'dialectically.' That is, he must leave him life and consciousness, and destroy only his autonomy. He must overcome the adversary only insofar as the adversary is opposed to him and acts against him. In other words, he must enslave him."[28] In this resolution of the film's struggle, it is Sam who has achieved the position of the master, a fact whose "recognition" depends on Cady's continued existence. With Sam looming over him, the once again shirtless and now prostrate Cady tells him to kill him. Hesitating for a moment, Sam then declares, "No, no. That would be letting you off too easy, too fast. Your words, remember? . . . You're gonna live a long life—in a cage! That's where you belong, and that's where you're going. And this time, for life! Bang your head against the walls; count the years, the months, the hours, until the day you rot!" With this, the various fears that motivate the narrative action of the film—the fear of an interventionist federal government, the fear of the unleashed potential of the black man, and the fear of losing sexual authority—are, at least for the moment, laid to rest. Of course, as Hegel stresses as well, this is by no means the end of the story.

3

There are a number of ways that Scorsese's remake attempts to distance itself from its filmic predecessor. One interesting, and apparently minor, change occurs in the figure of the Bowden maid. In the original film she is one of only two African Americans ever to appear on-screen (the other being the janitor Cady hails). However, in Scorsese's film, this figure—whom earlier we could assume to have been a life-long resident of the South—has been transformed into a Latina named Graciella (Zully Montero), whose heavily accented English betrays her "foreign" origins (figure 12). This detail unveils a much more dramatic reorientation that takes place in the film, as the regional bounded location of its predecessor is now expanded into the fully integrated so-called New South, several of whose major urban centers of transnational economic and cultural flow—Charlotte, Raleigh, and Atlanta—provide the spatial coordinates for the film's action.[29]

A similar evacuation of older racial significations occurs in the figure of Cady. In a number of ways, this latest manifestation of the narrative menace seems a return to that found in the novel; or more precisely, this is how the other characters first perceive him. Rather than the white negro hipster evoked by Mitchum, Robert De Niro's once more hatless Cady is described as being "from the hills," "a Pentecostal cracker," and "white trash." With his distinctively rural Appalachian accent and dramatic religious tattoos, this Cady appears to meet these expectations. However, while Cady himself notes that he was housed in prison with poor rural whites, he later emphatically declares, "I'm no white trash piece of shit." And indeed, we are presented with much evidence throughout the film that would suggest Cady's distance from a clichéd vision of poor white Southern culture. His confession to Sam of being "sodomized" and forced into the role of a "fat hairy ugly hillbilly's wet dream" brings to mind the infamous rape

12 The maid Graciella arrives at the Bowden home, from *Cape Fear* (1991).

scene in John Boorman's *Deliverance* (1972), one of the classic American film fantasies about the menace of the white rural South. But here, Cady is identified with the urban victims in this earlier film rather than with its mountain-men perpetrators. Moreover, his self-education while in prison—a fact borne out by his repeated citations from Thomas Wolfe, Henry Miller, Friedrich Nietzsche, Dante, and the U.S. legal codes—further removes him from the stereotype of the ignorant and backward rural Southerner. The film figure of the "hostile redneck" finds its roots, Paul Loukides suggests, "in the television and newspaper accounts of the violent years of the civil rights movements."[30] The distancing of this latest incarnation of Cady from both his white predecessor in MacDonald's novel and his "black" one in the first *Cape Fear* thus signals the historical ground traveled from precisely those "violent years."

The referential dislocation that occurs in terms of this latest Cady makes the issue of how to "read" him one of the film's central concerns.[31] The solution offered to this dilemma similarly points toward the nature of the complex allegorical investments found in the narrative as a whole. In the latest version of the strip search scene, the police officer Lieutenant Elgart—played in a bit of film-historical self-referentiality by Mitchum—offers the most direct statement of this problem: on the exposure of Cady's heavily tattooed body, Elgart admits, "I don't know whether to *look at* him or *read* him." This opposition between "looking" and "reading" bears a striking resemblance to the contradiction at work in MacDonald's novel between "law" and "order." The first Sam's bureaucratic obedience to the letter of the law is structured like the act of looking, a passive acceptance of a world constituted by alien institutions. In later admitting the law to be "just a tool" to be deployed or set aside as one's changing needs require, Sam becomes a reader of his environment, able to shape it in a way that ensures the continuation of the social order he so deeply values.

However, the most recent *Cape Fear* departs dramatically from both its predecessors in suggesting that Sam's reading of the law is the root of the conflict. In this version, we learn that Sam, who has been transformed into the defense attorney at Cady's rape trial, decided to bury a key report concerning the sexual promiscuity of Cady's victim—an act that Sam acknowledges to be a violation both of the Sixth Amendment and of the American Bar Association rules of professional conduct—to guarantee that Cady would receive a long prison sentence. Early on, Sam remains confident that Cady would never learn what he had done because he believes his former client to be illiterate. However, the film viewer already knows that Sam is mistaken, for on his release from prison, Cady asserts that he had "already read" the books littering his cell. During the subsequent events, the positions of Sam and Cady are further reversed: Sam becomes the passive looker (through a two-way mirror during the police interrogation; from behind a trash bin during the assault on Cady; and later, through a boat window as his family is abused) and Cady the apparent maker of their world. Cady himself will render explicit the film's equation of the act of reading with power when he asserts, "I'm better than you all. I can out-learn you. I can out-read you, I can out-think you, and I can out-philosophize you. And I'm gonna out-last you."

Pam Cook has pointed out a gender coding of these two opposed states that recalls similar structures found both in *The Executioners* and in Mailer's essay: to be passive, a looker, is to be feminized, while the power to shape one's world is presented as a masculine attribute.[32] While the further significance of Cook's observation will become evident momentarily, there is also a way in which each of the film's three major female characters are guilty, along with Sam, of initially misreading Cady. Each of them first believes to have found in him an ally in their personal struggles with Sam: a drunk Lori Davis picks up Cady in a bar to punish Sam for standing her up; Danielle believes Cady to support her efforts to break free from her parent's authority; and Sam's wife, Leigh Bowden (Jessica Lange) expresses an admiration for Cady's success in frightening Sam and even later acknowledges that she empathizes with his feelings of loss, because she, too, has been betrayed by her husband, the viewer earlier having been informed that the family left Atlanta because of Sam's infidelities there. Cady, on the other hand, proves to be an expert reader of these women, and his ability to interpret their desires allows him to present himself as acting on their behalf—only to turn against them, like Sam, when it suits his own ends. And the fate of Lori Davis, as in the Diane Taylor incident in the first film, shows the terrible price women pay for their misreadings.

The act of properly reading Cady, or of unveiling his true nature, thus involves accurately locating the origin of the menace he embodies. In both *The Executioners* and in the first *Cape Fear*, the threat to the existing social order comes from the outside: respectively, from those living beyond the "charmed circle" of white middle-class suburbia and from the joint actions of a distant federal government and the racial Other. In the most recent film, however, the danger appears to be an internal one. This shift is beautifully illustrated in a brief scene directly preceding Cady's murders of Kersek and Graciella. Sam awakens to see Cady standing menacingly over him. When he comes to full consciousness, Cady has disappeared, but he tells his wife that he now realizes that all along Cady had been "in the house."

There are a number of possible ways of interpreting this change. In a conventional psychoanalytic reading, to which the film does at times invite us, Cady appears to be an emanation of the unconscious, a manifestation of Sam's incestuous desires for his daughter; or instead, a figure, linked with Sam, of Danielle's divided, ambivalent feelings about her father.[33] Equally plausibly, we could read Cady as the figural embodiment of an ethical struggle taking place within Sam—a struggle that further marks the distance of this remake from both of its predecessors. When we first see Sam on-screen, he is shown in conversation with his senior partner Tom Broadbent, played by the one-time Tennessee Republican Senator and 2008 presidential candidate, Fred Dalton Thompson. Sam informs him that he has successfully petitioned for a twenty-one-day postponement of Broadbent's daughter's divorce hearing, giving them the time needed to discover in which "S and L's and municipalities" the son-in-law has hidden his assets. As fragments of this discussion surface during the course of the subsequent action it becomes increasingly evident that Sam's actions on his partner's behalf will involve him once again in breaking the law. This new situation thus directly parallels Sam's earlier actions during Cady's

trial: in both cases Sam must circumvent the law to do what he has decided is right. Not surprisingly, then, Cady's actions ultimately lead Sam
to link in his mind past and present events. When Sam returns to his law
offices following the failed ambush of Cady, he informs Broadbent that he
will not do what was requested of him because "I've pulled a fast one and
it's come back and bit me on the ass in a major way." Although Broadbent
continues to rationalize their wrongdoings, Sam has learned to call his actions by their true names: "It's perjury, and it's bullshit, and I'm not going
to do it." In the same vein, Cady could be read as a manifestation of Sam's
guilt over his budding affair with Lori. As a figure from his Atlanta past,
Cady appears precisely at the moment at which Sam considers repeating
infidelities that had taken place in that city. Cady's brutal disfigurement
of the young woman again "saves" Sam by assuring this will not come to
pass.

While completely valid, I would argue that each of these interpretations has a function analogous to that of what Sigmund Freud describes
as "screen memories," distracting our attention away from and thereby
occluding from view the deeper social and political contents of the film.[34]
Moreover, neither the psychoanalytical nor the various ethical decodings
of the film's allegorical structure allow us adequately to account for the
additional woman in the Bowden household: the maid Graciella. By reading this character we can gain access to the film's displaced social and historical contents. Graciella, like her original in the Thompson film, remains
a marginal screen presence during most of the action. Even in her one significant scene, she turns out not to be herself: Cady, dressed in the maid's
clothing, sneaks up on and garrotes Kersek (figure 13). Only after the fact
do we learn that Cady has already killed the woman. However, in this way,
Graciella differs from the other three women in the film in that while
Cady may claim he "identifies" with the latter, he quite literally becomes
the former. Moreover, the contiguity of these two characters already had
been suggested earlier in the film, in a manner reminiscent of the visual
identification established in the first film between Cady and the African
American janitor. Cady's aggressive march into the camera on his release
from prison is followed by an abrupt cut to the Bowden household. There,
Graciella appears to emerge on-screen from the very camera eye entered
only a moment earlier by Cady.

This image of the cross-dressing murderer bears an obvious affinity to

13 Cady dressed in drag as Graciella, from *Cape Fear* (1991).

Alfred Hitchcock's *Psycho* (1960) and thereby again recalls the context of its filmic predecessor.[35] However, in Scorsese's film, the trajectory between the two characters has been reversed, so that much of the scene's terror arises from the momentary suggestion that the maid herself has been possessed by the spirit of Cady to enact a murderous vengeance on the family. Moreover, in *Cape Fear*, the link between the two characters is not Hitchcock's Oedipal one, but instead lies in their common social distance from the world of the Bowdens. In other words, what differentiates both Graciella and Cady from Sam, his family, and even Lori, is class position. In Scorsese's *Cape Fear*, we are thus witness to a veritable "return-of-the-repressed" of anxieties about class conflict, to an explosive resurfacing in the immediate post–Cold War world of these long-repressed fears.

However, the originality of this version of *Cape Fear* lies in the glimpses it offers of the new dimensions of class antagonism as they develop in the context of what has been variously described as an emergent postindustrial, post-Fordist, or service economy, one in which the New South indeed plays such an important role.[36] In his remarkable book *Throwaways*, Evan Watkins points out how the restructuring of the post–Second World War U.S. industrial economy—with its relatively high-wage, lifetime factory jobs and homogeneous (i.e., white and male) labor force—into a service economy defined by decreasing wages, part-time and piece-work employment, and the infusion of whole new categories of workers into the primary sectors of the economy has been accompanied by a dramatic reorganization of social space. The former distinctions between the place of work and the home have become increasingly blurred, Watkins argues, as the once sacrosanct domestic space has become both a primary site of wage labor in the service economy and the place where its products are consumed, often directly in the form of the labor itself. Moreover, in this new cultural and economic regime, the differentiation between public and private spheres also begins to break down. Under the Fordist economy ascendant in the three decades following the Second World War, "real" work had been located exclusively in the public sphere, as all forms of domestic labor were delegitimated—while the private sphere had been reserved for leisure activities, often involving new forms of commodity consumption.[37] In the service economy, on the other hand, "Leisure time is not necessarily time spent by yourself or with family and friends, but is often spent in situations where the space is crowded by any number of service workers performing any number of tasks."[38] The "destabilization" of these older boundaries, Watkins goes on to suggest, "brings together, in the same social spaces, people who occupy those spaces across multiple and often conflicting interests, values, and behaviors. And it thereby creates conditions that can lead to intense antagonisms, which are only heightened by the breakdown of categories that no longer supply the norms of behavior in the situation. Even the simplest, most routine everyday behavior can become a 'problem' requiring negotiation. . . . In a service economy, social space is anxious space."[39]

The anxieties produced by these restructurations are ratcheted up to a nightmarish intensity in Scorsese's *Cape Fear*. The presence of Cady and the class-coded source of conflict he embodies makes every public space the family moves through—from the movie theater to an ice cream parlor, from a city street to a Fourth of July parade—fraught with heretofore unexpected dangers; while the identification of Graciella and Cady locates a new site of potential class conflict within the home as well. Moreover, the very first image we are given of the Bowden home bears out Watkins's observation that in a service economy the boundary between the home and the place of wage labor has disappeared: Graciella is shown arriving to perform her cleaning duties while Leigh works in their home as a commercial illustrator (the latter another of the film's nods to *Vertigo*). The two also interestingly occupy opposite ends of the economic spectrum of the postindustrial economy, each producing an "immaterial good": on the one hand, that of a service, and on the other, information.[40] The family's apparent inability to escape Cady—a marked departure from both earlier narratives, where it is only Sam's decision to trap Cady that first allows the menace into the private sphere—signals the ways in which all space in our supersaturated consumerist economic fabric has become to varying degrees "anxious space."

Similarly at work in the allegorical narrative of this *Cape Fear* are what Watkins refers to as the "technoideological codings" of this emergent social formation: an ideological ensemble that writes older fixed or apparently natural categories such as race and gender, as well as the conflicts to which they have given rise, as "obsolete," while at the same stroke displacing productionist notions of determinate class position with a consumption-based model of "class-as-lifestyle, which features instead a mobile, performative individual agency as its central term of identification."[41] The figure of Cady in this most recent film exemplifies this transformation as well: no longer the overdetermined Other of the novel nor the equally determinate hypermasculinized "white *negro*" of the first film, this Cady moves rapidly between any number of different identity positions, including, apparently, that of a woman of color. Paradoxically, however, in this way Cady comes to be identified less with the subject position of the worker in a service economy—figured most prominently by Graciella who, after all, only inhabits a single identity in the film narrative, that of a gendered and racialized working body—and more with what Watkins describes as that of the consumer: for the activity of a performative making of the self, what above I described as a "reading" of the world, is fundamentally structured as one of consumption. Cady has thus learned to maximize the resources he has acquired to negotiate the service economy's "encounter structures of performance"—those formed between the service provider and consumer—in a way that would seem to turn any apparent older "natural" class hierarchies on their head: the underclass Cady seizes the site of active reading-consumption, while the upper-middle-class Bowdens become relegated to a position of passivity.

The presence of this allegorical narrative content suggests an additional twist to the persistent gender codings remarked on by Cook: for in this emergent social formation, Watkins notes, there has occurred a transvaluation of an older gender hierarchy, such that the role of the worker increasingly "appears relatively feminized in relation to the masculinization of consumer positionality."[42] In the final confrontation on the Cape Fear River, these two positions are reversed one final time. Sam's chaining of Cady's foot to a piece of wreckage determines the ultimate fate of his opponent, whose repositioning as a passive "looker" is then visually reinforced by a close-up of his eyes as he sinks into the dark waters of the Cape Fear River. As in both earlier texts, Sam resumes the masculine role only through an utter and complete "feminization" of Cady. However, the nature of the masculine role he assumes differs dramatically from that found in either predecessor. Sam now holds the power to perform in his world, and in so doing, he becomes a version of the service economy's ideal consumer.

The figure of Graciella unveils the limits of such an ideological formation: for although gender and race take the form of mobile categories within the film, in this text, as in the contemporary real-world service economy, the class-positioned subject who is denied access to the resources necessary for a performative play of selves is precisely the person who also inhabits the now "obsolete" identity categories of woman and person of color. That is, while Cady can become Graciella or even Sam himself, Graciella lacks the performative resources to become either. As an apparent residuum of an older fixed or natural coding system, she becomes as "disposable" as the other obsolete objects in the narrative, such as those racist ideologies that I looked at in the beginning of this chapter expressed by and through Kersek—a disposal operation that the film neatly performs in both cases through the actions of Cady.

This fundamentally contradictory tension plays itself out again on a second level in the narrative. The suggestion of Sam's guilt, his burden of responsibility for creating the menace, provides a critical gesture absent from the pedagogical machinery of the film's two predecessors. In terms of the latest film's allegorical structure, Sam represents the middle classes whose often criminal manipulations of the economy exacerbated the growing inequities of the current economic and social arrangement— especially by way of those 1980s commonplaces, insider trading, corporate buyouts, and the savings and loan scandal briefly alluded to in the film. (Such schemes are, as is well known, also at the root of the personal wealth of the most recent Bush president, and they are given breathtaking visual form in the massive pencil drawings of Mark Lombardi's Narrative Structures series.)[43] Late in the film, Cady tells Sam, "Now you and I will truly be the same." The irony here is that they always already were the same, Sam's violences perhaps more covert, but having no less devastating consequences for his victims. The explosive appearance of Cady in the Bowdens' world thus signals the growing anxiety on the part of these classes about what will happen when their victims begin to come to consciousness of the crimes committed against them. The chickens of the excesses of the 1980s, the film suggests, are by the 1990s already coming home to roost, a fact borne out perhaps nowhere more dramatically than in one of the first major conflagrations of the post–Cold War world, the 1992 Los Angeles uprising, an event whose roots lie in the economic re-structurings alluded to above and that was thus, as many commentators pointed out, "about" class in the ways its 1965 predecessor seemed to be focused on race.[44] Of course, as this most recent version of *Cape Fear* makes explicit, race and class (and gender) are in this new world order, as much as in the old, still inextricably linked. Moreover, as in the real-world case of Los Angeles, the film hints that the lessons from this event have yet to be learned: with the successful suppression of the uprising of Cady, the incident, as Danielle's final monologue suggests, is rapidly repressed back into the depths of the collective political unconscious, giving the illu-sion, at least, of another awakening from the nightmare of history.

The film, however, ultimately retreats from the import of this critique, reinscribing Cady's menace by way of one final natural, or more precisely, as we shall see in the following chapter, "naturalist" coding. That is, the film suggests that the real origins of Cady's violence lie beyond the hori-zon of human history, in an elemental force that seems to spring, like the storms raging during the final confrontation, from the earth itself. This ultimately populist equation of Cady's violence with the inhuman forces of the natural world rewrites the film's historical narrative as a mytho-logical one, the family's murder of Cady thus becoming a version of the repressed primal act of violence that founds civilization. Ontologizing vio-lence in this way, the film negates even the possibility of imagining any alternative to the current social arrangement, thereby replicating the im-passe of much of contemporary liberal thought when faced with the reali-ties of class conflict given rise to by the new economies (again exemplified in the response to the events in Los Angeles). Indeed, by suggesting that any kind of order, even an unjust one, might be preferable to the anarchy that would follow the unleashing of such natural forces—be it Cady or the service economy's underclass—the film's pointed liberal critique falls into a cynicism that makes it hard to distinguish from the overt conservatism

Five

WHERE THE PROSPECTIVE HORIZON IS OMITTED

Naturalism, Dystopia, and Politics in *Fight Club* and *Ghost Dog*

Everything living, says Goethe, has an atmosphere around it; everything real in general, because it is life, process, and can be a correlate of objective imagination, has a horizon. An inner horizon, extending vertically as it were, in the self-dark, an external one of great breadth, in the world-light; and the regions behind both horizons are filled with the same utopia, are consequently identical in the Ultimum. Where the prospective horizon is omitted, reality only appears as become, as dead, and it is the dead, namely naturalists and empiricists, who are burying their dead here. Where the prospective horizon is continuously included in the reckoning, the real appears as what it is in concreto: as the path-network of dialectical processes which occur in an unfinished world, in a world which would not be in the least changeable without the enormous future: real possibility in that world. Together with that Totum which does not represent the isolated whole of a respective section of process, but the whole of the subject-matter pending in process overall, hence still tendential and latent. This alone is realism, it is of course inaccessible to that schematism which knows everything in advance, which considers its uniform, in fact even formalistic, stencil to be reality. Reality without real possibility is not complete, the world without future-laden properties does not deserve a glance, an art, a science any more than that of the bourgeois conformist.

ERNST BLOCH, *The Principle of Hope*

THIS LONG EPIGRAPH is taken from Ernst Bloch's monumental inquiry in *The Principle of Hope* into the irrepressibility of the utopian impulse.[1] According to Bloch, the naturalists and empiricists, with their careful schematic mappings of an apparently fixed and closed social reality and their assumptions about the law-governed structure of human nature, deny the presence of history, of the real possibility of change, located within any present. Although Bloch is referring to a much larger philosophical and aesthetic debate, the opposition he sets up here —

that between naturalism and utopia—also usefully recalls an important event in the literary history of the latter part of the nineteenth century. Fredric Jameson argues that the dramatic reemergence of utopian fiction in the late nineteenth century needs to be understood, at least in part, as a response to the asphyxiating historical closure of the then reigning literary naturalisms.[2] This is as much the case for William Morris, whose *News from Nowhere* (1890) constitutes a reply to the work of the great English naturalist writer George Gissing, as it is for Morris's other primary interlocutor, Edward Bellamy, the latter decrying the "profound pessimism of the literature of the last quarter of the nineteenth century" and writing his hugely influential narrative utopia, *Looking Backward* (1888), as an attempt to provide an alternative to it.[3]

If this latest manifestation of the literary utopia thus represents a dialectical negation of the vision of literary naturalism, might we then be able to speak of what G. W. F. Hegel names the negation of the negation, a third form that recapitulates and subsumes elements of both aspects of what should now be understood as an initial contradiction?[4] In other words, what happens when the thoroughgoing pessimism about the present moment is suddenly transported into the otherworldly space of the utopian fiction? It is precisely such a negation of the negation, I want to argue here, that gives rise in the late nineteenth century and the early twentieth to perhaps the most influential and productive subgenre of the modern narrative utopia: that of the *dystopia*.

Any discussion of the dystopian form must now come to grips with the history of its development and transformation in the course of the past century offered in Tom Moylan's *Scraps of the Untainted Sky: Science Fiction, Utopia, Dystopia* (2001). Challenging many of the conventional assumptions about these works, Moylan argues that dystopian fictions are not "texts that temperamentally refuse the possibility of radical social transformation"—and in this they could be understood to be as dialectically other to what Bloch and Jameson see as the "Anti-Utopianism" of literary naturalism as they are to their more properly utopian predecessors. "Rather," Moylan maintains, "they look quizzically, skeptically, critically not only at the present society but also at the means needed to transform it."[5] Moylan's focus then moves from the more general category of the dystopia to what he calls the "critical dystopia," a textual practice first emerging in the late 1980s in response to the conservative political retrenchments of the Reagan-Thatcher late Cold War period, and exemplified for him by Kim Stanley Robinson's *Gold Coast* (1988), Octavia Butler's *Parable* novels (1993 and 1998), which I discuss in chapter 8, and Marge Piercy's *He, She, and It* (1991). The "strongly, and more self-reflexively 'critical'" stance of these texts, Moylan crucially maintains, does *not* signal the emergence of "an entirely new generic form but rather a significant retrieval and re-functioning of the most progressive possibilities inherent in dystopian narrative."[6] Moylan then concludes that such texts "negotiate the necessary pessimism of the generic dystopia with an open, militant, utopian stance that not only breaks through the hegemonic enclosure of the text's alternative world but also self-reflexively refuses the anti-utopian temptation that lingers like a dormant virus in every dystopian account."[7]

There are two crucial points that I would like to take from Moylan's reading. First, he helps us recognize a difference between the utopian and dystopian forms that goes deeper than the familiar "good place–bad place" opposition. Of the new critical dystopias, Moylan notes, "As an anticipatory machine in that new context, the critical dystopias resist both hegemonic and oppositional orthodoxies (in their radical and reformist variants) even as they refunction a larger, more totalizing critique of the political economy itself. They *consequently inscribe a space for a new form of political opposition*."[8] Such an "inscription" of a new space for political opposition is, in fact, I would argue following Moylan's lead, characteristic of *all* dystopias (something then "formally and politically foregrounded in the recent works").[9] In short, the subject of utopian desire in the dystopia is *politics* itself—of agency and of a kick-starting of the engine of history in a moment when it seems to many to be terminally stalled. To put this another way, utopia is always already a politics *in potentia*, what Slavoj Žižek, in turn drawing on Alain Badiou, describes as an Event: "An intervention that cannot be accounted for in the terms of its pre-existing 'objective conditions,'" and indeed whose success (pace Bellamy) or failure in "seizing the masses" then helps to define these very conditions.[10] On the other hand, the dystopia, and especially the recent critical dystopia, defiantly holds open, in the conditions of dimmest radical political possibility—as in the years of the global neoliberal onslaught—precisely the hope that such a politics might reemerge. In this way, the critical dystopia becomes a self-consuming text, one that narrates the desired abolition of the very conditions of its own emergence, such that politics once again see emerging a fundamental and often irresolvable contradiction between the author's or the text's explicit political orientation and what Jameson calls the "ideology of form" — that is, "'form' apprehended as content . . . formal processes as sedimented content in their own right, as carrying ideological messages of their own, distinct from the ostensible or manifest content of the works."[13]

As I noted above, Moylan locates the paradigmatic expression of the modern dystopia in Forster's short story "The Machine Stops," showing in great detail precisely how this text sets the formal pattern that will be taken up by the works following it. In a long footnote near the beginning of his discussion of this particular text, Moylan explains why he views Jack London's earlier *The Iron Heel* (1908), "though politically preferable to Forster's" work, as outside the bounds of the subgenre of the dystopia proper: "It is *almost* a dystopia, or perhaps a 'proto-dystopia.' . . . To put it more formally, the dystopian genre (complete with its eutopian surplus of the future Brotherhood of Man, encoded, as in Orwell and Atwood, in the textual apparatus of the text — in this case a footnote) is born within the pages of this text."[14] While the dialectical history I outlined above would relocate works like *The Iron Heel* within the tradition of the modern dystopia (which is not the same thing as denying Moylan's insights into the role Forster's story plays in the later formal codification of the subgenre), it is precisely its status as such a liminal case, wherein the seams between its various components remain evident on the surface, that makes it so useful for my purposes here. For the tension Moylan notes in London's fiction makes evident the contradiction between London's left-wing socialist political impulses and the despairing claims of his naturalist form — a naturalism even more readily apparent in the fictions *The Son of the Wolf* (1900), *The Call of the Wild* (1903), and *White Fang* (1906), by which the turn-of-the-century American author is best remembered today. This contradiction manifests itself in the text of *The Iron Heel* in terms of a formal dislocation, the utopian space literally located on the narrative's horizons, in a series of footnotes written by the future historian Anthony Meredith to the older rediscovered manuscript narrating the adventures of Avis and Ernest Everhard. Utopia then becomes no more than a ghostly frame to the detailed naturalistic portrait of the world located in the main body of the text.

However, an even more significant absence in *The Iron Heel*, and one that will also be a central part of the subgenre to which London's text helps give rise, is any vision of revolution, either as a specific punctual event or a series of tendencies within the near future, by which the radically other human situation haunting the borders of the narrative might become material. Indeed, the radical party on which London pins so much hope resolves itself into a figure for the emergent corporate and state bureaucracies that would come to cast such deep shadows across the history of the then new century.[15] Vanishing in London's text is thus any mediatory link between the dystopia and absent present utopian future—indeed, as the former becomes ascendant during the course of the narrative, the latter resolves itself into little more than a formal placeholder, an expression of desire rather than hope, for something that London finds increasingly unimaginable. (A similar dilemma is apparent in one of the other most influential dystopian visions of the twentieth century, Yevgeny Zamyatin's *We* (1921), the text's utopia located in the horizon "world" of the "infinite revolution."[16]) A dawning realization of the terrible power of the narrative apparatus he sets into motion here is indicated by London's inability, or unwillingness, to complete his central narrative, the text literally breaking off in midsentence: to do so, he necessarily would have to show the imminent defeat of the global alliance of socialist parties, the final victory of the Iron Heel, and the full emergence of a three hundred–year-long dystopian future of oligarchical rule. Indeed, such a narrative completion would sunder utterly the link between the utopian and naturalist tendencies at work in the text.

The link between dystopia and the formal properties of naturalism is also made explicit by London's and Zamyatin's direct descendant, George Orwell, who, in a May 1947 letter to F. J. Warburg, the British publisher of *Nineteen Eighty-Four*, writes, "I will tell you now that this is a novel about the future—that is, it is in a sense a fantasy, but in the form of a *naturalistic novel*. That is what makes it a difficult job—of course as a book of anticipations it would be comparatively simple to write."[17] Moreover, Orwell already had acknowledged a deep admiration for the work of Gissing, and there is even evidence that he had his English predecessor in mind when developing his vision of Oceania.[18] In one of his last essays published before his most famous novel, Orwell describes the Victorian England pictured in Gissing's fiction in terms that bear an uncanny resemblance to the "future" dystopian world of *Nineteen Eighty-Four*: "The grime, the stupidity, the ugliness, the sex-starvation, the furtive debauchery, the vulgarity, the bad manners, the censoriousness — these things were unnecessary, since the puritanism of which they were a relic no longer upheld the structure of society. People who might, without becoming less efficient, have been reasonably happy chose instead to be miserable, inventing senseless taboos with which to terrify themselves."[19]

While their socialism teaches Gissing, London, and Orwell that such a situation must always be viewed as the consequence of human "choice," and hence open to the possibility of change, their fascination with the dark determinism of naturalism threatens to blot out this insight altogether, grounding the present catastrophe in human nature itself, something expressed in both London's and Orwell's cases as a deep human lust for power that will inevitably derail any project of radical transformation. Of course, Orwell will push these tendencies to their final conclusions, making *Nineteen Eighty-Four* for so many of its readers a full-blown formal anti-utopia — "a non-existent society described in considerable detail and normally located in time and space that the author intended a contemporaneous reader to view as a criticism of utopianism or of some particular eutopia," as Lyman Tower Sargent usefully defines the practice.[20] I wonder, though, if anti-utopia is a position that any human being can inhabit for very long and if such a pure form of an assault on the utopian imaginary exists. For indeed, most anti-utopias on further inspection turn out to be — and this is something very much the case in *Nineteen Eighty-Four* — what Karl Mannheim calls "conservative utopias," a form of "counter-utopian" thinking wherein "not only is attention turned to the past and the attempt made to rescue it from oblivion, but the presentness and immediacy of the whole past becomes an actual experience."[21] In works such as Orwell's, it is these nostalgically longed-for past utopias that are likewise located on the textual horizons — think of Winston Smith's childhood, his golden country, the sanctuary above Mr. Charrington's shop, and the glass paperweight containing the Indian Ocean coral — while the naturalist vision remains the dominant note in the text.

Equally significant, these later dystopias betray another deep formal link to the traditions of nineteenth-century naturalist fictions, and this turns on the figuration of radical political agency itself. Does any one anymore (or indeed ever) really find I-330's calls for "infinite revolution" or Smith's dogged faith in the Proles — the latter devastatingly named by Raymond

Williams a "stale revolutionary romanticism"[22] — an effective rebuttal to the deeply naturalist visions of the essential viciousness, selfishness, and cowardice of human nature offered by Zamyatin's Benefactor or Orwell's O'Brien? These classical texts thus establish a pattern that will haunt the tradition of dystopian writing throughout the twentieth century: desiring a radical change of affairs, but pulling short of endorsing any mechanism or agency by which such a change might come about, these dystopias oscillate between the radical openness of the utopia and the asphyxiating closure of naturalism. Indeed, as we shall see, it is exactly this dilemma that marks the two popular recent film dystopias that I will examine in the pages that follow.

I

What makes the two 1999 films I will discuss — David Fincher's surprise hit *Fight Club* and Jim Jarmusch's *Ghost Dog* — so interesting is the way they adapt the formal strategies of the dystopia, as well as its precursors in naturalist fiction, to the new situation of what has been variously described as an emergent global postindustrial, post-Fordist, or service economy. To be precise, both narratives are located on the horizons of dystopia proper — *Fight Club* is more akin to what Moylan calls the "proto-dystopia," focusing on the emergence of a truly dystopian (and perhaps, utopian) "near-future situation," while *Ghost Dog* is deeply related to the more recent generic kin of SF and the dystopia, and one deeply mined in recent years in film treatments, the superhero comic-book narrative.[23] Moreover, these two films express a particular kinship to one of the currently dominant strands of dystopian fiction, what Jameson describes as the postmodern "dirty realism" of cyberpunk, in which "what is implied is simply an ultimate historicist breakdown in which we can no longer imagine the future at all. . . . Under those circumstances . . . a formerly futurological science fiction . . . turns into mere 'realism' and an outright representation of our present."[24] (The great 1990s literary example of such a "realist" critical dystopia is Leslie Marmon Silko's *Almanac of the Dead* [1991]). The blasted urban landscapes of both films are very much those of cyberpunk fiction: postindustrial urban cores, filled with abandoned buildings, decaying factories, and the waste products and "throwaway" populations of twentieth-century capitalist culture. *Ghost Dog* is shot in a decaying and nearly empty Jersey City, and we learn that the decrepit Victorian home of the central characters in *Fight Club*, constructed specifically for the film, has "no neighbors, just some warehouses and a paper mill." Moreover, both films are deeply critical of contemporary corporate and consumer culture. And finally, like the true critical dystopias examined by Moylan, both films work to move beyond this negative critical gesture and to (re)imagine history in the form of the collective political agencies that would lead us beyond the present impasse.

I want to begin my discussion of *Fight Club* elsewhere, however, with an image that has been very much on the minds of many people since September 2001: that of skyscraper towers falling down. In the final movement of the film, members of the paramilitary terrorist organization, Project Mayhem, under the direction of the film's protagonist, the schizophrenic "Tyler Durden" (whether Tyler is actually his name, or simply that of his fantasy double, is never made clear), have planted explosives in the corporate skyscraper towers of the credit card companies. This task is undertaken in the belief that the destruction of the global debt record—read in this context as a figure of finance capital in toto—will eradicate the current order and open up history to the possibility of a new beginning. In the one direct statement of a utopian vision in the film (and bearing out Moylan's point that these texts always contain such a horizon), Brad Pitt's Tyler Durden tells his double, the injured and recumbent "Jack" (Edward Norton)—in a scene whose visual presentation recalls the interview with a T. S. Eliot–quoting Colonel Kurtz in Francis Ford Coppola's *Apocalypse Now* (1979)—that he dreams of a world where the skyscrapers are overrun with vines, where cornfields have been planted in the city plots, and where we all wear leather clothing meant to last a lifetime: a primitivist utopia not unlike that found in the "scraps of the untainted sky" seen at the end of Forster's "The Machine Stops," the Mephi garden world of Zamyatin's *We*, Winston Smith's mythic golden country, the Uganda of Ignatius Donnelly's *Caesar's Column* (1890), the postapocalyptic landscape of George R. Stewart's *Earth Abides* (1949), or the various reverse evolutions of J. G. Ballard's dystopias (the latter to which the film's vision seems especially indebted). All these examples, as well as the original studio version of *Blade Runner* to which I alluded in chapter 3, raise some interesting questions about the persistence of primitivist nostalgia in the dystopian narrative form. Indeed, we might ask to what degree dystopias, like their natural-

14 Twinned towers collapse as Tyler and Marla look on, from *Fight Club* (1999).

ist predecessors, are first and foremost responses to, and expressions of the desire to move beyond, the general modern condition Henri Lefebvre describes as "urbanization": "Not only has capitalism laid hold of preexisting space, of the Earth, but it also tends to produce a space of its own. How can this be? The answer is: through and by means of urbanization, under the pressure of the world market; and in accordance with the law of the reproducible and the repetitive, by abolishing spatial and temporal differences, by destroying nature and nature's time."[25]

In the film's final scene, Norton's character stands holding hands with his girlfriend, Marla Singer (Helena Bonham Carter) (figure 14). Together they watch from their skyscraper perch the buildings around them imploding and then falling to the ground, an image that now cannot but recall the collapse of the two towers of the World Trade Center (uncannily enough, after all the other buildings around them have collapsed, two identical towers remain in the center of the frame, frozen for an instance before they, too, begin their downward plunge); however, in the moment of its original release, what this image would have brought to mind most readily was what had been until 2001 the single greatest act of non–state sponsored terrorism in U.S. history, Timothy McVeigh's April 19, 1995, bombing of the Alfred P. Murrah Federal Building in Oklahoma City.

Oddly enough, at this moment, we also get a brief flash of a penis, a film still image apparently crudely spliced into the main narrative action. This is meant to recall Tyler's earlier confession that he used his employment as a theater film reel changer as an opportunity to splice into Disney and children's animation pictures still images from pornographic movies: the audience does not consciously "see" these images, but they do have the powerful effect of upsetting their consumerist slumbers, if only for the briefest of moments. (The DVD copy of the film launches with a similarly detourned version of the FBI warning and copyright notice, overlaid by the manic laughter of Tyler.)

Both the image of the skyscraper "coming down" and the strategy of *détournement* represented by Tyler's guerilla action (we also see him urinating into the soup at the upscale hotel at which he works as a waiter) are figures that have become something of mainstays of contemporary cultural studies analysis. Indeed, one of the now classic texts of cultural studies, Michel de Certeau's "Walking in the City," opens with an image not unlike that seen in *Fight Club*'s narrative frame. In his essay, Certeau imagines the intellectual-critic standing on the 110th floor of the World Trade Center. In this privileged location, he is "lifted out of the city's grasp" and transfigured into a voyeur, consuming the abstract image of the city as "a universe that is constantly exploding."[26] The intellectual fiction at work in this scene, according to Certeau, is that we can be transformed into "a viewpoint and nothing more," a passive witness to an aestheticized image of the ongoing catastrophe that is modernity. Such a position, however, is one that makes politics unimaginable. Thus Certeau issues a call for intellectuals to come "down" from these heights and into the space of the "ordinary practitioners of the city," those who "make use of spaces that cannot be seen" from the perspective at the top of the system, and those to whom the book is dedicated—"To the ordinary man."[27]

In a brilliant engagement with Certeau's essay, as well as with a number of other cultural studies texts, Meaghan Morris notes that this now commonplace "intellectual ritual of renouncing the heights" bears a striking parallel to what she calls a populist art of comic reduction (comparing corporate towers to penises and dildos to "deflate" their pretensions) and indeed betrays the *populist* political resonances of so much current cultural studies work, as in, for example, Laura Kipnis's influential reading of the transgressive "class-antagonistic" politics of *Hustler* magazine.[28] Such gestures, Morris goes on to argue, more often than not miss "the point about the role of the 'urbanization of capital' in creating economic and social inequalities, precisely at a time when its operations in our cities are reaching new heights of intensity and savagery, directly affecting our lives."[29]

That the political identifications of Fincher's film are deeply populist as well is made explicit early on. We have two veterans of popular neopopulist cinema at work here: Fincher, whose earlier *Aliens 3* (1992) contains an assault on a Japanese-identified corporate power, and Edward Norton Jr., who until this film was best known for his chilling portrayal of a young demagogic Southern California white supremacist in *American History X* (1998, dir. Tony Kaye). Moreover, the Chuck Palahniuk novel on which the film is based also makes clear its links to an earlier tradition of populist skyscraper fictions. The climactic scene in the novel differs from that in the film in that in the former we find our protagonist *on* the roof of the world's tallest building (in this case, the single structure Project Mayhem plans to destroy); his apparent suicide attempt is then interrupted by the appearance of Marla and a group of his supporters—a scene that recalls the rooftop climax of Frank Capra's depression-era populist classic, *Meet John Doe* (1941).[30]

Crucially, however, Fincher's film offers us a new kind of populist mass, one produced by the particular conditions of the postindustrial service economy: the members of the Fight Club are, as Tyler describes them, "an entire generation waiting tables and pumping gas—slaves with white collars . . . working jobs we hate so we can buy shit we don't need." Later, he informs the police chief who dares to challenge this nascent revolutionary collective: "The people you are after are the people you depend on. We cook your meals, we haul your trash, we connect your calls, we drive your ambulances, we guard you while you sleep." They, like the second *Cape Fear*'s Leigh and Graciella before them, are all involved in what Michael Hardt and Antonio Negri call "production as *immaterial labor*—that is, labor that produces an immaterial good, such as a service, a cultural product, knowledge, or communication."[31] Moreover, while the endless cycle of consumerism that was so central to the post–Second World War Fordist economic and cultural revolution continues unabated, the older "guaranteed" and high-wage positions that had also been such a fundamental part of this mode of regulation and regime of accumulation have disappeared without a trace.[32] The depths of alienation and dissatisfaction of these men have thus drawn them first into the cult of sensation represented by the Fight Clubs, and then into the organized, highly disciplined, and lethally effective terrorist organization, Project Mayhem. That the Fight Clubs themselves draw on some of the central tropes of naturalist fictions, especially in its U.S. manifestations (London, for example, wrote newspaper articles and fiction about boxing), is borne out by Henry Giroux in his critical analysis of the film: "Violence in *Fight Club* is treated as a sport, a crucial component that lets men connect with each other through the overcoming of fear, pain, and fatigue. . . . Violence in this instance signals its crucial function in both affirming the natural 'fierceness' of men and in providing them with a concrete experience that allows them to connect at some primal level."[33]

Yet the film itself is finally not really about these men: throughout they remain largely nameless presences, classically naturalist representatives of what Georg Lukács calls social stereotypes rather than full characters.[34] Indeed, after the shooting death of one of their founding members, a new mantra arises in the group: "Only in death does a member of Project Mayhem have a name." Our protagonist, on the other hand, does have a name—at least one for his followers—and, even more important, he has a history. He is, when we first meet him, firmly ensconced within the young urban middle class, working as a "recall coordinator"—one of the new post-Fordist information managers engaging in the second of Hardt and Negri's three types of immaterial labor, "the immaterial labor of analytical and symbolic tasks"—traveling across the country investigating gruesome automobile crashes and evaluating the cost effectiveness of general recalls for the auto manufacturers.[35] However, he, too, is trapped in the depths of alienation: he is an insomniac, finding no reward or pleasure in his work, detached from everyone around him (he becomes addicted to support groups because "when people think you're dying they really listen to you instead of just waiting for their turn to talk"), and, most important, deeply dissatisfied with the consumerist ethos in which he lives. He is someone who, as his schizophrenic double tells him, is "looking for a way to change [his] life." He, or rather his double, accomplishes this by blowing up his upper-floor condo dwelling, as well as all his material possessions (he later tells an investigating detective, "this wasn't just stuff, it was me"), moving into an abandoned structure in the city' decrepit and nearly abandoned industrial district (another sign of the post-Fordist reality the characters inhabit) and ultimately launching the Fight Club movement. The film's main characters thus replicate Certeau's gesture of coming down from the tower's heights. And indeed, the film opens with Norton's character and his Tyler Durden persona already in the tower, the main body of the narrative taking the form of an extended flashback of his movement down from these former heights. In this way, too, he appears to become one with the very different alienations of the "common man."

This populist gesture of "coming down" into the world of the "people" is a central one of both naturalist and dystopian fiction: think of Frank Norris's or London's regular evocations of "the People" or Orwell's romanticization of the Proles—and the last line of *Meet John Doe* is, "There they are Norton, the People; try and lick that." However, this gesture is a deeply ambivalent one that finally maintains an unbridgeable gap between the "us" of the middle-class protagonist and the "them" of the people. In his discussion of Gissing's *The Nether World*, Jameson argues that the "conceptual and organizational framework" of naturalist fiction "is not that of social class but rather that very different nineteenth-century ideological concept which is the notion of 'the people,' as a kind of general grouping of the poor and 'underprivileged' of all kinds, from which one can recoil in revulsion, but to which one can also, as in some political populisms, nostalgically 'return' as to some telluric source of strength."[36] The same combination of fascination and revulsion—a schizophrenia of the naturalist populist form as deep as that of the film's protagonist—is evident in *Fight Club*. For precisely when the original Fight Clubs metamorphosize into Project Mayhem, that is, from a therapeutic movement of de-alienation to a political one of collective action and social change, the film's attitude toward it changes dramatically. Suddenly, the sympathetic image of a deeply alienated public becomes one of a secret underground fascist organization, threatening to consume society in a maelstrom of violence and destruction à la the then haunting image of McVeigh. It is from this reality—one that he is responsible for—that our protagonist rapidly retreats, slaying his populist double and returning to his old middle-class self (the concluding pages of Palahniuk's novel are in fact far more ambiguous about the nature of this return). In a symbolic reversal of Certeau's gesture, he has returned to the heights of the tower and from there bears witness to an aestheticized destruction of the city, the window of the building serving as a double to the television screen through which so many in the United States and elsewhere remained captivated in rapt fascination throughout September 11, 2001, and the days that followed by the seemingly endlessly repeated footage of the attacks and the two towers' collapse. Žižek, in his analysis of the film, notes of this final image, "in accordance with late capitalist global commodification, *Fight Club* offers as an 'experiential commodity' the very attempt to explode the universe of commodities; instead of concrete political practice, we get an aestheticist explosion of violence."[37] Or to put this another way, while toying with what Badiou now identifies as a deeply modernist "passion for the real" — manifest in whatever terribly misguided way as well in both the McVeigh and the al-Qaeda attacks (and it is only these fundamentalist others, Žižek maintains, who seem to "believe" in our moment) — the film finally leaves us with what Jameson identifies as a Cold War "late modernist" aesthetic ideology and its privileged trope of irony.[38]

It is at this point then that we finally arrive at the real political center of this film. The protagonist's schizophrenia is a classic example of the narrative device of splitting Sigmund Freud discusses in his analysis of E. T. A. Hoffmann's "The Sandman."[39] But here we have moved from Freud's individual psychoanalytical framework into a larger social and cultural one, where the Other serves as the screen image onto which Norton's character, as well as the film's audience, can project their deepest and most dangerous political desires. Indeed, his double Tyler tells him, "You were looking for a way to change your life. You could not do this on your own. All the ways you wished you could be, that's me."

And yet the film remains fundamentally divided in its view of these desires. In a way, then, critiques of the film such as those advanced by Giroux miss a crucial point about *Fight Club*. To say that film "mimics fascism's militarisation and masculinisation of the public sphere with its exultation of violence as a space in which men can know themselves better," and to critique its blatant "misogynistic representation of women, and its intimation that violence is the only means through which men can be cleansed of the dire effect women have on the shaping of their identities" (which would make Fincher's film, *The Panic Room* [2002] appear as an attempt to redress these shortcomings), is in fact to ignore the fundamental disavowal of these representations and politics that occurs not only in the climactic scene in the tower but throughout.[40] The film is as easily seen as a parody of exactly this hypermasculine and protofascist imagery as it is of all other forms of self-help discourse. In other words, any approach that imagines that the film takes its own vision seriously heals the division that structures both the psyche of its protagonist and its larger narrative.

Thus the general assault on social and cultural alienation that has been the focus of much of the conversation about this film actually serves as a pretense for investigating a far more troubling issue plaguing our present: a more fundamental sense of *political* alienation, the radical sense of otherness that too many feel when faced with the prospects of their own potential for action—or at least this is the view this film attempts to reinforce. The fundamental structure here is an ethical rather than a political one—and it may be this ethical stance that constitutes part of the legacy of naturalism to dystopian fictions (and it is thus no surprise that the latter form flourishes precisely in the post–Second World War context of late modernism), a legacy that the best of the critical dystopian fictions work to overcome.[41] Locating these political desires within the fundamentally alien Other, the film can conveniently also maintain its disavowal of them. Moreover, by conveniently taking up the existential burden of (political) action, the fundamentally Other populist underclasses of this film—alien invaders not unlike those in *Independence Day*, the film I will discuss in my following chapter—do the dirty work of "beginning" history once again, fusing a new collective in opposition to them. The real fascism hinted at in this film is thus not that found in Project Mayhem, but in that found in the state reaction that would surely arise as a response to its appearance. And indeed, after the events of September 2001, too much of this dystopian fantasy becomes actuality.

2

Although there are no towers in *Ghost Dog*, this film also opens with an invocation of the scopic view from above, as we "see" the landscape of the city from the aerial perspective of a pigeon flying overhead. The viewer then once more comes down from this distanced viewpoint, diving back into the urban texture of the city and meeting this film's central protagonist, the African American samurai, Ghost Dog (Forest Whitaker). This gesture of taking the viewer/reader into the lives of the "other half" is, of course, also very much part of the tradition of literary naturalism (Stephen Crane's *Maggie, A Girl of the Streets* [1893] is exemplary in this regard), and the decayed urban setting of this film, as well as the brutally violent contest between two opponents, meets some of the basic expectations of the form as well.

The film makes its links to the original historical context of naturalism explicit in a number of other ways. *Ghost Dog* is the second part of a 1990s diptych by Jarmusch exploring the environmental, social, and cultural consequences of industrial modernization in the United States. The first installment, *Dead Man* (1996), is set in an 1870s U.S. West in the midst of its transformation by modern industrial capitalism and follows the adventures of an Eastern clerk, "William Blake" (Johnny Depp), and his Native American companion, Nobody (Gary Farmer), as they encounter the "dark Satanic mills," violence, cannibalism, and other destructive energies of the emerging industrial and mercantile economy. *Ghost Dog* then takes us to the other end of both the continent and this history, as the factories of the first film now lie in silent ruin. The central protagonists of the first film are very much like those in *Ghost Dog*, cultural hybrids caught between worlds in which they have no place (and the character of Nobody also makes a brief cameo appearance in *Ghost Dog*).[42] Together, both films offer a devastating revisionist commentary on the violences — environmental, racial, and cultural — of both capitalist modernization and our dominant popular cultural forms, unveiling both as terrible dystopias in their own right.

However, *Ghost Dog*'s connection to the traditions of literary naturalism is even more direct: for this film can be read as an adaptation of London's classic work of naturalist fiction, *The Call of the Wild*. Ghost Dog is, after all, the name the former sled dog Buck is given by the Alaskan Yeehat Indians in the novel's concluding pages: "They are afraid of the Ghost Dog, for it has cunning greater than they, stealing from their camps in fierce winters, robbing their traps, slaying their dogs, and defying their bravest hunters."[43] Such a description is equally apt for the film's protagonist as he engages in a brutal war of extermination with the local Mafia, the Vargo family, after they have turned on him, their former contract employee (labor flexibility in the realm of organized crime), to cover up the execution they ordered of one of their members. His technological, military, and strategic prowess is truly staggering: Ghost Dog effortlessly penetrates into every crevice of the Mafia crime network, even invading the family's countryside estate and murdering all the senior bosses and their guards. Later, in a scene adopted, as are other elements of the film, from Seijun Suzuki's cult classic *Koroshi no rakuin* (*Branded to Kill*) (1967), he shoots another Mafioso through the drainpipe in his bathroom sink. Both Ghost Dogs, too, are caught in a desperate struggle with their deep

from different ancient tribes, and now we're both almost extinct. Sometimes you gotta stay with the ancient ways, the old school ways." What this film is thus centrally about is the passing of these "old school ways." (Moreover, the samurai film tradition on which Jarmusch draws here is also about a similar moment of monumental social and cultural transition in the passing of the pre-Meiji era "old school ways.") Earlier Louie had complained that "nothing makes any sense anymore"; and one of the Mafiosi shot by Ghost Dog confesses with his dying breath that Ghost Dog has restored a certain sense of pride in him, "sending us out in the old way, like real fuckin' gangsters." It is this sense of disorientation, of the destruction of a certain set of masculine cultures, that pervade this film. And in its concluding scene, it does appear as if these two "ancient tribes" will be continued, in a much diminished capacity, through young women, the daughter of the Vargos (who had witnessed Ghost Dog's murders) and Pauline, a young African American girl who has befriended Ghost Dog and who in the final image of the film is seen reading his copy of *The Way of the Samurai*, quotations from this quintessential professional's manual appearing throughout the film.

Auerbach's description of the anxieties at play in London's text thus offer us an important clue as to the central ideological contents of both this film and *Fight Club*: "London's progressive disenchantment with work registers the growing fear felt by many turn-of-the-century American men that the market, increasingly abstract and rationalized, could no longer offer the grounds to define manhood, particularly in terms of those ideals of self-reliance, diligence, and mastery at the heart of nineteenth-century liberalism. Once the workplace diminishes in significance in the new century, then masculinity threatens to become primarily a performance or a pose for its own sake."[46] Both films, I would suggest, finally give expression to current middle-class and deeply masculine anxieties about their own insecurity in an emerging global political economy—anxieties that have only been driven to new levels of intensity in the economic aftermath of September 2001. And yet, whereas *Ghost Dog* can offer us a brilliant critique of the destructive nature of these older cultures, very much like its contemporary *Fight Club* (and like Scorsese's *Cape Fear* eight years earlier), it never attempts to portray movements or a politics that would help move us beyond this impasse. In the end, both films pass beyond the engagements of the critical dystopia and give way to the "resigned

A NIGHTMARE ON THE BRAIN OF THE LIVING

Messianic Historicity, Alienations, and *Independence Day*

Men make their own history, but they do not make it just as they please; they do not make it under circumstances chosen by themselves, but under circumstances directly encountered, given and transmitted from the past. The tradition of all the dead generations weighs like a nightmare on the brain of the living. And just when they seem engaged in revolutionizing themselves and things, in creating something that has never yet existed, precisely in such periods of revolutionary crisis they anxiously conjure up the spirits of the past to their service and borrow from them names, battle cries and costumes in order to present the new scene of world history in this time-honored disguise and this borrowed language.

KARL MARX, *The Eighteenth Brumaire of Louis Bonaparte*

And how is it that a discourse of this type is sought out by those who celebrate the triumph of liberal capitalism and its predestined alliance with liberal democracy only in order to hide, and first of all from themselves, the fact that this triumph has never been so critical, fragile, threatened, even in certain regards catastrophic, and in sum bereaved?

JACQUES DERRIDA, *Specters of Marx*

One film was more explicit than all others: *Metropolis*. In it, the paralyzed collective mind seemed to be talking with unusual clarity in its sleep.

SIEGFRIED KRACAUER, *From Caligari to Hitler*

IN PERHAPS HIS SINGLE most well-known adage, G. W. F. Hegel wrote in the preface to *The Philosophy of Right*, "The owl of Minerva spreads its wings only with the falling of the dusk."[1] It is from such a position of historical retrospection that we can say that Francis Fukuyama's conservative Hegelian essay, "The End of History?," is one of the inaugural texts of the period of the 1990s. Fukuyama's essay is significant, among other reasons, for signaling a return to the kinds of universal and global claims that, as I suggested in my first chapter, had been largely in abeyance in the heyday of postmodern theory. Fukuyama—a student of Allan Bloom, a former analyst at the RAND Corporation, and at the time of the publication of this essay, a minor bureaucrat in the first President Bush's State Department—inaugurated a wide-ranging debate in the summer of 1989 with his assertion that history had come to end with the "unabashed victory of economic and political liberalism," thereby fulfilling Hegel's proclamation of nearly two centuries earlier.[2] Relying on Alexandre Kojève's landmark lectures on Hegel's *Phenomenology of Spirit*, Fukuyama argues that the "idea" of Western liberalism, along with its material political and economic institutions, has emerged as the only real basis for the organization of the totality of global society. The "universal homogenous state" that is emerging might best be summarized "as liberal democracy in the political sphere combined with easy access to VCRs and stereos in the economic."[3] Fundamental contradictions, the motor of all history for Hegel, no longer exist. The most significant contradiction of liberal societies, that between capital and labor, has been resolved such that "the egalitarianism of modern America represents the essential achievement of the classless society envisioned by Marx"; the persistence of global poverty and the widening throughout the 1980s of the gap between the rich and the poor "do not have to do with the underlying legal and social structure of our society, which remains fundamentally egalitarian and redistributionist." Poverty is rather, Fukuyama maintains, a residual formation, a product of obsolete "social and cultural characteristics of the groups composing it."[4] Therefore he concludes that when these contradictions no longer exist, history itself comes to an end.

However, interestingly enough, there is little triumphalism in Fukuyama's declaration of victory. For while he does draw on a Hegelian notion of history, there is no sense of any dramatic dialectical *Aufhebung* (lifting up / sublation / canceling and preserving) giving rise to this transformed social totality. Rather, the energies of history have in the past decade simply dissipated: liberal democracy and market capitalism emerge victorious because of the defeat and collapse of the only two competing universal ideas, that of fascism and, even more important, of communism. Indeed, Fukuyama will later assert that he believes in the "essential correctness" of Hegel and Kojève's claim that history ended in 1806 "insofar as the vanguard of human history arrived at the end on that date"; thus, from our position of historical retrospection, it appears that the "experiment" initiated by Karl Marx was no more than "a 150-year detour," and the later "unexpected" emergence of fascism and communism simply "delayed the arrival of the universal homogenous state by a couple of hundred years."[5] Moreover, the two remaining ideas that might appear as challenges, nationalism and religious fundamentalism, are insufficiently universal in their claims and appeal. "In the contemporary world," Fukuyama notes, "only Islam has offered a theocratic state as a political alternative to both liberalism and communism. But the doctrine has little appeal for non-Muslims, and it is hard to believe the movement will take on any universal significance."[6] Crucially, Fukuyama maintains, "at the end of history it is not necessary that all societies become successful liberal societies, merely that they end their ideological pretensions of representing different and higher forms of human society."[7] This said, however, the triumph feels like a hollow one: for rather than engaging in the dynamic struggles of history, the residents of the posthistorical world will serve as mere caretakers of the memory of past achievements. The master's willingness to risk life itself for some grand idea is replaced by banal "economic calculation, the endless solving of technical problems, environmental concerns, and the satisfaction of sophisticated consumer demands."[8]

The two texts that are at the center of this chapter—Jacques Derrida's *Specters of Marx* (1993) and Roland Emmerich's blockbuster film, *Independence Day* (1996)—can be understood as responses of sorts (explicitly so in Derrida's case) to Fukuyama's neoliberal fantasies. While the two works move to opposite ends of the political spectrum—Derrida marks the space that the "New International" of the late-1990s counterglobalization movement will soon occupy, while the film gives expression to what will be shortly thereafter codified as the neoconservative Project for the New American Century (to which Fukuyama also signed on)—both forcefully demonstrate that the 1990s, while marking the conclusion of Cold War history, by no means guarantee the end announced by Fukuyama, the posthistorical global neoliberal dispensation. Rather, both recognize that the present is a moment of intense political struggle over precisely the identity of the world that is coming into being—a struggle, of course, in which Fukuyama's essay participates as well. It is to the lessons both works have to offer concerning the nature of that struggle that I want to turn my attention in this chapter.

Specters of Marx and *Independence Day* share an interest in figures who disrupt the closure of the status quo: ghosts in the case of Derrida's work and alien invaders in the film. Both works also imagine these figures sheathed from head to toe in metal: the first ghost we encounter in Derrida's text, that of Hamlet's father, makes his appearance onstage in full armor, while the alien invaders in *Independence Day* enter human history clothed in sophisticated military hardware. However, before turning to the significance of these two figures, I want first to briefly invoke another set of popular culture aliens: Kang and Kodos, the drooling, one-eyed, tentacled space invaders who dutifully make a bid for the takeover of the earth each year on the episode of *The Simpsons* celebrating that most ghostly of holidays, Halloween. In the 1996 installment, first appearing a few months after the theatrical release of *Independence Day* and only weeks before the U. S. presidential election—an election in which the candidates from both parties struggled to claim *Independence Day* as their own—the pair hit on a brilliant idea: they kidnap the presidential candidates Bob Dole and Bill Clinton and take their place on the campaign trail, thereby assuring that regardless of which one of them is elected, they will end up in control.[9] Although people do note some oddities during the campaign—including the fact that the two major party candidates are seen repeatedly in each other's company, usually holding hands (to exchange protein strings, they inform us)—all goes according to plan, until Homer Simpson stumbles on their interstellar ship. After inadvertently jettisoning the real Clinton and Dole into outer space, Homer turns up and exposes the plot. However, the unmasked aliens now gleefully declare that his efforts have been to no avail: after all, given the American two-party system, citizens have no choice but to vote for one of them. When someone in the gathered crowd suggests that he might vote for a third-party candidate, Kang, echoing election-year sentiments of pundits on both the left and the right, says, "Go ahead, throw your vote away" (at the announcement of which we cut to an angry Ross Perot seen punching his fist through his campaign hat). The final scene of the episode is set sometime after the election that has installed the Dole-substitute Kang in the White House. The invaders are shown herding about an enslaved human population, forcing them to con-

against the tepid apocalyptical discourse we find in the Fukuyama essay that gave the repetitious discourse of the "end of history/end of ideology" (Karl Mannheim begets Daniel Bell begets . . .) its most recent cachet.[11]

It is precisely this latter form of conservative apocalypticism that Derrida confronts head-on in *Specters of Marx*, a work whose significance lies not the least in the wide-ranging and energized conversation it sparked, creating a context in the post–Cold War world for reflections on the contemporary state and future possibilities of Marxism itself.[12] In what might be taken as much as a rebuke to the apocalypticism of Baudrillard as to that of Fukuyama, Derrida maintains, not unlike Morris, that such ritualized invocations of the end are forms of "conjurations," "exorcisms" that consist "in repeating in the mode of an incantation that the dead man is really dead."[13] Beginning with the "holy alliance" Marx envisioned in the opening pages of *The Communist Manifesto* (1848) and extending through its descendants in contemporary neoliberalism, the purveyors of these various forms of teleological narratives — with their vision of an end at which history must arrive, or perhaps has already arrived (the full and total victory of global capitalism) — betray a desire for ontological purity, for the full self-presence of a present purged of any ghosts that may haunt it. It is a present, as Jameson describes it, "that has already triumphantly exorcized all of its ghosts and believes itself to be without a past and without spectrality, late capitalism itself as ontology, the pure presence of the world-market system freed from all the errors of human history and of previous social formations, including the ghost of Marx himself."[14]

Thus, in place of these ontological visions of the present, Derrida offers what he describes as a "hauntology" that emphasizes — in a way similar to the contemporary interventions of Ernesto Laclau and Chantal Mouffe and Slavoj Žižek — the irreducible antagonisms and nonsuturability of any historical present: "Haunting belongs to the structure of any hegemony" (*SM*, 37). Choosing among the multiplicity of Marxisms now made available after the collapse of the institutional state and party orthodoxies, and yet refusing the depoliticization of Marx's work that follows in the wake of some of its academic institutionalizations, Derrida then invokes the vital Marxist specter of a very different vision of history. Such a historical sensibility finds kinship with the late work of Walter Benjamin, the single most influential Marxist critic of the ontologies of teleological, progressivist, and Hegelian "bad-side-of-history" dialectics.[15] This alternative Marxist vision of history incorporates what Derrida calls a "messianic without messianism," and Benjamin a "weak messianic power," the understanding that *every* present moment (*Jetztzeit*) contains within it the explosive possibility of a radically other future—or, as Derrida describes it, the faith in "the coming of the other, the absolute and unpredictable singularity of the *arrivant as justice*" (*SM*, 28).

Derrida's conceptualization of the messianic without messianism, as well as Benjamin's earlier formulation, serves not only as a critical tool to be deployed against conservative end-of-history narratives but also as an invitation to reimagine the Marxist problematic of history. Derrida does not dispense with the Marxist concept of revolutionary rupture—"the messianic, including its revolutionary forms (and the messianic is always revolutionary, it has to be)" (*SM*, 168)—but rather with two aspects of what he takes to be Marxism's historical ontology. Derrida's work is thus fundamentally concerned with the politics of representation, with the consequence of certain ways of imagining history and the present—something that is, as we shall see momentarily, also central to *Independence Day*. On the one hand, Derrida's work can be understood as an extension of Louis Althusser's project, with its aims of purging a certain Marxism of any residual Hegelian teleologism (a universal goal toward which history moves), of mechanistic determinism (a necessary set of stages through which we must pass on the way toward that goal), and of progressivism (the "bad-side" dialectics that I will discuss shortly): for Derrida, this lingering species of Hegelianism has had the effect of canceling the materiality of history itself.[16] However, unlike certain strands of structuralist Marxism emerging out of Althusser's work, Derrida offers the messianic as "another historicity—not a new history or still less a 'new historicism,' but another opening of event-ness as historicity that permitted one not to renounce, but on the contrary to open up access to an affirmative thinking of the messianic and emancipatory promise as promise: as *promise* and not as onto-theological or teleo-eschatological program or design" (*SM*, 74–75). For Derrida, it is not only the future, or what had been labeled in classical Marxism as socialism or state communism, that must not be "pre-determined, prefigured, or even pre-named" (*SM*, 168)—and in this Derrida reiterates the Marxist resistance to the thoroughly idealist utopian project of representing a new social order before its collective achievement (a ban beginning with Marx and Engels and finding its fullest expression in the work of the Frankfurt School theorists, the latter to which Derrida's argument here bears a striking resemblance. It is also the very historical process that will produce a situation of revolutionary struggle that is subject to Derrida's prohibition. Marx himself violates this ban, for example, in the preface to *A Contribution to the Critique of Political Economy* (1859) in his confident formulation that a conflict between the development of "the material productive forces of society" and "the existing relations of production" will inevitably open up onto "an era of social revolution."[17] Derrida, on the other hand, maintains, "This future is not described, it is not foreseen in the constative mode; it is announced, promised, called for in a performative mode" (*SM*, 103).

While such an emphasis on the performative realization of the future finds its deepest resonances in Benjamin, there is also a striking similarity between Derrida's argument and one advanced in the late 1950s by Roland Barthes in his classic work of ideological semiology, *Mythologies*. If the fundamental work of what Barthes describes as myth is to naturalize and universalize a certain (bourgeois) historical reality—and in doing so, to mask the political aims of such a pedagogical process—then the one kind of language that by definition cannot be mythical is that of revolution: "Revolution is defined as a cathartic act meant to reveal the political load of the world: it *makes* the world; and its language, all of it, is functionally absorbed in this making. . . . revolution announces itself openly as revolution and thereby abolishes myth."[18] Barthes goes on to argue, however, that to the degree that the "Left is not revolution," that is, to the degree that it is distanced from this active performative making of the world, it becomes more and more susceptible to the process of mythologization, certain dimensions of the leftist project—its parties, statist bureaucracies, historical teleologies, ideologies, and so forth—become reified institutions and orthodoxies that in turn mark any questioning or challenge to its now fixed "universal" truths with the sign of "deviations."[19]

In a crucial way then, the "deviant" projects of Benjamin, Barthes, and Derrida all converge in their goal of restoring to Marxism its revolutionary energies. While Benjamin negatively and critically invokes this revolutionary historicity in opposition to both 1930s Stalinist orthodoxy and social democrat progressivism and, as I argued in my introduction, in response to the closure of the modernist 1920s,[20] and Barthes against the institutional rigidity of the mid-century French Communist Party, Derrida affirmatively takes advantage of the historical opportunity made available in the 1990s by the collapse of these older orthodoxies, states, and parties — what Warren Montag describes as "the externalized material form in which [Marxism] was alienated from itself" — to issue a call for a "New International" (SM, 85).[21] Cautious of "totalizing in advance" and thereby transforming the performance of the New International into its own orthodoxy or myth (SM, 37), Derrida defines this "link of affinity, suffering, and hope" largely in terms of what it will be without: "Without status, without title, and without name, barely public even if it is not clandestine, without contract, 'out of joint,' without coordination, without party, without country, without national community (International before, across, and beyond any national determination), without co-citizenship, without common belonging to a class" (SM, 85). The alliance that will then emerge Derrida describes only as a "counter-conjuration," unified "in the (theoretical and practical) critique of the state of international law, the concepts of State and nation, and so forth: in order to renew this critique, and especially to radicalize it" (SM, 86). "In this way," Montag notes, "the spirit or a spirit of Marxism, that is, one of its promises, will survive the parties, unions and mass organizations, all the practical forms that Marxism has so far taken, one day, in the future, to be realized in new, perhaps better, forms."[22]

That such a conjuration of the messianic in response to the "state of emergency" of the present is not limited to theoretical texts such as Derrida's Specters is made evident by films like Independence Day. The film opens by invoking the same posthistorical malaise located by the episode of The Simpsons, Baudrillard, and Fukuyama, and to which Derrida responds in Specters. Each of the film's four central characters, representatives, we can assume, of a cross-section of contemporary American masculinity, appears trapped in his own form of paralytic stasis, inhabiting a twilight region in which any form of effective and decisive action seems inconceivable. Indeed, it is precisely the masculine anxieties about social positioning and political agency that I discussed in the previous two chapters that will serve as a motor for both the narrative and the pedagogical movement of the film.[23] In the opening scenes, we are first introduced to U.S. President Thomas J. Whitmore (Bill Pullman), a former Gulf War fighter pilot faced with plummeting approval ratings and an inability to pass his legislative agenda — a consequence, as his press secretary, appropriately enough, informs us, of his "message" getting "lost" amid "too much politics, too much compromise." Later, we meet David Levinson (Jeff Goldblum), a Jewish television cable repairman in New York City, a brilliant former MIT student who has accomplished little in life and who invests much of his energy pining for his estranged wife (he still wears his wedding ring four years after their separation), who is now the above-mentioned press secretary to the president. Next to appear on-screen is Captain Steven Hiller (Will Smith), an African American fighter pilot—not coincidentally, as I will suggest later, based in Los Angeles—who is caught in a double bind of being forced to choose between a professional dream of becoming a member of the U.S. Space Program and commitments to his single-mother, exotic-dancer girlfriend (another pilot informs him, and us, that there is no way the United States will accept a shuttle pilot who is married to a stripper). And finally, we encounter Russell Casse (Randy Quaid), a Vietnam veteran and self-proclaimed alien abductee, now reduced to the pathetic existence of an alcoholic trailer park–inhabiting crop-duster living in the desert of Southern California's Imperial Valley. As the film presents it, the current problem of historical and political stasis has shaken masculine identity to its very foundations, irrespective of class or race positioning. All of this will change with the appearance of the aliens who force these men out of their paralyzed existences and ultimately enable them to reclaim an active control of their destinies.

If these men embody a lived sense of historical paralysis, it will be the film's alien invaders who offer a dramatic figuration of Derrida's and Benjamin's messianic (figure 15). Thus what Derrida describes as the "coming of the other" and an "absolute and unpredictable singularity" (SM, 28) one of the characters in the film labels a "historic and unprecedented event" that will blow to pieces the stasis of the present and free it from Benjamin's homogenous "continuum of history."[24] And as in both Derrida's and Benjamin's analyses, the film shows that any substantive change in the present can come about only through a dramatic revolutionary rupture in the temporal-historical continuum.

The messianic aliens accomplish this unsticking of history by destroying the world's great urban centers: we witness the apocalyptic consummation of New York, Los Angeles, and Washington, D.C., and we are told the same thing occurs in Chicago, Atlanta, Philadelphia, Paris, London, Berlin, Moscow, and Bombay (figure 16). There is something deeply shocking in the

15 The alien space ships first appear over New York City, from *Independence Day* (1996).

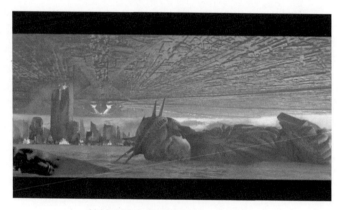

16 New York City lies in ruins after the aliens' attack, from *Independence Day* (1996).

contemplation of these casual images of the destruction of the world's cities, and this is not simply because of the staggering loss of life it would entail: for what the film also implies here is the near total eradication of a worldwide archive of cultural heritage, stored in the urban centers as a consequence both of the histories of their production and of their accumulation, imperial or otherwise.[25] At the same time, however, there is also an undeniable libidinal charge that accompanies such an image of purifying destruction (even more anarchistic and joyfully apparent in Tim Burton's contemporary *Mars Attacks!* [1996]): for it is precisely this cultural heritage, Benjamin's famous "documents of civilization" that are always already "documents of barbarism," that stands as the material embodiment of the accumulated dead weight of history that has rendered any real change impossible. Marx calls this heritage the "nightmare on the brain of the living" that continuously thwarts any effort to create "something that has never yet existed," and Benjamin describes it as the "pile of debris" endlessly growing skyward, produced by the "one single catastrophe," the storm blowing from paradise "we call progress."[26] Freeing us from this catastrophe and awakening us from this nightmare, the alien attack—here nothing less than a figure of revolution itself—finally enables the long dreamt-of new beginning.

It is no surprise that Derrida's invocation of the messianic looks back to Benjamin's work (and Barthes's to Brecht's): for while the vision of posthistory is part of the cultural baggage of a postmodern present, this idea of a revolutionary rupture might more properly be described as a central dimension of the modernist past, with its deep "passion for the real" theorized by Alain Badiou. Indeed, the conviction that the obliteration of the urban cultural heritage is necessary to free up the energies of change is given voice in one of the other central documents of the modernist moment, the Italian "Futurist Manifesto": "So let them come, the gay incendiaries with charred fingers! Here they are! Here they are! . . . Come on! Set fire to the library shelves! Turn aside the canals to flood the museums! . . . Oh, the joy of seeing the glorious old canvasses bobbing adrift on those waters, discolored and shredded! . . . Take up your pickaxes, your axes and hammers, and wreck, wreck the venerable cities, pitilessly!"[27] Like F. T. Marinetti's "gay incendiaries," the equally pitiless aliens in the film will accomplish their messianic rupture through the use of a cleansing fire that envelops the cores of the great cities in a visually spectacular wave of rolling flame. The "independence" celebrated in the film thus comes as much from the aliens' arrival as from their ultimate defeat.

In suggesting these parallels, my intent is not to diminish the importance of the "weak messianic power" articulated each in its own specific way by Derrida and Benjamin. I take it, as Benjamin writes, as a force that can fan "the spark of hope" in moments of the dimmest political possibility where at every turn it appears that the "enemy has never ceased to be victorious."[28] Moreover, it has long been a central part of the heritage of Marxist cultural criticism to illuminate the spectral traces of this power in all kinds of cultural documents and forms, as well as to make us aware of the constitutive unevenness (*Ungleichzeitigkeit*) of history, what Derrida labels the hauntology disrupting any imagined or desired ontological closure. With all these thinkers I mean to emphasize exactly how widely felt in this period were the desires that Derrida and Benjamin label the messianic: the power of the film (something misunderstood, or perhaps unconsciously too well understood, by many reviewers who sneered at its trivialities and plot flaws) arises precisely to the degree that it is able to tap into these contemporary desires for a radical change of affairs.

However, the messianic historicity as it is articulated in the work of Benjamin and Derrida potentially opens up onto another set of dilemmas. The significance of Benjamin's messianic historicity similarly is stressed by Étienne Balibar in his valuable short book, *The Philosophy of Marx*. Balibar points out that Benjamin's intervention is aimed at what was in the late 1930s a doctrinaire acceptance of the Hegelian "dialectic of the bad side" embodied in Soviet proletarian ideology: the understanding that history steadily and necessarily progresses by way of what appears on the surface as a sequence of struggles, clashes, conflicts, and even catastrophes. It is in opposition to this way of thinking that Benjamin offers his famous angel of history, who critically suggests, as Balibar puts it, that "History not only advances 'by its bad side,' but also *to the bad side*, the side of domination and ruin" — to fascism, but also to Joseph Stalin's show trials and the gulag. Benjamin's goal is thus nothing less than the complete dismantling of any remnants of the myth of history as necessary progress, whether this myth is expressed in its bourgeois, Hegelian, or Marxist form.

However, Balibar goes on to point out the tremendous price to be paid for this critical stance: for Benjamin's weak messianic thought, the *faith* that the future is immanent in every moment of the present represents "a prospect which still presents itself as revolutionary but not as dialectical, primarily in that it radically disqualifies the idea of practice, or of liberation as transformation by one's own labours."[29] In other words, while offering an indispensable critical refusal of both historical determinist self-confidence and the posthistorical sensibility of any form of ontological history, weak messianic thought can end up continually deferring an engagement with the vexed questions concerning the formation of the concrete and particular collective political agents that will help usher in such a future. Although Benjamin's death shortly after completing his famed theses meant that he never had the opportunity to address this dilemma, we find the full realization of the logic implicit within his text in Max Horkheimer and Theodor Adorno's *Dialectic of Enlightenment*, a text deeply influenced by Benjamin's final essay: "It is not the portrayal of reality as hell on earth but the slick challenge to break out of it that is suspect. If there is anyone today to whom we can pass the responsibilities for the message, we bequeath it not to the 'masses,' and not to the individual (who is powerless), but to an imaginary witness—lest it perish with us."[30] Derrida's list of "withouts" similarly fills the place of political agency with such an "imaginary witness," a move that risks, as Gayatri Spivak suggests, "a transformation of militancy into religion."[31]

The separation of militancy and religion is not a simple one, however, and Derrida works very carefully throughout *Specters* to show the central role that religion plays in Marx's thought. Balibar also reminds us of the deep influence that the Hegelian critique of religion, first articulated by Ludwig Feuerbach, had on the early work of Marx. Feuerbach maintains that it is through religion that real, sensuous human beings project their "essences," their potential for self-creation in this world, into another supersensuous domain. These potentialities then come back to them in the form of an Other, or an alien—and religion for Feuerbach is the most fully realized form of alienation.[32] I would argue that, similarly, the messianic invaders in *Independence Day*, along with the "imaginary witness" invoked by Derrida, Benjamin, and the Frankfurt School, express the depths in the present (as well as the past of the 1950s—another moment, as Derrida points out, when the death of Marxism, the end of ideology, and the end of history itself were proclaimed [*SM*, 14]) of what we might call *political* alienation: the radical sense of otherness too many feel when faced with the prospects of their own potential for action. Thus at once the sign of the inextinguishable desire for historical rupture *and* the necessary impossibility of consciously—that is, politically—acting in a way that might bring it about, the aliens in the film inhabit the same contradictory and impossible space as Benjamin's angel: "The angel would like to stay, awaken the dead, and make whole what has been smashed. But a storm is blowing from Paradise and has got caught in his wings; it is so strong that the angel can no longer close them. This storm drives him irresistibly into the future, to which his back is turned, while the pile of debris before him grows toward the sky."[33] The question of what the angel might do to break free of such an irresistible force, and thus embark on a historical path that would enable him to accomplish his intended task of awakening the dead, remains one the messianic vision of history alone is unable to answer.

These visions of the coming of the messianic Other mark out a more fundamental existential anxiety as well. There is comfort to be found in ontological, deterministic, apocalyptical, and even alienated messianic narratives of history, for all of them legitimate what Erich Fromm long ago described as the "flight from freedom." In any free collective action, in any radical project of actively remaking history, lies the terrible possibility that things may turn out badly, that they move to the bad side, a lesson the events of the previous century bring home again and again: the messianic rupture may open up onto either paradise or the abyss, and, as Derrida's and Benjamin's works forcefully demonstrate, there is no a priori guarantee as to which destination we will arrive at. A similar sense of historical contingency marks the alienated political agency we see in *Independence Day*, a certain frisson and cinematic suspense arising from the possibility that the aliens may in fact succeed in wiping us out. But of course, as the existentialists also remind us, inactivity is itself a form of action, enabling the continuation of a status quo that all of these narratives I have touched on suggest is unbearable; indeed, as in the parables of Franz Kafka, these narratives give substance to the sense that sometimes "the worst thing is better than nothing at all."[34] Caught between the Scylla of the fear of political catastrophe and the Charybdis of inactivity, we turn toward the only avenue of possibility that appears to remain available: the affirmation of the messianic, of the *potentiality* of otherness in history.

However, as figures for an alienated political agency, the film aliens offer another resolution to these various existential dilemmas: they at once rupture the terrible continuum of history, goad the collective into action, and, conveniently, bear the burden of responsibility for any ill consequences (wide-scale suffering, death, violence, and destruction) that arises during the moment of transition. The film's aliens thus serve as a placeholder for a figure who will achieve its full real-world incarnation on September 11, 2001.

The appearance of the aliens also provides a magical solution to one of the other most pressing political questions of the 1990s, one that similarly could not be answered by an appeal to a messianic historicity: how to forge, and even more important *sustain*, a political bloc from the fragmented interests and competing microgroups inhabiting the political landscape? The film's vision of the global collective unity that arises in response to the invasion is represented in a number of ways: first, in a fleeting but crucial image of what are identified as Iraqi and Israeli fighter pilots now forged into an alliance (the film's repeated references to the Middle East—indeed, the first appearance of the alien ships is over northern Iraq—betrays an awareness, shared by Fukuyama, that in this region at least, history still appears very much to be possible);[35] second, in the opening lines of a speech by the president in the moments before the climactic counterattack on the aliens: "Mankind—that word should have new meaning for all of us today. We can't be consumed by our petty differences anymore. We will be united in our common interests"; and finally, and most obviously, in the heroic character couple of a Jew, Levinson, and an African American, Hiller, symbolically transcending the notorious summer 1991 events in Brooklyn's Crown Heights to save the planet.[36]

The process by which this unification comes about offers a textbook illustration of Laclau and Mouffe's claim that all collective political agency is fundamentally constituted in negativity: the aliens in the film present us with the one form of the antagonistic Other big enough to subsume all the peoples of the earth into a collective whole.[37] This device is an old one in the traditions of science fiction literature. It is no coincidence that H. G. Wells's great catastrophic works, such as *The War of the Worlds* (1898), precede his later imagining of "modern utopias" of global harmony: in Wells's vision, too, the invasion of the aliens enables the formation of a new global collectivity.[38] And in Murray Leinster's classic Cold War short story "First Contact" (1945), the beginnings of a new connection between the human and alien spaceship crews, inadvertently first encountering each other in the deepest reaches of interstellar space, is enabled through the discovery of an even more alien Other they have in common: "And we were together for a couple of hours before the two ships separated and we'd nothing in particular to do. So I became convinced that humans and aliens are bound to be good friends if they have only half a chance. You see, sir, we spent those two hours telling dirty jokes."[39]

In *Independence Day*, it is the alien's own voice that marks it as this Other. During the film, only one alien ever has the opportunity to "speak"—or more precisely, to communicate telepathically (a plot device beautifully

17 An encounter with a death-drive alien, from *Independence Day* (1996).

parodied in the conclusion of the antijingoistic science fiction film, *Starship Troopers* [1997, dir. Paul Verhoeven]). When the president asks this alien what his species wants "us" to do, it chants, "die, die" (figure 17). In this way, the aliens become the very embodiment of the Freudian "death drive." Lee Edelman argues that in a mainstream political symbolic logic that fetishizes the image of the child as the reproduction of the present in the future—"the child has come to embody for us the telos of the social order and been enshrined as the figure for whom that order must be held in perpetual trust"—it is the queer subject position that embodies for that order the death drive, "rupturing . . . our foundational faith in the reproduction of futurity."[40] Following Edelman's lead, we might read the aliens in the film as figures for this queer subjectivity as well—giving a new resonance to Marinetti's "gay incendiaries." A similar logic is evident in the monstrous alien figures of Ridley Scott's *Alien* (1979) and *The X-Files: Fight the Future* (1998, dir. Rob Bowman): in both films, the respective aliens' menace arises from a "queer" asexual reproduction, using human bodies as incubators, that threatens to demolish the reigning symbolic order. And in *Mars Attacks!* the Martians' queerness is marked in a number of places: in a failed attempt to assassinate the president, the Martian appears in high drag; and the symbol on the Martian flag that is later planted in the president's prone body recalls the logo of ACT UP!. Edelman goes on to speculate on the potentialities opened up by a queer politics that embraces this imaginary, and I would extend his insight to all politics that take themselves to be radical: for what is the messianic in the view of the symbolic order if not the death drive? Or, as Derrida notes, "Some, and I do not exclude myself, will find this despairing 'messianism' has a curious taste, a taste of death" (*SM*, 169).

Interestingly, the one explicitly gay-coded character in the film, David's boss, Marty Gilbert (Harvey Fierstein), is killed off during the initial attack on New York City. Michael Rogin suggests that this character represents the possibility for David of a "same-sex flirtation" (and indeed, in an early scene cut from the film, Marty plants a celebratory kiss on David's lips), a temptation that must be overcome in "the growth toward heterosexual manhood" (below I will discuss further the implication of this vision of masculine maturity for the film's women characters). In this way, Rogin argues, the film "plays with forbidden desire in the service of normalization."[41] I would suggest that something similar occurs in terms of the figure of the aliens, as the film rechannels the "curious taste" of radical desires they embody into some very different directions.

The film begins this recontaining operation by placing the death-driven aliens in direct opposition to a human desire for life: late in his climactic speech, the president tells the assembled troops, "You will once again be fighting for our freedom. Not from tyranny, oppression, or persecution, but from annihilation. We are fighting for our right to live." The aliens thus serve as a "vanishing mediator" between the fragmentary, alienated condition of the present and the state of collective unity the film invites us to imagine will exist after they have been vanquished.[42] That is, once they have performed the task of dissolving the unbearable stasis of the past, the aliens, like Marty, along with the threatening open-ended messianic possibilities each embodies, must disappear. In their place, a new world symbolic order emerges. But what exactly is it that the film imagines will live?

These political alienations are not the only ones imagined to be overcome by the radical singularity of the attack. I have already pointed out the similarity between the fantasy of urban cultural destruction found in *Independence Day* and that expressed in such quintessential modernist works as Marinetti's "Futurist Manifesto."[43] But there is another striking resonance between the futurist vision and that offered by the film: both appear to embrace the transformative possibilities of modern technological warfare, again as a way of effecting a break with the dead weight of the past. Among its other aspects, Marinetti writes that, "war is beautiful because it inaugurates the dreamed-of metallization of the human body."[44] A similar image of a metallicized body appears in the film; yet here it takes the form of the terrible figure of the alien Other, sheathed in what we are told is biomechanical armor.

Thus, at this central narrative juncture, the film's vision effects a crucial departure from the modernism embodied in Marinetti's manifesto. After Hiller captures a downed alien pilot, a secret xenobiological research team opens up the armor. The head of the team (Brent Spiner, the actor who also played the android Data in *Star Trek: The Next Generation*) observes that these entities are "not all that dissimilar to us" and that to realize this, all one has to do is "get through their technology." The doctor pays for this misreading with his life—the entire medical staff is slaughtered by the freed alien—and we learn in this brief moment of cross-cultural contact just how savagely different the aliens are from us. Crucially, this difference is presented as being a consequence of their total instrumental "enframing" (*Ge-stell*), to use Martin Heidegger's concept, by technology—a fate that the film, making evident its soft environmentalist agenda, warns may await us as well.[45] In the modernist moment—marked as in the case of the futurist's early twentieth-century Italy by a sputtering and frustratingly incomplete technological modernization—this total enframing appears as a utopian possibility; however, in our fully modernized world, the same vision comes back to us as a figure of a potential apocalyptical catastrophe, technology itself now embodying the alien Other that menaces the human. (Of course, this anxiety too, as I pointed out in earlier chapters, has long been an important dimension of the science fiction imaginary.) The aliens in the film appear as a technological "return-of-the-repressed," invading our world, as we learn, to strip it of all its natural resources. And, in a vision that harkens back to the first *Terminator*, even our machines seem early on in the film to have turned against us, as our enframing global web of communication satellites are used by the invaders to coordinate their initial attack.

Independence Day is hardly alone in offering this type of critical vision of contemporary technological alienation, something also at play, for example, in John Carpenter's *Escape from LA* (1996). However, there are some crucial differences between these two narratives that are worth emphasizing as well. In the conclusion of the Carpenter film, the protagonist Snake Pliskin (Kurt Russell), having been forced into another irresolvable political bind (where the only choices are a decadent, out-of-control consumerism, the "senseless" violence of third world revolution, and religious fundamentalist totalitarianism), ends up literally pulling the plug on modernity (by turning off the planetary power grid), a messianic gesture that, as one character in the film observes, wipes away five hundred years of Western modernity's "achievements." *Independence Day*, on the other hand, ultimately presents a much less apocalyptical fantasy, calling not for the total rollback of technological modernization, but rather for what we might call its de-alienation. (The shift in vision that occurs as we move from *Escape from LA* to *Independence Day* is similar to that which occurs between the first two *Terminator* films.) Understanding how such a de-alienation unfolds in terms of the film's narrative is thus crucial for grasping its ultimate political content.

The film presents three distinct stages in the human counteroffensive against the technologically figured menace. The first, immediately coming on the heels of the destruction of the world's major cities, takes the form of a massive wave of U.S. military aircraft sent to blow out of the sky an alien ship near Los Angeles. This fails because, as we soon learn, the alien craft are protected by an impenetrable force field—an image revived in the post-9/11 film version of Wells's *War of the Worlds* (2005, dir. Steven Spielberg)—and the result is that most of the U.S. planes are destroyed. The second counterattack follows the revelation of the invaders' ultimate agenda ("die, die"), which leads the president to consent to a nuclear strike against another of their ships. This effort fails as well and, in fact, does the aliens' work for them by obliterating the city of Houston. However, in the third, and finally successful, counterattack, the humans follow a very different strategy: Hiller pilots a salvaged alien scout vehicle (apparently the very ship taken from the infamous 1950s Roswell, New Mexico, crash site) into the core of the orbiting mothership, where Levinson introduces a virus into the aliens' computer system. This momentarily shuts down the force fields (apparently the hubris of the invaders made them forget to install any back-up system), thereby enabling a carefully coordinated, global strike by the surviving military forces. They succeed, and in the process they enable the heroic redemption of Vietnam veteran Casse, who— in what appears, in one of the film's many visual borrowings, to be a reprisal of Slim Pickens's famous nuclear missile ride in Stanley Kubrick's *Dr. Strangelove* (1964)—flies his fighter plane into the heart of one of the ships. Meanwhile, Hiller and Levinson guarantee that the alien forces will not have any opportunity to regroup by spectacularly blowing up their interstellar mothership with a nuclear bomb.

Many critics complained about the implausibility of this resolution. However, to simply reject this narrative climax as a silly one is to miss the more significant work that it performs. For finally the film suggests that it is only old-style, big industrial technology that is the inhuman, alien Other; and whatever form this takes—be it the unrestrained use of military hardware, the bomb, or even the alien ships themselves—this technology is revealed to be both a threat to human existence and, ultimately, a failure. Over and against this form of technology, however, the film offers a redeemed image of another kind of technology: a friendly, user-based one of smart, "clean" information machines like the personal computer. Indeed, even the ur-form of clean electric information technology, the telegraph, plays a key role in the film's reassertion of the human, enabling a global communicational network to spring up that the aliens are unable to detect. Moreover, this same lesson is reiterated in the making of the film itself, involving as it did groundbreaking computer simulation technologies that replaced any cumbersome and costly physical staging of the battle sequences.

Here, then, we can see how the messianic narrative structure of the film, playing on some of the deepest utopian and radical political desires at work in our present, gradually turns over into an ideological one, ultimately performing the crucial work of cultural hegemonic pedagogy in reinforcing a series of notions about technology (including the idea that there is a qualitative difference between dirty and clean technologies, something to which the growing problem of the disposal of computer monitors and cell phones has given the lie) that are central to what was in the 1990s an emergent information-based economy. Moreover, the film teaches us that success comes to those who have mastered the skills and ideals necessary to flourish in these emergent realities: the film's heroes are those who combine a performative flexibility and skill in informational technologies with a soft environmentalism (one of the first appearances of Levinson onscreen shows him picking aluminum cans out of an office trash barrel and throwing them into a nearby recycling bin) and a vaguely global sensibility. Thus it should come as no surprise that what begins as an allegorical vision of revolutionary rupture folds back over the course of the film into an extended advertisement for Apple computers, the very folks who broke the ground for this recoding strategy with their now legendary use of Orwell's *Nineteen Eighty-Four* for their initial marketing salvo in 1984 for the Macintosh line. This can occur because finally there is no real contradiction between a global corporate vision and the vision of the film.

The truly pressing questions concerning the new information technologies are those that the film cannot even begin to bring into view and that have nothing to do with some ideological vision of the cleanness of informational technologies versus the dirtiness of older industrial forms (although we would do well to reexamine the reifications implicit even in this opposition, haunting those forms of environmental politics that view the so-called second-wave industrial economies of the various third worlds as the greatest menaces to the planetary ecosystem). Technology is, as Jameson points out, always already "a figure for something else."[46] Likewise, I would argue that the more fundamental issues about the new information technologies concern the role they will play in the organization and maintenance of a worldwide corporate capitalist marketplace, a marketplace that itself has helped produce the sense of posthistorical malaise to which the film represents a response in the first place; and who will, and (equally significantly) who will *not*, have access to these technologies (the latter being what Jean-François Lyotard describes as postmodern forms of proletarianization).[47] Nor, however, does this exhaust the possibilities of these technologies, as Derrida notes the potential role they can play in the formation of "another space for democracy" (*SM*, 169). Jameson extends this point even further: "For the cybernetic possibilities that enable post-Fordism along with financial speculation, and generate the extraordinary new wealth that constitutes the power of the postmodern business establishment, are also available to intellectuals today on a world scale."[48] I will directly take up the issue of the radical potential of these technologies in my next chapter.

This vision of technology similarly points toward another narrative operation of redemption at work in the film. The sequence of three counterattacks offers an allegorical thumbnail sketch of changes in U.S. military philosophy following the Second World War. In the first assault, we see the outmoded military thinking operative in the Vietnam War, an attempt to overwhelm the enemy with a sheer volume of technological overkill—with, not surprisingly, the same humiliating results. The second attack represents the obvious self-destructive bankruptcies of any nuclear exchange; and indeed, at one point Levinson reminds us that even if an all-out nuclear attack destroyed the aliens, the subsequent fallout and nuclear winter would render the planet uninhabitable and thereby effectively "end life as we know it." By the time of the third attack, the lessons of these earlier failures have been assimilated. In the last attack we see the combination of smart information-based stealth technologies with old-fashioned military gumption; and the multinational nature of the strike force is repeatedly driven home by the film. Such a strategy thus resembles nothing less than that employed in the then recent real-world U.S. "victory" over what had been presented as another expansionist, death-obsessed, antienvironmental, and world-threatening alien: Saddam Hussein. Moreover, the heroic redemption of the Vietnam War veteran Casse reinforces the widely shared belief that the Gulf War was somehow a similar redemption of Vietnam; and even the destruction of the mother-ship offers a fantasy scenario of what should have been the conclusion of the Gulf conflict. The film's vision of the first Gulf War is perhaps best summarized by President Whitmore (who, remember, is himself a hero of that war) in the moments of tense immobility between the alien's arrival and their first attack on our cities: "In the Gulf War we knew what we had to do. It's not that simple anymore." The film then harkens back to what have already become for many the nostalgically longed for "simpler" days of the Gulf War, before the opening of the new-old 1990s quagmires of Somalia and Bosnia: for it is the Gulf War that represents the film's model of a workable political mobilization in the new world.

This, then, suggests the ultimate work of ideological recontainment per-formed by the film. Earlier in this chapter, I pointed out that the political paralysis experienced by President Whitmore was presented as a conse-quence of his vision getting lost in the haze of "politics" and "compro-mise." The aliens provide a means for getting us beyond these messy com-plications of a democratic form of government by creating what Giorgio Agamben calls the "state of exception" that enables a massive expansion of the president's power.[49] This is figured in the film when later we are informed that the aliens have killed the vice-president and the cabinet; and we can be assured that the destruction of Washington has wiped out both the legislative and judicial checks on presidential power. Moreover, later in the film we see the president fire his secretary of state, who we learn had formerly been the director of the CIA—the organization that had served in the post-1960s popular cultural imagination as a figure of an out-of-control "big" government. Indeed, the film goes out of its way to inform its viewers of what most of them probably already know: that the CIA has long been involved in the illegal appropriation of U.S. funds to finance covert operations like the base in Nevada where the alien wreckage recovered at the Roswell crash site had been stored for more than four decades (as one character rhetorically asks, "You don't think they actually spend $20,000 on a hammer or $30,000 on a toilet seat?"). However, the film also suggests that neither the president nor the "legitimate" military leadership had any idea about these practices—granting both of them, as the former CIA director tells us, "plausible deniability." Thus, in what can only be viewed as a deft political balancing act, the film manages to redeem the images of both George Bush I, the heroic and decisive leader of the Gulf War, and of Bill Clinton, the idealistic young president whose agenda is undermined by Beltway politics. It is not our leaders, the film suggests, but the system in which they are forced to work that needs to be disposed of.

The alien invasion in the film allows a similar operation of political simplification to take place on the global level as well. The president's stirring speech before the final victory is revealing in this regard. While he invokes a new form of global community, it is one in which the United States, as in the planning and staging of the counterassault itself, remains decidedly in control. The president asserts that it is "fate" that the final battle happens to fall on July 4; henceforth, he tells the assembled throng, the day will "no longer be known as an American holiday," but instead will commemorate the birth of a brave new world order. Crucially, however, it is a globe remade in the image of the United States, where all the world's interests and values are subsumed under American ones, and where Americans still get to call all the shots. They even get to make up the holidays.

In this way, the film offers a figuration of the vision of the post–Cold War U.S. global hegemony that would shortly be articulated in the neoconservative Project for the New American Century: "The Project is 'dedicated to a few fundamental propositions: that American leadership is good both for America and for the world; that such leadership requires military strength, diplomatic energy, and commitment to moral principle; and that too few political leaders today are making the case for global leadership.'

. . . Though recognized as distinctive American values, these principles are presented as universals, with terms like freedom and democracy and respect for private property, the individual, and the law bundled together as a code of conduct for the whole world."[50] What is already evident in this document, and something that *Independence Day* makes clear, is a fascinating reversal that takes place in conservative discourse during the course of the 1990s. For an older conservatism, the state, the euphemistic "big government," is in fact the enemy—something apparent, for example, in the "states' rights," antidesegregation imaginary of the first *Cape Fear* film I discussed earlier, and a stance central to the conservative revolution of the Thatcher-Reagan 1980s, which Salman Rushdie in his novel *Fury* (2001), a scathing portrait of the neoliberal 1990s Manhattan, suggests represents an extension of the radical antistate positions of the 1960s: "Thatcherite Conservatism was the counterculture gone wrong: it shared his generation's mistrust of the institutions of power and used their language of opposition to destroy the old power-blocs—to give the power not to the people, whatever that meant, but to a web of fat-cat cronies."[51] However, in the neoconservatism that takes shape in the 1990s in response both to the end of the Cold War and to neoliberal globalization, the state once again is viewed as central, but it is a state utterly stripped of its progressive welfare functions and reformed into a military-police machine. And, of course, it would be the events of September 11, 2001, that would provide the neoconservative proponents of this view with a real-world alien invasion, thereby relaunching the history, now in the form of a "clash of civilizations," or more precisely, a "clash of fundamentalisms," the neoliberal Fukuyama declared to have ended.[52]

In this film, one of the great dangers Derrida's work so carefully guards against thus in fact comes to pass: the messianic desire becomes embodied in an "identifiable messiah," a figure that takes the form of a recentered, patriarchal U.S. leadership. Significantly, none of the three major women characters in the film—the current, former, and future wives, respectively, of Whitmore, Levinson, and Hiller—play any real role in the victory over the aliens, save that of being wellsprings of support for their mates. The longed-for restoration of masculine political authority, the film teaches us, is contingent on the return to "traditional" gender divisions of labor. Indeed, by the end of the film, all three women have been decisively removed from the public spheres in which they circulated at the beginning (as press secretary, stripper, and active political leader) and are either killed off or reinserted into their "proper" domestic settings. On both the East and West coasts, the African American and Jewish yuppie households are restored; meanwhile, the career-minded and child-abandoning Hillary Clintonesque wife of President Whitmore (the latter shown in the opening of the film gently caring for their daughter as his wife attends a political meeting in Los Angeles) is made to confess her sins on her deathbed: "I'm so sorry I didn't come home when you asked me to." "We're going to live on; we're going to survive," Whitmore declares in the chilling conclusion to his speech: for in the narrative construction of the film, this "we" takes on a decidedly neoconservative hue.

In the end, then, the film follows a narrative parabola not unlike that found in Fritz Lang's classic *Metropolis* (1926), as the latter was first so brilliantly described by Siegfried Kracauer: "The whole composition denotes that the industrialist acknowledges the heart for the purpose of manipulating it; that he does not give up his power, but will expand it over a realm not yet annexed—the realm of the collective soul. Freder's rebellion results in the establishment of totalitarian authority, and he considers this result a victory."[53] (This too might suggest a disturbing homology between Lang's 1920s Weimar Germany and the 1990s United States.)[54] Bringing into the light of day the frustrated political desires and messianic energies of our moment, *Independence Day* similarly provides a narrative mechanism for their rechanneling into a support for what only now can we recognize as an emergent hegemony.

There are a number of important lessons for politically engaged intellectuals to be gathered from this tracing of the film's narrative trajectory. However indispensable may be the critical recovery of the messianic specters haunting the closure of our own present, such an endeavor always must be accompanied by much more risky and dangerous acts: the concrete and specific reimagining and reinvention of the forms of collective political agency—a question that, as we saw in the previous chapter, is often passed over in cultural studies celebrations of populist oppositionality. Montag too, in describing what he calls the "helmet effect" of Derrida's work, notes the necessity for a specific materialization of the spirit of Marxism so brilliantly invoked by Derrida: "Can there be a spirit of Marxism that is not always already realized in practical forms, that can appear in the world in any other way than arm(or)ed from head to foot?

. . . The movements of struggle and the diverse organizations that take shape within them, far from killing the spirit of Marxism, are the sole form in which it can, in its irreducible diversity, live."[55] It is this lesson of Marx's work, and, as Montag suggests, of Derrida's project, that is too often ignored. What seems to be the unspoken assumption, if not the desperate hope, of many invocations of both messianic and populist oppositionalities is that they will somehow in and of themselves give rise to political forms and goals that are amenable to the project of creating a new *and better* society. However, as the repeated invocations in this chapter of the fascist modernist Marinetti (as with the case of Timothy McVeigh in the previous) bear out, there is no guarantee that such political energies, such a "passion for the real," cannot as equally be yoked for reactionary as for progressive goals.

This also gives voice to a specific anxiety on the part of contemporary left intellectuals: our fear, given the lessons of the preceding century, of taking an active role both in the formation of these new radical political movements and in helping develop their long-term goals. As Žižek puts it, "An Act always involves a radical risk, what Derrida, following Kierkegaard, called the *madness* of a decision: it is a step into the open, with no guarantee about the final outcome—why? Because an Act retroactively changes the very co-ordinates into which it intervenes. This lack of guarantee is what the critics cannot tolerate: they want an Act without risk—not without empirical risks, but without the much more radical 'transcendental risk' that the Act will not simply fail, but radically misfire."[56]

As is still often the case, we have much to learn in this regard from the work of Antonio Gramsci. Everyone is an intellectual, as Gramsci famously maintains; however, he goes on to point out that there nevertheless must exist a specific social group that takes up the "professional" role of intellectuals.[57] Such a stratum is in Gramsci's vision indispensable for any political, economic, social, and cultural transformation to occur: "Critical self-consciousness means, historically and politically, the creation of an *élite* of intellectuals. A human mass does not 'distinguish' itself, does not become independent in its own right without, in the widest sense, organizing itself; and there is no organization without intellectuals, that is without organizers and leaders, in other words, without the theoretical aspect of the theory-practice nexus being distinguished concretely by the existence of a group of people 'specialized' in conceptual and philosophical elaboration of ideas."[58] The "elitism" and "specialization" that Gramsci speaks of here should be understood first and foremost as privilege: an allocation of social resources necessary to engage in this complex, time-consuming, and vital work. Moreover, such an activity never takes place in isolation, but as part of a constant dialogue and pedagogical exchange with the "masses" (and here, too, Derrida's reminders of the dangers of premature totalization are indispensable). However, these privileges also entail significant responsibilities: responsibilities that include a continuous, open-ended formulation and reformulation of political strategies and alternative visions of the future; the education of people in the real possibility of realizing these other futures; the creation of safe spaces where these kinds of conversations and energies might be fostered; and finally, the taking up of an active role in shaping some of the directions, strategies, and tactics of these movements, including, as Bruce Robbins forcefully argues, a critical strategic defense of the remnants of the welfare state that historically made such work possible.[59] "The mode of being of the new intellectual can no longer consist in eloquence, which is an exterior and momentary mover of feelings and passions, but in an active participation in practical life, as constructor, organizer, 'permanent persuader' and not just simple orator."[60] Such a work of "persuasion," what Derrida described in a passage I cited earlier as the "performative" rather than the constative mode of intellectual labor, is as indispensable today as it was in Gramsci's moment: for as *Independence Day* shows us, just as there is no determinate connection between a moment of revolutionary temporal rupture and the social organization that will follow it—something of which Marx himself was clearly aware in his later writings[61]—so, too, there is no necessary relationship between the critical energies of messianic historicity and any specific form of political action. Rather, political organization and mobilization only comes about through a difficult, painful, and gradual process of education and action. What this film also shows us is that if we do not undertake this arduous labor, if we leave the question of political agency hanging in the air for too long, we can rest assured that others will take up the task, filling the placeholder of the messianic with a very different content.

This also suggests the dangers of the conspiracy vision of September 11, 2001—that the U.S government or some other organization planned and staged the destruction of the World Trade Center and other events of 9/11—promulgated by groups such as Scholars for 9/11 Truth.[62] Such a view at once grants too much and too little agency: too much in that it entertains the possibility of pulling off a conspiracy of this scope and magnitude without any leaks, and too little in that it ignores the real success of conservative intellectuals and media in the hegemonization, or what Žižek calls the "proper politicization," of the *passage à l'acte* that is 9/11.[63] As I hope this chapter and others in the present book demonstrate, this is a work that had begun long before the towers were struck, and that continues on into the present. The real challenge thus facing us is precisely the construction of an alternative to this pedagogy.

In my final two chapters I thus turn my attention to a number of cultural and theoretical projects that in the 1990s took up exactly this challenge, and this essential risk, by working to imagine new progressive forms of community and agency.

Seven

AS MANY AS POSSIBLE, THINKING AS MUCH AS POSSIBLE

Figures of the Multitude in Joe Haldeman's *Forever* Trilogy

Perhaps the central contradiction of globalization at this point in our history is the way in which it brings to the fore its own nemesis in terms of a fundamental reconception of the universal right for everyone to be treated with dignity and respect as a fully endowed member of our species.

DAVID HARVEY, *Spaces of Hope*

But for a clearer understanding of these things, we must note here that we live in continuous change, and that as we change for the better or worse, we are called happy or unhappy. For he who has passed from being an infant or child to being a corpse is called unhappy. On the other hand, if we pass the whole length of our life with a sound mind in a sound body, that is considered happiness. And really, he who, like an infant or child, has a body capable of very few things, and very heavily dependent on external causes, has a mind which considered solely in itself is conscious of almost nothing of itself, or of God, or of things. On the other hand, he who has a body capable of a great many things, has a mind which considered only in itself is very much conscious of itself, and of God, and of things.

BARUCH SPINOZA, *The Ethics*

Maybe to get rid of war, we have to become something other than human.

JOE HALDEMAN, *Forever Peace*

FREDRIC JAMESON OPENS his first discussion of the aesthetic practice he will name "cognitive mapping" with the astonishing confession that it is "a subject about which I know nothing whatsoever, except for the fact that it does not exist."[1] He goes on to argue, echoing a classic formulation of Louis Althusser, that the essay that follows will involve nothing less than an attempt "to produce the concept of something we cannot imagine."[2] The project

Jameson begins here, and which continues in his books *Postmodernism; or, The Cultural Logic of Late Capitalism* (1991), *The Geopolitical Aesthetic: Cinema and Space in the World System* (1992), and beyond, thus offers less a fully articulated vision of this aesthetic practice than an allegory, or a prefiguration, of something of which only the earliest intimations might now be glimpsed. Jameson does, however, go on in this inaugural essay to outline some of the fundamental coordinates of this cultural work: its deeply pedagogical function, as it teaches us something about what would be involved in positioning ourselves in the world; its thoroughly spatial and collective orientation; and, finally, its totalizing movement: "The project of cognitive mapping obviously stands or falls with the conception of some (unrepresentable, imaginary) global social totality that was to have been mapped."[3]

A similar set of imperatives is at work in the concept of World Bank literature articulated by Amitava Kumar, as it, too, grapples on a number of different fronts with the political task of constructing adequate representations of our own "unrepresentable, imaginary global social totality." Indeed, the three fundamental dimensions of the project of cognitive mapping described by Jameson are echoed in the question posed by Kumar, "How, then, do we elaborate a pedagogy that connects the 'here' and the 'there'?"[4] Kumar's agenda is, on the one hand, to spark a rethinking of the current configuration of postcolonial studies, and, on the other, to displace "the obsolete and inadequate category of 'World Literature' that has exercised so much influence over the literary discipline."[5] The latter's inadequacy arises because, as Franco Moretti reminds us, its focus in practice has remained "fundamentally limited to Western Europe, and mostly revolving around the river Rhine"; this inadequacy, in turn, renders the analytical methods it has produced obsolete in the face of an emergent global reality.[6]

The insertion of "bank" into the mix—playing as it does on the title of one of the central geopolitical institutions of the current moment—also has the effect of highlighting the limitations of both earlier intellectual endeavors. First and foremost the concept of the bank reminds us of a fundamental absence of issues of political economy in many conceptualizations of both world literature and postcolonial studies; and indeed, Kumar notes, "My own questions spring from the understanding that postcolonial studies, as practiced in lit. crit. establishments, have been primarily literary (rather than broadly cultural, and certainly economic) in their focus and practice."[7] Moreover, the notion of the bank also implies another fundamental shift in terms of how the very identity of culture itself is imagined. It is no coincidence that the first articulations by J. W. Goethe of the concept of *Weltliteratur* occurred precisely at the moment of the explosive rise of nationalism in Europe and the Americas. World literature—and something similar can often be said of work in postcolonial studies—adopts a conceptualization of different cultures as spatially bound and discrete entities, more often than not imagined on the scale of the nation-state.[8] In contrast, the figure of World Bank literature turns our attention to the deep *relationality* of both spaces and levels within the contemporary form of the capitalist world system—on the one hand, the continuous interchange among the "levels" of the economic, the political, and the cultural; and, on the other, the ceaseless flow of finance, commodities, information, and populations through the various networks that now link disparate locales in the world system. In short, World Bank literature is a form of "totalizing" thinking, which, as Jameson notes, "often means little more than the making of connections between various phenomena, a process which . . . tends to be ever more spatial."[9]

At the same time, however, to think totality relationally and relationality in a totalizing fashion is not, as goes the tired charge, to collapse difference into a homogenous identity. Indeed, even to think relationally presupposes the recognition of difference in the forms of levels, scales, and the constitutive unevenness of various cultural spaces. Moreover, the related practices of cognitive mapping and World Bank literature guard against the tendency toward identity often embedded in the converse and what became during the course of the 1990s the increasingly central concept of globalization. David Harvey, who has already done a great deal to sensitize cultural and critical theory to the continuously evolving spatial dimensions of the capitalist mode of production, offers a similar challenge to what he views as the potentially debilitating political conclusions that might be drawn from certain ways of imagining the processes and structures of globalization. He argues that while the attention given to globalization puts the issues of space and cultural geography on center stage, this concept can also be a deeply ideological one, as much as earlier and related notions like that of postindustrial society. Indeed, Harvey points out that "the answer to the question 'who put globalization' on the agenda is, therefore, capitalist class interests operating through the agency of the U.S. foreign, military, and commercial policy."[10] (This reality has become only more evident in the shift Harvey notes in his more recent book, *The New Imperialism*, from a Clinton era "neoliberal" to a Bush regime and post-9/11 "neoconservative" global imperialism.[11]) The figure of globalization thus often occludes the particular agency and interests involved in the process of spatial reterritorialization—both more readily evident in its conceptual precursors, Americanization and neocolonialism—while also performing the same pedagogical role as its temporal twin, the so-called end of history, which teaches us to think of it as a baleful and inexorable process of universal commodification and cultural homogenization.[12] Harvey thus proposes, in a fashion similar to the challenge Kumar issues to postcolonial studies, that we shift our "language from 'globalization' to 'uneven geographical development,'" thereby placing emphasis on the fact that our present moment is witness to a rearticulation on a new spatial scale of the contradictory logics of capitalism, only the latest in a historical series of "spatial fixes" and reterritorializations, rather than any kind of more fundamental break.[13] It is precisely this situation of uneven geographies on a global scale that both necessitates and makes possible new ways to imagine oppositional political organization and activities.

Thus both Kumar and Harvey emphasize not only the question of the representability of the new global system but also the deeply political nature of representation itself. And with this Jameson concurs: "This is surely the most crucial terrain of ideological struggle today, which has migrated from concepts to representations."[14] A similar attention to the political force of different kinds of representational acts is also at work in Jameson's much-debated thesis concerning third world literature: "Third-world texts, even those which are seemingly private and invested with a properly libidinal dynamic—necessarily project a political dimension in the form of national allegory: *the story of the private individual destiny is always an allegory of the embattled situation of the public third-world culture and society.*"[15] One of the more underappreciated dimensions of Jameson's reading here is the degree to which it unfolds as an exercise in generic thinking, genres, as he earlier defined them, being "literary *institutions*, or social contracts between a writer and a specific public, whose function is to specify the proper use of a particular cultural artifact."[16] Developing this point further in the essay on third world literature, he argues that one

of the greatest dangers in any approach to "non-canonical forms of literature" is to read them in terms of the canon itself (by which he means the
forms and rhythms of a hegemonic European realism and modernism):
not only is such an approach "peculiarly self-defeating because it borrows
the weapons of the adversary" but it also passes "over in silence the radical
difference" of these works.[17] Thus I think much of the debate surrounding
Jameson's essay dissipates if we view it not as offering ontological claims
about the nature of all cultural production in the "third world, but rather
as a strategic intervention aimed, like all genre criticism, at constituting
both a set of interpretive practices, pegged in fact to a particular spatial
scale, and an alternative corpus of texts on which these will go to work.
The function of Jameson's generic reframing of these texts is, like Kumar's
substitution of World Bank literature for postcolonial studies or Harvey's
uneven geographical development for globalization, to enable us to read
overly familiar phenomena in a new ways. Moreover, such an approach
to his analysis turns the tables on his critics, demanding that they make
explicit both the alternative they offer and its political, that is, its readerly,
import.

In the final footnote to "Third-World Literature in the Era of Multinational Capitalism," Jameson observes that one of the fundamental
philosophical underpinnings of his description of the genre's cognitive
aesthetics is Georg Lukács's model of class consciousness, or standpoint
epistemology, wherein a "'mapping' or the grasping of the social totality is
structurally available to the dominated rather than the dominating classes"
(the other underpinning is G. W. F. Hegel's master-slave dialectic).[18] Moreover, he goes on to suggest that his concept of "national allegory" represents a subgenre of the larger aesthetic of cognitive mapping, this essay
thus serving as "a pendant" to his influential 1984 work, "Postmodernism;
or, The Cultural Logic of Late Capitalism" (a slightly modified version of
which is reprinted as the first chapter of the book of the same title). In the
course of this latter essay, Jameson does two very different things. First,
he offers a symptomology of various semi-autonomous dimensions of a
properly first world, and particularly U.S. (as well as a specifically class-
based) experience of the postmodern (the collapse of critical distance, the
waning of affect, the weakening of historicity, the dissolution of the centered subject, the new centrality of the image, the inability to map our
place in this new reality, and so forth).[19] It is on this first dimension that

most of the critical discussion surrounding the essay focuses. However, Jameson then concludes with another call for the development, in terms of the original situation of the postmodern, of a new "pedagogical political culture"—the aesthetic practice of cognitive mapping.

Filling in the absent place of the Symbolic in Althusser's adaptation of the Lacanian tripartite schema (ideology famously described by Althusser as "the imaginary relationship of individuals to their real conditions of existence"),[20] such a new political art "will have to hold to the truth of postmodernism, that is to say, to its fundamental object—the world space of multinational capital—at the same time at which it achieves a breakthrough to some as yet unimaginable new mode of representing this last, in which we may again begin to grasp our positioning as individual and collective subjects and regain a capacity to act and struggle which is at present neutralized by our spatial as well as our social confusion. The political form of postmodernism, if there ever is any, will have as its vocation the invention and projection of a global cognitive mapping, on a social as well as a spatial scale."[21] The rest of the larger book then moves between these two projects, analyzing privileged symptomatic texts—for example, the experience of space in the Bonaventure Hotel, nostalgia films, the experimental video *AlienNATION*, new historicism, and free market rhetoric—to see what aspects of the postmodern condition they might illuminate; *and* exploring other allegories of the cognitive mapping process such as the "thinking" of Frank Gehry's house, of Robert Gober's installation projects, and of the genre Jameson names "allegorical encounter" films for further lessons about what such a new political aesthetic might look like.

Thus when read in conjunction with the third world literature essay, we see Jameson gradually expanding the aesthetic category of cognitive mapping to incorporate different kinds of representational acts—acts, moreover, that originate in different locations, Harvey's unevenly developed geographies, within the global totality. Such a proliferation of perspectives then continues in the collection of essays that make up the first part of *Signatures of the Visible*: the films that serve as the central objects of analysis here originate in the U.S. Hollywood system (*Jaws* [1975, dir. Steven Spielberg], *The Godfather* [1972, dir. Francis Ford Coppola], *Dog Day Afternoon* [1975, dir. Sidney Lumet], *The Shining* [1980, dir. Stanley Kubrick]); France (*Diva* [1981, dir. Jean-Jacques Beineix]); West Germany (Hans-Jürgen Syberberg's documentary trilogy of the 1970s); Poland (*Fever*

[1980, dir. Agnieszka Holland]); Venezuela (*La casa de agua* [1980, dir. Jacobo Penzo]); and Colombia (*Cóndores ne entierran todos los dias* [1984, dir. Francisco Norden]). The second part of the book then offers a dialectical diachronic complement to this synchronic or spatial mapping, rehearsing Jameson's periodizing schema of realism-modernism-postmodernism in terms of the particular and foreshortened history of the sound film.

In this book, as in the diptych he suggests is composed of the third world literature and postmodernism studies, the various perspectives offered on an emerging global reality remain relatively detached from one another. However, in Jameson's next film study, *The Geopolitical Aesthetic*, we see a self-conscious attempt to coordinate these various perspectives to produce a more systematic mapping of the present. Jameson opens the book with a discussion of U.S. conspiracy films. This expands on an observation in the original "Postmodernism" essay that "conspiracy theory (and its garish narrative manifestations) must be seen as a degraded attempt— through the figuration of advanced technology—to think the impossible totality of the contemporary world system."[22] He then reads films from a particular set of sites, all of which might best be characterized as transitional zones: the Soviet Union in its final hours (*Days of Eclipse* [1988, dir. Alexander Sokurov]); Taiwan, or the "newly industrialized First-World tier of the Third World or Pacific Rim" (*The Terrorizer* [1986, dir. Edward Yang]);[23] France, as it faces subsumption into the transnational entity of the European Union (Godard's *Passion* [1982]); and the Philippines, imagined as a privileged site for the recognition of a relentless modernization that effects a European first world as well (*Perfumed Nightmare* [1978, dir. Kidlat Tahimik]). Not only do these various sites remind us of the insufficiency of the older national cultural categories through which we continue to think the present—those also at work in much of postcolonial and world literature studies—but their multiple cartographic projections, when brought into coordination, also begin to illuminate the horizon of an emergent "geopolitical unconscious." In this way, Jameson argues, the earlier "national allegory" becomes refashioned "into a conceptual instrument for grasping our new being-in-the-world. It may henceforth be thought to be at least one of the fundamental allegorical referents or levels of all seemingly abstract philosophical thought: so that a fundamental hypothesis would pose the principle that all thinking today is *also*, whatever else it is, an attempt to think the world system as such. All the more true will this be for narrative figurations."[24]

It is this emphasis on the multiplication of perspectives, as well as their necessary coordination, in an attempt to think the contemporary geopolitical framework that I want to suggest stands as one of the most significant lessons of Jameson's work for the collective project Kumar names World Bank literature. The construction of World Bank literature as a field of investigation requires not only new reading strategies — sensitized to ways various texts grapple with the representational problem of bringing into focus the relational, spatial, unevenly developed, and total system of global capitalism — but also a new canon of texts. Kumar points toward both dimensions of this project in his observation about much of the work now celebrated under the aegis of postcolonial fiction: "I have been hard-pressed to find amongst these writings much about the new global realities. Searing critiques of the semi-feudal, semi-capitalist existence in rural India, yes; shallow, glitzy portrayals of city life in modern India, well, lots of that. But to date, I have read only one Hindi short story that could be described as a self-conscious critique of life under the World Bank–I.M.F. dictates of the past decade. Where is the literature of the New Economic Policy?"[25] And yet World Bank literature cannot simply be a transformation of the emerging canon of postcolonial studies, as important as such an undertaking remains; rather, it needs to open up U.S. and first world canons as well, fluid and recently achieved as these, too, may be, to a variety of nonliterary, in all senses of this term, texts that take up the political task of bringing into view various aspects of "life under the World Bank–I.M.F. dictates" (something Kumar in fact already does by introducing into his discussion the video documentary, *Degrees of Shame* [1998, dir. Barbara Wolf]).

⌇

To further advance this endeavor, I would thus like to suggest an additional generic site that promises to make a singular contribution to the thinking of the present we have been calling World Bank literature: the equally noncanonical and nonliterary genre of science fiction.[26] Indeed, it may be that, within the particular context of the former first world, mass cultural genres and other similarly marginalized practices best perform the labors of cognitive mapping demanded by the situation of the present. I take my lead here from Jameson as well, whose numerous writings on science fiction are sites, I want to argue, where significant aspects of the concept of cognitive mapping were first worked out.[27] Jameson claims that the interest of science fiction lies neither in the ways it prepares its readers for the "demoralizing impact of change itself" nor in the "accuracy" of its projections of the future—indeed, he suggests that one of the genre's "deepest vocations," as is that of its precursor, the narrative utopia, "is over and over again to demonstrate and to dramatize our incapacity to imagine the future, to body forth . . . the atrophy in our time of what Marcuse has called the *utopian imagination*, the imagination of otherness and radical difference."[28] However, alongside this "deconstructive" operation of the genre, Jameson argues that science fiction also succeeds in offering an important allegorical mapping of the present, one that unfolds along both diachronic and synchronic axes. On the one hand, the strategies of indirection in science fiction, similar to those employed in the detective story, bring into focus "the ultimate object and ground of all human life, History itself."[29] Jameson argues that the genre's "multiple mock futures serve the quite different function of transforming our own present into the determinate past of something yet to come" and thus enable us to perceive the present as history.[30]

Jameson offers an exemplary case of this strategy in his reading of Philip K. Dick's novel, *Time Out of Joint* (1959). The novel's presentation of late-1950s U.S. small-town life as a fantasy reconstruction in the very different "reality" of 1997 has the effect of starkly illuminating the historicity of the novel's contemporary moment. At the same time, Jameson argues, "the very structure of the novel articulates the position of Eisenhower America in the world itself and is thereby to be read as a distorted form of cognitive mapping, an unconscious and figurative projection of some more 'realistic' account of our situation . . . the hometown reality of the United States surrounded by the implacable menace of world communism (and, in this period to a much lesser degree, of Third World poverty)."[31] This, then, brings us to the form's second fundamental operation, that of providing mappings of space.[32] Echoing the claims made in "Third-World Literature," Jameson observes that science fiction eschews the pleasures and demands of canonical forms of literature—those of complex psychological portraits of "realistic" characters and "well-formed plots"—and thereby frees itself for this operation of spatial figuration: "The collective adventure accordingly becomes less that of a character (individual or collective) than that of a planet, a climate, a weather, and a system of landscapes—in short, a map. We thus need to explore the proposition that the distinctiveness of SF as a genre has less to do with time (history, past, future) than with space."[33]

This double project is already evident in H. G. Wells's founding work in the genre. *The Time Machine* (1895) undertakes a temporal figuration as it projects a far-flung evolutionary future for which the class divisions of capitalist Great Britain are imagined as determinate preconditions; whereas, *The War of the Worlds* (1898), through its self-conscious allegory of the violences of contemporary imperial conquest, here returned with a vengeance on the metropolitan center, offers one of the earliest attempts to cognitively map a previous project of global reterritorialization. Wells's conclusion to the latter novel is of interest to us here as well, as he shows how the very violences of the Martian conquest fuse disparate interests into an anti-imperial bloc, imagined on a global rather than a merely national level. And yet, while in this labor Wells offers an effective prefiguration of later anticolonial movements, he can imagine these collective formations in this historical moment only through an allegorical representation of the then contemporary European nation-state system, the "Earth" as one nation in an interplanetary system of nations. Such a failure to imagine the otherness of a collective subject on a truly global plane would mark both Wells's own subsequent utopian fiction, *A Modern Utopia* (1905), and, far more tragically, as Frantz Fanon foresaw, the various real-world decolonization projects.

Jameson's own writing on science fiction has long been attentive to these spatial-allegorical or figurative dimensions. For example, in his earliest SF essays, he explores the indirect engagement in Brian Aldiss's *Starship* (1958) with the contemporary questions of "the relationship between industrialized and so-called underdeveloped societies of our own planet."[34] And later, he looks at how the "character systems" in Philip K. Dick's *Dr. Bloodmoney* (1965) bring into focus "the replacement of the older compromised world of empirical activity, capitalist everyday work and scientific knowledge, by the newer one of communication and messages of all kinds with which we are only too familiar in this consumer and service era."[35] He also investigates the operations of the recurrent spatial figure of the door in the short fiction of A.E. Van Vogt "as a virtual allegory of the brutal and abrupt world-displacements of Americans at war."[36]

Jameson's work thus poses a number of interesting questions for a properly World Bank literature science fiction scholarship: in what ways might current efforts in the genre present allegorical figurations of the contemporary processes and spaces of globalization? And, even more significant—a concern also central in Harvey's and Kumar's discussions—what is the relationship between these mappings and any possible renewal of the capacity to imagine, and subsequently to produce, new collective political agencies?

One recent example of this double operation of allegorical figuration can be found in the 1990s triple-crown (Hugo, Nebula, and John W. Campbell) award-winning novel by Joe Haldeman, *Forever Peace* (1997). Haldeman's first science fiction novel, and also a multiple award winner, *The Forever War* (1974), offered its own effective mapping of an earlier moment in the history of the present. *The Forever War*, along with Ursula K. Le Guin's *The Word for World Is Forest* (1972) and Thomas M. Disch's *Camp Concentration* (1968), ranges among the great science fiction allegories of the Vietnam War. In this work, Haldeman, who was injured while serving in the U.S. military in Vietnam, focuses on an intergalactic war between Earth's highly technologized military force (an allegory for that of the United States in the 1960s) and a technologically primitive alien Other, the Taurans. What initially appears to be a hopelessly outmatched struggle ends up dragging on for centuries, as the Taurans' fighting capabilities evolve in response to the human assault. This novel centers on the experiences of the soldier William Mandella, who we learn is one of only a few of the original late-1990s draftees to survive the entire war. Because actual combat involves travel by "collapsar jump" to remote interstellar outposts, Mandella ages only a few years during his service as centuries pass back on Earth: although he actually fights in only a handful of battles, the Forever War itself lasts for 1,143 years.

The narrative alternates between episodes of Mandella's increasingly bewildered encounters with human social, cultural, and sexual mores that have changed dramatically during this time period—as well as the growing distance between himself and later, "younger" recruits, "these people who at times seemed scarcely less alien than the enemy"—and brief explosive scenes of the brutality, chaos, and horror of actual combat: "Suddenly a laser flared through the Taurans from the other side, somebody missing his mark. There was a horrible scream, and I looked down the line to see someone—I think it was Perry—writhing on the ground, right hand over the smoldering stump of his arm, seared off just below the elbow. Blood sprayed through his fingers, and the suit, its camouflage circuits scrambled, flickered black-white-jungle-desert-green-gray."[37] Juxtaposing in this way vast temporal and spatial scales with the more local individual-phenomenological ones, Haldeman's novel offers a superb early figuration of the utterly disorienting and alienating experience of what we now recognize to be an emerging postmodernism: a situation wherein the subject lacks the cognitive organs to map, or to situate itself within, both a dramatically expanded spatial totality and rapidly increased rates of change, the "future shock" of contemporary popular sociology. As Haldeman's novel allegorically presents the latter, transformations that formerly took centuries now occur within the span of only a few years, outstripping the subject's ability to cope with them: "It was dawning on me that I had not the slightest idea of how to conduct myself socially. So much of my 'normal' behavior was based on a complex unspoken code of sexual etiquette. Was I supposed to treat the men like women, and vice versa? Or treat everybody like brothers and sisters? It was all very confusing."[38] (A similar image of the disorienting effects of accelerated change is central to Dick's masterpiece, *Ubik* [1969]).

The war comes to an abrupt end when humanity evolves into a postindividual group subject, Man, who can finally come into contact with the similar collective consciousness of the Taurans: "The 1143-year-long war had been begun on false pretenses and only continued because the two races were unable to talk."[39] Deploying an image he will return to once again in *Forever Peace* (as well as in such works as his marvelous 1994 short story "None So Blind"), Haldeman shows, in a way that also effectively captures the war veteran's sense of alienation from the community to which he finally returns, how these changes have rendered obsolete older, centered, and monadic subjects such as Mandella: "I asked a Man to explain what it meant, what was special about clone-to-clone communication, and he said that I *a priori* couldn't understand it. There were no words for it, and my brain wouldn't be able to accommodate the concepts even if there were words."[40] In the end, Mandella along with other veterans of the Forever War who refuse to become assimilated into the collective consciousness of

Man, are resettled on an isolated planet named Middle Finger—"a kind of Coventry for heterosexuals. They call it a 'eugenic control baseline'"—to live out the rest of their natural life spans.[41]

This conclusion offers us the palpable relief of a utopian horizon—while also reminding us that the radical otherness of utopia cannot but invoke disquiet, if not sheer horror, in those of us, like Mandella, who were formed within a different historical situation (a point borne out even more explicitly in Soviet utopian and science fictions, ranging from Andrei Platonov's *Chevengur* [1926–29]—a work Jameson explores in *The Seeds of Time*—through Arkady and Boris Strugatsky's *Roadside Picnic* [1972] and *The Ugly Swans* [1972]). However, such a resolution to the narrative conflict also confronts the reader with a fundamental dilemma: for while the novel does teach us that the struggles, violences, and exploitations of the present will only come to an end with the emergence of a new posthuman (no longer Western, bourgeois) subjectivity, it opens up a yawning chasm between the conditions of our present and those of this necessarily unimaginable other situation. In short, the novel offers no image of human *action,* collective or otherwise, that would play a role in bringing about these necessary changes. Once again, then, Mandella becomes another kind of allegory of our present situation: unable to adjust to an utterly transformed present situation, his "capacity to act and struggle . . . is at present neutralized by . . . spatial as well as . . . social confusion."[42] The conclusion to *The Forever War* thus also offers a figuration of the sense of deep political paralysis that will quickly emerge as another constitutive feature of the post-1960s, postmodern experience—a fact that gives a very different, and more bittersweet, resonance to the novel's title.[43]

In his opening *caveat lector* to *Forever Peace*, Haldeman points out, "This book is not a continuation of my 1975 novel *The Forever War*. From the author's point of view it is a kind of sequel, though, examining some of that novel's problems from an angle that didn't exist twenty years ago."[44] This later novel also focuses on a seemingly interminable military struggle between two opponents whose technological developments are dramatically uneven. Moreover, like its predecessor, this is also a novel explicitly about the problems of mapping the present. In the opening of the narrative, the protagonist, Julian Class, an African American physicist and a military platoon leader, appears to be similar to Mandella, in that both lack the capability to situate themselves within their respective worlds:

"It's harder to see a pattern when you're part of it" (FP, 35). Interestingly, this statement by the novel's third-person narrator follows close on the heels of Julian's own commentary on the hero of Stephen Crane's naturalist classic, *The Red Badge of Courage* (1895): "The confused protagonist, Henry, was too deeply involved to see this simple truth, but he reported it accurately" (FP, 35). If we read this last statement as Haldeman's own self-reflection on his earlier fiction — where the consistent use of a first-person point of view also suggests a deep identification between the author and his central character — then the "new angles" this later work explores are indeed those made available by, among other things, nearly two decades of distance from the horrific immediacy of his own experience (a distance also signaled by a willingness in the later novel to move between first- and third-person narrations).

There are a number of other significant structural changes between the two novels. First, the setting of the war has been relocated from the interstellar expanse of *The Forever War* back exclusively to our planet. In the middle of the twenty-first century, a multifront war is being waged between the forces of the Alliance, mostly northern hemisphere nations under the leadership of the United States, and the Ngumi, a loose confederation of rebel forces in Africa, South America, and parts of Asia. Prefiguring the real-world events of September 2001, we learn that the war begins after a terrorist strike on the United States itself, in this fictional case, the nuclear bombing of Atlanta. Moreover, here too, suspicions are raised as to whether the Alliance knowingly "sacrificed" the city's people to justify the subsequent war (see FP, 11, 37). All the actual combat in the novel takes place exclusively within the homelands of the Ngumi, and Class's platoon operates in Costa Rica. The omniscient narrator succinctly summarizes this new situation: "It was partly an economic war, the 'haves' with their automation-driven economies versus the 'have-nots,' who were not born into automatic prosperity. It was partly a race war, the blacks and browns and some yellows versus the whites and some other yellows. . . . And of course it was an ideological war for some — the defenders of democracy versus the rebel strong-arm charismatic leaders. Or the capitalist land-grabbers versus the protectors of the people, take your pick" (FP, 36). This reduction in the spatial imaginary between the two novels is significant because it registers a fundamental shift that has occurred in the time period between U.S. actions in Vietnam and contemporary forms of military adventurism: what has diminished is the perception of the distance between the spaces and cultures of our world, distances that were given dramatic figuration in Haldeman's earlier text. Thus moving from one novel to the other reinforces the sense that over the course of the last decades of the twentieth century the globe had, to invoke the popular image, "shrunk."

One of the fundamental causes for this transformation is then brought into focus in the next significant change between the two books. In the earlier novel, war is still waged primarily through the traditional means of human infantry—although these modern soldiers, both men and women, are completely encased in highly sophisticated and dangerous (to their wearers as much as to anyone else) "fighting suits."[45] Yet by the time we arrive at *Forever Peace*, the nature of this technological "enframement" (*Gestell*) has changed: "All ten people in Julian Class's platoon had the same basic weapon—the soldierboy, or Remote Infantry Combat Unit: a huge suit of armor with a ghost in it" (*FP*, 11). The ghost is the controlling consciousness of this complex killing machine, a human "mechanic" "jacked" into and sharing a sensory and neurological feedback with the unit that enables it to be operated at a distance (and, as we later learn, thereby also enabling its operator to be killed at a distance if the machine is destroyed or even severely damaged before the link between it and the operator has been severed). Superior both to regular infantry, in their massive destructive capacity, and to robots, because of the presence within them at all times of human decision-making capacity, these war machines also "represented a technology that was out of the enemy's grasp" (*FP*, 13). These two figures of military technology thus stand as allegories of the shift in U.S. military strategy between the Vietnam and the first Persian Gulf War—the latter almost exclusively fought at a distance through a cyborg union of stealth and other advanced (and wildly expensive) aircraft technology and their elite cadre of operators.

However, Haldeman adds another twist that moves the second figure beyond a simple allegory of the first Gulf War military technologies. Not only are all mechanics jacked into their individual soldierboy but they also share an intimate link with all the other members of the platoon and thus tap into each other's deepest memories, fantasies, and experiences. During the ten days of the month of their active military duty, all privacy disappears for the mixed-gender group of mechanics, and the memories of this link linger the rest of the time. Moreover, this technology has allowed memories and experiences to be stored and accessed by anyone else possessing a jack; and although only military personnel and other government-approved researchers are officially cleared for jacks—put into place through a highly risky surgical procedure—a thriving black market for their installation, largely based in Mexico, has arisen. Needless to say, this technology has produced a whole set of subindustries, including new forms of prostitution (jack hookers are known as Jills). In this way, the allegorical resonances of the older soldierboy figure expand to encompass the new "information" technologies and thereby also offer a fuller figuration of the situation of the southern hemisphere in the "hot" 1990s global economy. For as *Forever Peace* reminds us, the fundamental condition of this forcibly underdeveloped space is one of wide-scale scarcity, at once of basic human necessities—"in the United States, luxuries were just that: entertainments or refinements. In the Canal Zone they were things like medicine or meat" (*FP*, 65)—and of advanced technologies, not the least of which now includes informational ones (the postmodern global forms of proletarianization I discussed in the preceding chapter).

Haldeman's narrative then adds an additional element to this rich allegorical portrait of uneven geographical developments. Early in the novel, the situation in the first world is described in this way: "Most jobs having to do with production and distribution of goods were obsolete or quaint. Nanotechnology had given us the nanoforge: ask it for a house, and then put it near a supply of sand and water. Come back tomorrow with your moving van" (*FP*, 45). The nanoforge serves first as a figure of commodity fetishism and of the alienation of life under capitalism, goods apparently arising without human intervention. Interestingly, the only form of productive labor that appears to occur in this space in the world system is that of professionals—scientific researchers, such as Class and his colleagues, medical doctors, military personnel, bureaucrats, and other intellectuals, one of whom later declares, "Sitting around consuming would drive us crazy" (*FP*, 151). However, once again, Haldeman deepens the allegorical resonances of the nanoforge figure so that it also stands in for the very technologies of production whose access to and control of by the subaltern peoples would ameliorate southern "unevenness." While nanoforges can

also produce nanoforges, the U.S. government maintains a strict monopoly on them. Hence, we learn, "Panama was a 'most favored nation,'
but not a full Alliance Member, which in practical terms meant it had limited use of American nanoforges, but there weren't any of the machines
within its boundaries" (*FP*, 64). It is thus the absence of both productive
and reproductive (informational) infrastructures that produces the situation of dramatic political and social instability in these zones of the world
system: "The unrest that led to the massacre was directly traceable to its
lack of the magic box" (*FP*, 65).

Jameson, Harvey, and Kumar each in their own way suggest that these
kinds of mappings are a necessary precondition for imagining new sites of
and possibilities for political mobilization in the present; and I want to argue that a similar insight emerges in Haldeman's fiction. In his later work
he will attempt precisely the kind of figuration that was impossible at the
end of *The Forever War*—and it is precisely this last operation that makes
the later novel a "sequel" to and a completion of its predecessor. In this
way, *Forever Peace* also diverges from other, and—as with the postcolonial fictions pointed out by Kumar—better-known contemporary science
fictional mappings. The figuration of the new informational technologies
has become a central, indeed some would argue dominant, aspect of postmodern science fiction since the rise in the early 1980s of the cyberpunk
movement, especially in the work of its most celebrated member, William
Gibson. In his discussion of cyberpunk as the quintessential form of a
postmodern "dirty realism," Jameson notes that in such works, "*dirty* here
means the collective as such, the traces of mass, anonymous living and
using."[46] In this representation, both the "traditional values of privacy"
and "public space as such" disappear, replaced by a new vision of the "no-
man's-land": "the space of adventure that replaces the old medieval landscape of romance with a fully built and posturban infinite space, where
corporate property has somehow abolished the older individual private
property without becoming public."[47] Whatever its libidinal and utopian
resonances, such a vision is also always already a deeply ideological one,
making manifest class interests similar to those that Harvey points out
are at work in many current conceptualizations of globalization. Moreover, this representation of "meat" or bodily space serves as the contradictory Other to the cyberpunk vision of informational technologies as a mechanical prosthesis: that is, an extension of *individual* consciousness and

capabilities—an image, then, also deeply related to the romanticization in these texts of the enhanced and individualized free agent "hired gun," be she a ninja assassin or he a hacker: a cool figure, in short, of the postmodern corporate professional, loyal to no interest beyond those of the self.[48] (There are also popular film representations of this same opposition, for example, in Paul Verhoeven's classic Reagan-era cynical text, *Total Recall* [1990, dir. Paul Verhoeven].)

In Haldeman's work, however, something quite different occurs. Here, the technologies become a figure not so much of an extension of the individual subject but rather the means of its decentering by a new kind of *collective* existence.[49] "Jacking" in this novel serves first and foremost as a figure for an epistemological potential found in the collective, one unavailable to the isolated individuals Mandella or Class. Later in the novel, after he has first jacked with the secretive and radical pacifist collective, the Twenty, Class observes that only now could he "understand why the *totality* could become more clear as more people joined: all the information was already there, but parts of it were better focused now that Cameron's point of view had combined with Mendez's" (FP, 203; my emphasis). The greatly enhanced capacity this new epistemological condition brings about is also evident in the climax of the novel, as a now tremendously expanded collective is able to muster "an impressive display of intellectual force" and bring about a speedy resolution to the apparently monumental threat that has emerged (FP, 349).

In this new vision, Haldeman dispels the fear, at play in the figure of the clone-collective Man in *The Forever War*, that collectivity equals homogeneity. Indeed, the kind of collective epistemology he imagines here requires a dialectical sublation of the individual and the group: "It's sharing information, not transferring it. I'm a doctor, which may not be a huge intellectual accomplishment, but it does take years of study and practice. When we're all jacked together and someone complains of a physical problem, all the others can follow my logic in diagnosis and prescribing, while it's happening, but they couldn't have come up with it on their own" (FP, 255). Such a changed condition also contains ontological dimensions, some of which the following passage beautifully captures:

I basked in the wonder of discovery. It wasn't like the difference between blindness and sight, exactly, but it was as if all your life you'd been wearing thick tinted glasses, one lens opaque, and suddenly they were gone. A world full of brilliance, depth and color.

I'm afraid you get used to it, I felt. It becomes just another way of seeing. Of *being*, she answered. (FP, 94)

Finally, Haldeman suggests deeply ethico-political consequences of this collective experience, a kind of Sartrean recognition of the Other, the significance of which Julian Class is especially well-equipped to understand: "The people in his university life were mostly white but color-blind, and the people he jacked with might have started out otherwise, but didn't stay racist; you couldn't think black people were inferior if you lived inside black skin, ten days every month" (FP, 79).

All of this sets the stage for the dramatic utopian transformation narrated by the novel. Later, the Twenty reveals to Class the reason why the platoons never stay linked for more than ten days:

"What happens is that after a couple of weeks in the soldierboy, you paradoxically can't be a soldier anymore."

"You can't kill?" I said.

"You can't even hurt anybody on purpose, except to save your own life. Or other lives. It permanently changes your way of thinking, of feeling; even after you unjack. You've been inside other people too long, shared their identity. Hurting another person would be as painful as hurting yourself." (FP, 179)

They use the verb *humanize* to describe such a process (FP, 180), although as Class himself suggests in the statement that serves as one of the epigraphs to this chapter, such a collective experience means becoming other to any definition of the human earlier (Western) intellectual and cultural traditions have had to offer. The second half of the novel then traces out a plot on the part of a coalition of U.S. intellectuals—including the Twenty, some of Class's colleagues at the University of Houston, and a handful of other well-placed figures in the government and military—to humanize the soldierboy platoons, parts of the U.S. government, and, significantly, the thousands of Ngumi prisoners of war held in the detainment camps of the Alliance. A number of challenges to this revolutionary agenda arise, including that of a millenarian death cult, the Hammer of God, or Enders, as they are more popularly known, which also includes members in positions of significant power. However, by the novel's conclusion, the radical coalition has met with success and thereby changed things "forever."

Interestingly, the novel also suggests why such a transformation has become so necessary in the present global situation. This is figured in the novel through Class's work on the Jupiter Project, a supercollider encircling the giant gaseous planet that, when ignited a few months hence, will re-create conditions "when the universe was smaller than a pea, and filled with exotic particles that no longer exist" (FP, 25). However, Class and his partner and mentor, Amelia Harding, soon discover that to start the machine will almost definitely result in the complete annihilation of the current configurations of time and space, and thus end humanity. This leads to speculation about a possible telos of consciousness itself:

> "So if Belda's right," Amelia said, "physical law was all in place. Twenty billion years ago, someone pushed the 'reset' button."
>
> "And some billions of years before that," Belda said, "someone had done it before. The universe only lasts long enough to evolve creatures like us." She pointed a V of bony fingers at Amelia and me. "People like you two." (FP, 177)

These kinds of speculations on the cyclical nature of time have long formed a significant part of the science fiction genre: similar visions are at work, for example, in both Isaac Asimov's Second World War era short story "Nightfall" (1941) and, in the context of post–Second World War atom bomb fears, Walter Miller's classic of theological science fiction, *A Canticle for Leibowitz* (1959). In Miller's and Haldeman's cases, the images serve as the allegorical embodiment of more general anxieties about a ruthless human domination and consumption of the natural world, which have produced the global environmental crisis that currently threatens this planet. Moreover, the responses of various characters in Haldeman's novel to this traumatic realization recall the three possible replies to the "ecological crisis" that Slavoj Žižek has suggested are currently available: denial of its significance, "'I know very well, but just the same . . .'" (in the novel, this arises in part out of fear of a loss of institutional position and prestige); "obsessive activity"; and "grasping it as a sign bearing some hidden meaning" (the last especially evident in the Enders, who see this machine as the mechanism for bringing about what they take to be God's will). Žižek argues that each of these responses are "forms of avoiding an encounter with the Real," before offering another approach: "We must learn to accept the real of the ecological crisis in its senseless actuality, without charging it with some message or meaning."[50] This means accepting a capability to destroy the world as a fundamental dimension of reality itself and learning to stop trying to flee from this "traumatic kernel," and rather living with it. But then to do the latter, to live with death, would require that we become otherwise: that is, humanity as we know it, or the reigning symbolic order, would have to come to an end—exactly the kind of change envisioned in Haldeman's novel. That such an "evolution" can only be a global and total one is borne out by the character's recognition that to do anything else— to destroy the supercollider, even to expunge its memory from the world— would not guarantee that "in another ten or a million years, somebody else will [not] come up with it. Sooner or later, somebody will threaten to use it. Or not even threaten. Just do it" (FP, 177).

However, to bring about such changes also requires a rethinking of the nature of collective political mobilization. The novel does so through a series of negations, offering representations of what such an authentic collective will *not* be. On the one hand, this imagined form of a new collective differs from the "mob," here figured as the subaltern masses of the Ngumi nations, wherein all individuality, and hence all possibility for a profitable exchange of knowledge, disappears: "It was not the sort of political demonstration a rational mind might have conceived, since it demonstrated their brutality rather than ours—but it did speak directly to the mob, which collectively was no more rational" (FP, 135). This image also points toward the polar opposite possibility, that of fanaticism: a blind faith in the rightness of individual action, again negating the possibility of communication that Haldeman sees as so fundamental to our very survival. This latter pole is more concretely figured in the internal first world conspiracy, the Enders, whose actions take place in isolation from even most other members of the cult and are underwritten by a blind faith in their own singular vision of things.

There is an additional figure of the false collective presented in the novel, embodied in the institution that dominates all life in the mid-twenty-first century: the Universal Welfare State that both regulates the use of the nanoforges and wages unending war with the Ngumi. Class encounters this institution directly when he goes to the Luxury Allocation Board in

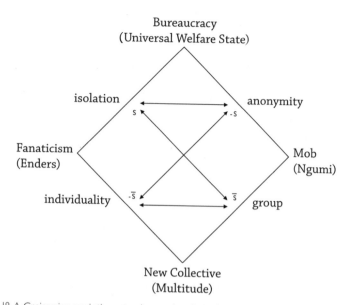

18 A Greimasian semiotic rectangle mapping the major groups in Joe Haldeman's *Forever Peace* (1997).

Dallas to request a gift for Amelia: "Door after door concealing people who sat at desks slowly doing work that machines could have done better and faster" (*FP*, 73). This is a vision, of course, of a state bureaucracy whose collective condition of work—chilly isolation and anonymity—is also a figure for the everyday experience of its interpellated subjects such as Class.

We might illustrate the relationship among these four figures—the Enders, Ngumi, Universal Welfare State, and the unnamed new collective—by deploying A. J. Greimas's semiotic rectangle (figure 18). Such a schematic presentation of the novel's vision proves productive in a number of different ways. First, in *Forever Peace* the true collectivity is presented as the utopian "neutralization," to use Louis Marin's term for this narrative process, of an "omnipotent and impersonal" apparatus, of which the "only experience people in the West have had," Jameson suggests, "is corporate capitalism itself."[51] However, such a negation of the welfare state is also one of the fundamental ideological operations performed by Reagan-era cyberpunk fiction (and before that, as we saw in chapter 4, of a neoconservative discourse more generally). The end product of this narrative work in cyberpunk is the two antinomic positions I traced out earlier: the opposition of the "dirty realist" mass urban living and the romanticized free-agent professional. Crucially, then, we can see how in Haldeman's work the limitations of these two solutions are made manifest, as they are allegorically represented by the negative form of the blind anonymity of the subaltern mass and a first world conspiracy, the Enders. Haldeman's vision thus pushes us beyond the global free market ideology of earlier cyberpunk, as it offers us a figure of an oppositional collectivity formed out of the union of the professional intellectual *and* the mass, of North *and* South, of intellectual and technological know-how *and* subaltern knowledge, with new information technologies playing a central role in this group fusion. What is being envisioned here is something both beyond politics and beyond social engineering—something for which we do not yet have the language: "There's no word for what we're doing" (FP, 238).

This representation of the thinking of Haldeman's novel also points toward a productive correspondence between the various levels produced in the Greimasian schema and in Jacques Lacan's three orders, a correspondence that in turn shines new light on the radical historical dimension of what is often understood as a static ahistorical structuralist device. Thus the figure in the novel occupying the place of Greimas's Complex term, the Universal Welfare State, corresponds to the Big Other (A) of the symbolic order itself, "the parasitic symbolic machine (language as a dead entity which 'behaves as if it possesses a life of its own')."[52] The second plane generated by the Greimasian schema, the binary opposition of the allegorical figures of the Enders and the Ngumi, occupies what Jameson describes as the "dual system" of the Imaginary, the antinomies whose very irresolvability constitute the lived experience of a particular situation (for us, that of globalization).[53] Finally, the new collective for which there is as of yet "no name," and which is thus strictly speaking unrepresentable, stands in the "impossible" place of the Real. Reading these figures allegorically—such that the Universal Welfare State is a figure of our current reality of global corporate capitalism and the Enders and the Ngumi of the contradiction of neoliberal free market individualism and a thoroughly urbanized post–welfare state collective life—also shows the way that Haldeman's narrative effectively marks what Alain Badiou names a potential "evental site" ("site événementiel") or the void of any specific situation, a situated opening to history or radical becoming that is absent in discussions that focus exclusively on the systemic closure (end of history and the colonization by capital of all internal and external space) of our global totality.

Perhaps it is needless to add that from the perspective of the dominant order itself, any figure occupying this place of the void of the Real will appear as Radical Evil, as that "which disrupts the pattern of the organic substantial whole": "Suffice it to recall Thomas More, the Catholic saint who resisted the pressure of Henry VIII to approve of his divorce. . . . from a 'communitarian' point of view, his rectitude was an 'irrational' self-destructive gesture which was 'evil' in the sense that it cut into the texture of the social body, threatening the stability of the crown and thereby of the entire social order. So, although the motivations of Thomas More were undoubtedly 'good,' *the very formal structure of his act was 'radically evil'*: his was an act of radical defiance which disregarded the Good of community."[54] This last position according to Žižek is also that of the "Hegelian notion of the infinite judgment" (as opposed to the merely negative judgment, represented in the case of Haldeman's novel by the Ngumi), and Hegel himself argues that "*crime* is the *infinite judgment* which negates not merely the particular right, but the universal sphere as well, negates *right as right*."[55] This fact is rendered dramatically evident in the Greimasian schema I offered in chapter 4, where this final place is filled by the diabolical figure of Max Cady, whose various allegorical resonances I outline there. What all this further suggests is the necessity to mark the sometimes barely perceptible but still absolute distinction between the destructive "irrationality" of fanaticism—that of the Enders and the Ngumi, or more concretely, of fundamentalist terrorism in our world, be it that of a Timothy McVeigh or of religious radicals—and the fidelity of authentic revolutionary formations.[56]

If in Haldeman's novel there is "no word" for this latter formation, the period of the late 1990s witnesses the reemergence of a concept that may in fact offer just such an appellation: I am referring here to Baruch Spinoza's notion of the "multitude." The most influential and widely discussed articulation of this concept in this moment is that offered by Michael Hardt and Antonio Negri in their landmark volume, *Empire* (2000). Indeed, one of the first descriptions found in their book of what they see as the fundamental opposition structuring the present could also characterize the problem being worked through in Haldeman's novel: "The multitude is the real productive force of our social world, whereas Empire is a mere apparatus of capture that lives only off the vitality of the multitude—as Marx would say, a vampire regime of accumulated dead labor that survives only by sucking off the blood of the living."[57] Moreover, their distinction of the figure of the multitude from that of the people also echoes Haldeman's differentiation of the true collective from some of its kin forms: "The multitude is a multiplicity, a plane of singularities, an open set of relations, which is not homogenous or identical with itself and bears an indistinct, inclusive relation to those outside it. The people, in contrast, tends toward identity and homogeneity internally while posing its difference from and excluding what remains outside of it."[58]

However, for our discussion an even more relevant characterization of the multitude is that offered by Étienne Balibar in his mid-1980s work, *Spinoza et la politique* (not published in English until 1998). Balibar makes explicit the nature of the bond joining together the members of this collective in ways that resonate with the vision in Haldeman's novel. According to Balibar, "the essential element in Spinoza's concept of democracy is freedom of communication. . . . the search for a strategy of collective liberation, whose guiding motto would be *as many as possible, thinking as much as possible*."[59] All "political regimes should be thought of as orders of communication: some of them are conflictual and unstable, and others are coherent and stable."[60] The history of the development of society from the least to the most free form of collective existence, that is from the hierarchical command structure of monarchy to the democracy of the multitude, is that of "the effort to transform the mode of communication, to move from relations of identification (that is, from the mode of *communion*) to relationships based on *exchange* of goods and of knowledge."[61] The figure of the multitude, much as the original collective imagined in Haldeman's novel, in effect resolves the fundamental opposition of the individual and the group: for since in Spinoza's conceptualization "no individual is rigorously 'like' any other, each having his own 'temperament,' multitude is then synonymous with exchange (in the broadest possible sense—exchange of properties is only one aspect of this idea) and with free communication between irreducibly singular individuals."[62] Moreover, as Spinoza argues in *The Ethics*, the individual is more free, that is more readily able to pursue his or her self-interest, in collective life, where he or she "lives according to a common decision, than in solitude."[63] For as he earlier notes: "To man, then, there is nothing more useful than man. Man, I say, can wish for nothing more helpful to the preservation of his being than that all should so agree in all things that the minds and bodies of all would compose, as it were one mind and one body; that all should strive together, as far as they can, to preserve their being; and that all, together, should seek for themselves the common advantage of all."[64] Such an end can best be realized in the context of unrestrained communication, which "can multiply the power of every individual, even if some individuals inevitably know more than others."[65] All regimes of control seek to restrict communication, for, as Haldeman's novel suggests, the opening up of these flows threatens them in the deepest ways. Similarly, the political struggles of the 1990s can be understood as being waged over the restriction or opening of these various modes of "communication," in Balibar's expanded sense of the term.

This figuration of the multitude in Haldeman's novel takes on additional resonance for those of us who spend our lives working within the university community. First, the novel argues for the possibility—indeed the necessity—of intellectuals, including those within the university, taking an active role in the creation of these new kinds of collective formations, deploying the resource of time we possess to perform this indispensable task: this is the task of the "professional intellectual" articulated by Antonio Gramsci I examined in my previous chapter. The intellectual's ethic is, Balibar adds, "not to prepare or announce the revolution but to take the risk of thinking in full view of his public. This is not a risk many revolutions have been prepared to take."[66]

Second, Haldeman's novel also represents the intellectual, scholarly, and research communities that we occupy as one of the best, if still only partial, intimations available of such a utopian collective experience: that is, one of the few places *already in our world* where some degree might occur of unalienated labor, noninstrumentalized activity (or, "play"), noncommercial exchanges, and democratic self-governance (which is something quite different from the current corporate administration favorite, "shared governance"). This is also the reason so much of the novel's action takes place within the various communities in which the research scientist Class spends his time, communities of unending conversation, speculation, and invention (this, too, resonates in some interesting ways with Jacques Derrida's passionate defense of the "university without condition," which he concludes, "is not situated necessarily or exclusively within the walls of what is today called the university").[67] However, it is only when these communities begin to transform their ideas into practice—the point being after all, the novel reminds us, to change the world—that their potential is realized.

Haldeman's double figuration of these communities may also help those of us working within the university better to grasp the nature of the attacks now, especially after the reheating of the so-called culture wars after 9/11, being directed against this institution and its labors. Those forces bent on dismantling the university often seem possessed by an excess of rage, not unlike that found in the figure of the anti-Semite as described by Max Horkheimer and Theodor Adorno in *Dialectic of Enlightenment*: a figure consumed by ressentiment, a deep and destructive envy directed at the "happiness"—the freedom of exchange and sense of community— imagined to be possessed by others, but never by himself: "No matter what the Jew as such may be like, their image, as that of the defeated people, has the features to which totalitarian domination must be completely hostile: happiness without power, wages without work, a home without frontiers, religion without myth. These characteristics are hated by the rulers because the ruled secretly long to possess them. The rulers are only safe as long as the people they rule turn their longed-for goals into hated forms of evil."[68] The university, along with a few other out-of-the-way sites in the world system, appears as one of the last bits of unfinished business in the global victory of neoliberal capitalism; and thus it is precisely its continued existence that offers at least one reminder of the possibility of living otherwise. One of the central political challenges that Haldeman's novel presents concerns not only the maintenance of this and other similar communities in the face of so much destructive rage (and also, as Bruce Robbins and Jameson argue, of their institutional contexts such as the welfare state) but also the question of how they might be extended outward to include more and more people.[69]

Finally, the novel suggests that such transformations will make the role of first world intellectuals obsolete, as it shows us the aroused subaltern collective itself as the only force really capable of negating the menace of the Enders and of the Jupiter Project. The prospect of being rendered obsolete takes on an even more poignant figuration in the fate of Class: as a result of his political activities he loses the ability to jack, and hence is condemned to remain, with the similarly "crippled" Amelia, outside the new global collectivity—a reminder that utopia, as Karl Marx once pointed out, is not for the likes of us. Unlike Mandella's, however, Class's sacrifice is not a futile one, for his efforts have helped bring about, finally, the end of the slavery of a "barbarism" described by Martin Luther King Jr. in the novel's epigraph: "When killing his fellow man was a normal condition of existence."

This event thus signals the end of what Marx calls "pre-history" and the entrance for the first time into the realm of true freedom, an image developed even more explicitly in Haldeman's final novel in the trilogy, *Forever Free* (1999). Here, Haldeman returns to the characters and settings of *The Forever War* and writes a true sequel to the earlier novel. Chafing at the restrictions placed on them in their colony "jail," Mandella and a group of other veterans of the Forever War commandeer a starship to travel twenty thousand light years beyond the known universe: because of the relativity effect, whereas on their return only a decade will have passed for them, they will have journeyed tens of thousands of years into the future. This device provides Haldeman with the opportunity for a moment of generic self-reflection about the limitations of science fiction to anticipate the radical otherness of the future, our imaginations being so deeply inscribed in what we already know:

> "So we go out for ten years, or forty thousand, and come back," said Lar Po. "Suppose Man's experiment has been successful. We'll be useless Cro-Magnons."
> "Worse than that," I said cheerfully. "They'll probably have directed their evolution into some totally new direction. We might be like house pets. Or jellyfish."[70]

Haldeman evades such a dilemma, as he shows their journey cut short by a series of unexplained events. When the voyagers return, they discover all the populated worlds bereft of human, Man, and Tauran life. Traveling to Earth, they encounter a mysterious race of superbeings, the Omni, who inform them that they had lived hidden on our planet for thousands of years and that they gave both humans and Taurans language and intervened in their histories in other ways, including setting "up the initial conditions" for the first contact of the races that culminated in the Forever War.[71] However, not even these beings are responsible for the mysterious events and disappearances. Mandella ultimately learns that his group's efforts to journey beyond the known universe provoked the "unnameable"—the god entity who established the laws of our physical universe and who also periodically intervened in our history—to end the "experiment" that is reality. In the end, however, this entity changes its mind: "'I don't guess I need to straighten up,' he said; it said. 'I'll just leave you on your own. Check back in a million years or so.'"[72] Moreover, before departing, the unnameable offers one final refutation of any lingering notions of a historical determinism: history, it tells the voyagers, "isn't a *line*. It's a table. There are all kinds of futures. Else why bother to experiment?"[73] The novel's closing line then gives playful expression to this new utopian situation where life seems to go on as before, though only now in a situation of real freedom: "Meanwhile, we chip ice, shovel snow, thaw pipes, scrape windows. Winter lasts forever on this god-forsaken world."[74] (A similar vision of the departure of "God" as a prerequisite to the entrance into a realm of freedom, as well as a play on the idea of multiple possible worlds, occurs in one of the other great fantastic trilogies of the period—a work with its own rich "Spinozan" resonances—Philip Pullman's *His Dark Materials* series [1995–2000].) This is the utopian situation sketched by Adorno in his *Minima Moralia*: "No differently will the world one day appear, almost unchanged, in its constant feast-day light, when it stands no longer under the law of labour, and when for homecomers duty has the lightness of holiday play."[75]

Only with this last novel of the trilogy does the full force of Haldeman's vision become clear: for now we can see that this supposedly comic resolution to the tragic plot of *The Forever War* was not possible without first passing through the vanishing mediator of *Forever Peace*—one final and especially powerful allegorical lesson offered to us by what can be understood as a truly unified trilogy.

Eight

WE'RE FAMILY

Monstrous Kinships, Fidelity, and the Event in *Buffy the Vampire Slayer*
and Octavia Butler's *Parable* Novels

We live within an Aristotelian arrangement: there is nature, and beside it right, which tries
as much as possible to correct, if needs be, the excesses of nature. What is dreaded, what
must be foreclosed, is what is neither natural nor amendable by right alone. In short, what
is *monstrous*.

ALAIN BADIOU, *The Century*

Is there a new world here?

FRANÇOIS RABELAIS, *Gargantua and Pantagruel*

IN HIS MAJOR WORK from the late 1990s, *The Ticklish Subject: The Absent Center of Political Ontology*,
Slavoj Žižek describes what he takes to be the "three
main leftist reactions to the process of globalization." The first, "liberal multiculturalism," operates
in fact as "the ideal form of ideology of this global
capitalism," occupying the "privileged empty point
of universality" from which the practices and values
of every culture are treated with respect: as long,
that is, as they do not "disturb the smooth circula-
tion of Capital—the moment some political intervention poses a serious threat to that, an elaborate
set of exclusionary measures quashes it."[1] The second
position, critical of this first, takes "the risk of endorsing neo-conservative populism, with its notions
of the reassertion of community, local democracy

and active citizenship."[2] Yet this position, too, one that very quickly comes near to the various postmodern fundamentalisms, is as much a product of global capitalism as the ecumenical multiculturalism against which it reacts. Finally, Žižek argues, there remains a traditional "critical theory" that rejects "both liberal multiculturalism and fundamentalist populism" and "clearly perceives the complicity between global capitalism and ethnic fundamentalism."[3] Yet this position turns out in fact to be the most "conservative" of the three, as it attempts to preserve "the domain of the *political*, the public space of civil society, of active responsible citizenship" that are the products of modernity and inseparably linked to the form of nation-state—an older order that is itself the fundamental target of globalizing capitalism.[4] All three responses, he thus concludes, are "inadequate," leaving us with the fundamental question, *"how are we to reinvent the political space in today's conditions of globalization?"*[5] Alain Badiou, whose work will play a central role in what follows, similarly argues that a fundamental project facing us today "is a matter of developing a different figure of politics from the figure of the revolutionary Party, as it has dominated things since October 1917. The experimental dimension is inevitable."[6]

It is precisely this project of reinvention, what Žižek elsewhere describes as a "repeating" of the great modernist projects of universal human liberation (a repetition, of course, that always occurs, as Gilles Deleuze has taught us, in difference), that occupies a number of the most important critical theoretical projects of the 1990s.[7] To take perhaps the most widely discussed example from that moment, Michael Hardt and Antonio Negri maintain that "in modernity the power of capital and its institutions of sovereignty had a solid hold on history and exerted their rule over the historical process. The virtual powers of the multitude in postmodernity signal the end of that rule and those institutions. Capitalist rule is revealed as a transitory period. And yet, if the transcendent teleology that capitalist modernity constructed is coming to an end, how can the multitude define instead a materialist telos?"[8] The beginning of an answer to this question, they suggest, occurs "when the virtuality of the multitude passes through possibility and becomes reality. The ontology of the possible is in this sense the central terrain of analysis."[9] The present, they stress again and again, needs to be understood as one of immense open possibility—and perhaps this is the most important lesson today of Hardt and Negri and of Negri's fellow Italian *autonomia* theorists. For they help us recognize that the post-9/11 escalation of systemic state, capitalist, and indeed imperial violence is itself fundamentally a reaction to the positive creative energies and mobilizations unleashed by the new global proletariat — "all those whose labor is directly or indirectly exploited by and subjected to capitalist norms of production and reproduction" — and in particular, to the unexpected and unplanned emergence in the latter part of the 1990s of a vibrant counterglobalization movement of movements.[10]

In this light, the present appears less as a situation of absolute catastrophe and more, as Hardt and Negri elsewhere argue, like that earlier moment, "between the 15th and 16th centuries, when modernity appeared in the form of a revolution." In such a context, "the revolutionaries imagined themselves as monsters. [François Rabelais's] Gargantua and Pantagruel can serve as emblems for all the giants and extreme figures of freedom and invention that have come down to us through the ages and proposed the gigantic task of becoming more free." Thus today, they conclude, "we need new giants and new monsters that bring together nature and history, labor and politics, art and invention to demonstrate the new power that the birth of 'general intellect,' the hegemony of immaterial labor, the new passions of the abstract activity of the multitude provide to humanity. We need a new Rabelais or, really, several."[11]

It is precisely these new Rabelaises, actively producing figures of "new giants and new monsters," that I argue we can also find in one of the most dynamic areas of cultural production today, that of science fiction and its generic kin such as fantasy and the gothic. Indeed, the figure of the monster is one the four coordinates — along with time, space, and the machine — through which Mark Rose argues that the genre stages its paradigmatic confrontation between the human and the nonhuman.[12] In particular, I want to begin to think about the "monstrous" forms of radical kinship — which, in Judith Butler's terms, seek "to extend legitimacy to a variety of kinship forms, and which, in fact, refuse the reduction of kinship to family"[13] — that we see taking form in two popular fantasy and science fiction serial texts that came into being in the late 1990s: the television series *Buffy the Vampire Slayer* (1997–2003) and Octavia E. Butler's two *Parable* novels, *Parable of the Sower* (1993) and *Parable of the Talents* (1998). These works offer a transvaluation of the pedagogical narrative paradigms of their nineteenth-century ancestors, such as Bram Stoker's

Dracula (1897), which, as Nancy Armstrong argues, offers "its readership a glimpse of alternative kinship practices only to demonstrate spectacularly that such alternatives dissolve gender differences and so produce monsters. . . . This is indeed the job of the nineteenth century gothic: to turn any formation that challenges the nuclear family into a form of degeneracy so hostile to modern selfhood as to negate emphatically its very being."[14] A similar narrative dynamic is at work, as we shall see, in these "*fin de* millennium" texts: only here, these monstrous kinship forms are taken as the promise of a new future.

It is necessary first to distinguish between two very different kinds of representational activities taking place in science fiction and other forms of fantastic literature. On the one hand, these works are ideally suited for allegorical representations, where social, political, and cultural materials may be confronted in a way that simply would be too traumatic for much of its audience if tackled head-on. It is through these kinds of allegorical structures that much of the more readily acknowledged critical pedagogical agendas of these works unfold. *Buffy* in particular is exemplary in its use of these kinds of allegorical representations. The first few seasons of the series deployed an allegorical structure to offer a representation, far more effective than most televisual realisms, of the tribulations of high school, adolescence, and youth culture in the fin de siécle United States. One commentator notes that "a consistent 'monster' that Buffy and the rest of the Scooby Gang encounter is the same one faced everywhere by high school students (past, present, and future): alienation."[15] While I would suggest that we need to be wary of the potential naturalization, or what Roland Barthes calls the mythification, of "alienation" implicit in this statement—indeed, the series remains quite aware of the historical and cultural specificity of the materials with which it grapples—it does highlight the way the allegorical structure of the show operates. The primary characters are—or, especially in the case of the former cheerleader Buffy herself, *become*—outsiders of various sorts: at times the show has even dabbled with the notion that Buffy's status as slayer might serve as an allegory of queer youth (her mother once quipping in exasperation that she was willing to march in the Slayer's Pride Parade). Moreover, as in a classical allegorical text such as John Bunyan's *Pilgrim's Progress* (1678), various affective states take on a concrete materialization in the show's monsters. To take a few examples, a young girl who feels she is ignored by

Moreover, as the *Buffy* series progresses, we witness a very interest-ing transformation in what we might call the "scale" of the show's set-ting—and hence an expansion of its allegorical critique—from the local, immediate high school context of the first three seasons, where, by the third season, the central opponents are the school principle and the city's mayor; through what I would describe as the national scale of the fourth transitional university season, where the primary conflict is with a secret U.S. government agency attempting to construct a hybrid-demon soldier (why many devoted viewers consider this to be the least successful season in the series is an interesting question in its own right); into a particular kind of global allegorical setting of the sixth and seventh seasons, where the referent is a post-September 11 environment of depression, anxiety, fear, suspicion, and escalating global violence. Indeed, in the seventh and final season, Buffy begins to construct a truly global army, with members from China, Europe, Africa, and elsewhere, of young "potential slayers"— their real power, we ultimately learn, kept in check by the patriarchal order of the Watchers, those assigned to oversee and direct the training of each generation's "Chosen One" (I will return to this crucial point shortly).

Octavia Butler too has long used allegory as a way of shedding new light on significant social and political concerns. Her great Xenogenesis trilogy, for example, and in particular its first volume, *Dawn* (1987), deploys alle-gory to explore the fraught issues surrounding "forced" desegregation and white Southern resistance to it (the alien Oankali standing in for the interventionist federal government and the humans for the white South-erners). The *Parable* novels, on the other hand, offer social and political allegories aimed directly at the present. In classical dystopian fashion, or more precisely in what Tom Moylan calls that of the "critical dystopia," Butler presents us with a near-future world—one of the distinctive fea-tures of SF as a genre lies, as Fredric Jameson reminds us, in its mapping of spaces—that arises out of an extrapolation of the social, economic, and cultural policies of its present: a world of widespread environmental despoilage and social disorder, where any kind of federal government has dissolved away, where fundamental services are privatized or have dis-appeared all together, where corporate-run townships reintroduce wage slavery, and where the remnants of the lower middle-class retreat into barricaded neighborhood enclaves wherein they provide whatever mini-mal schooling their children receive and fight an ongoing battle with the anarchic predatory individuals and groups surrounding them. Interestingly, the allegorical center of the series shifts with the second novel, as Butler now focuses her attention on a rising tide of fundamentalism that takes root in the United States through its promise of returning some semblance of order to this chaotic world. In this, Butler also offers an allegory of what David Harvey among others has characterized as the neoconservative response to the destructiveness, violence, and social instability of neoliberal global economic policies.[16]

While the allegorical dimension of these two texts offers the means of an effective critical engagement with the present—and again, in this displaced fashion, actually reaches a much wider audience than any straight-ahead social commentary might—it remains a fundamentally *negative* gesture, illuminating what might be most intolerable in our world without offering any effective vision of an alternative to it. (It is the exclusive focus on this negative critical dimension that I think also marks a more general limit of much of engaged cultural criticism.) To begin to bring into focus the intimations of an effective alternative vision, we thus need to turn our attention to what I take to be the much more interesting dimension of these works, their operations of figuration. I take the concept of figuration from Louis Marin's great work, *Utopiques: Jeux d'espace* (1973). With it, Marin means to suggest a process of allegorical representation for which there is not yet a referent, a giving of representational form to that which has not been named.[17] Marin describes the ways in which the "speaking picture" of classical utopian texts, his primary object of study being Thomas More's *Utopia* (1516), offer a schematic or preconceptual way of mapping emergent aspects of a new social reality (in More's case, the lineaments of a capitalist mode of production germinating within the body of European feudalism). In what follows, I want to extend Marin's fundamental insight further and suggest that the contemporary science fiction texts under discussion here may also offer us figurations of new ways of being and acting in the world—ways that crucially can only appear from within the closure of the present to be nothing short of monstrous. The figurations in these texts are thus a form of what Badiou names a Truth Event, a supplement to or "going beyond" the current situation, the "what there is," which thereby "compels us to decide a *new* way of being."[18] Such a radical opening up onto the void of the present situation cannot, Badiou crucially argues, "be communicated," but is instead encountered:

"It is an Ethics of the Real, if it is true that—as Lacan suggests—all access to the Real is of the order of an encounter."[19] Similarly, I would argue, science fiction and its generic kin do not so much "communicate" a representation along the lines of various realisms as stage the Event of an encounter with the void of the Real (Alfred Bester's great 1950s novels, *The Demolished Man* and *The Stars My Destination* are paradigmatic of this operation)—and it is in the genre's particular staging of such encounters that the best works composing it become so valuable.

I take a more general lead in this investigation from a number of recent critical projects, all of which mark a vital new turn in the period under question in work in cultural studies scholarship and attempt to read a variety of cultural productions for their intimations of new forms of collectivity. For example, in the climactic chapters of *The Geopolitical Aesthetic*, Jameson looks at the utopian figurations of the collective we find both in the late work of Jean-Luc Godard and in the naïf cinema of the Filipino filmmaker Kidlat Tahimik.[20] Meaghan Morris deploys Deleuze and Félix Guattari's concepts of "repetition" and "becoming" to uncover in the documentary film project, *A Spire* (1988, dir. Glenn Singleman), a reconfiguration of the entire imaginary of the "colonial 'voyage/home' opposition" and a vision of a new way of "practicing place."[21] Kristin Ross recovers the lessons to be found in the "improper" forms of collective struggle that emerge in the singular events—the "unplanned, unguided, formless revolution[s]"—of the Paris Commune and "May '68," as well as the figurations of radically original forms of collectivity that we find in the work of Arthur Rimbaud: Rimbaud's "swarm" is something other ("Je est un Autre") than the vanguard industrial proletariat of what will become a Marxist orthodoxy and which thus at the same time "escapes from any of those paranoid or colonial formations—what Nietzsche calls 'formations of sovereignty'—such as the armies whose discourse Rimbaud parodies."[22] And finally, Allen Feldman offers a breathtaking analysis of how the "radical deconstruction and reassemblage of the body" that occurs in the IRA hunger strike of 1981 effects a "resymbolization of the Republican movement": "The hunger strike as self-inflicted violence short-circuited the ritual partition of victimizer and victim that characterized and stereotyped political hegemony in Northern Ireland by interiorizing this exchange."[23]

However, the most immediate inspiration for my reading is to be found in some of the recent work of another Butler—Judith Butler. In her groundbreaking discussion of the "documentary" *Paris Is Burning* (1990, dir. Jennie Livingston), Butler challenges the critical dismissal of the film as simply another version of an imperialist ethnographic appropriation of the cultural Other. Such a reading, she maintains, naturalizes and rigidifies racial, gender, and class categories, denies the members of the drag communities represented in the film any agency (offering them up as no more than victims of another's predation), and, even more significant, misses the ways the particular narrative tableau *constructed* by the film becomes a site for radical invention—a site for the Event, in short, of the production of new monsters. In reorienting our approach in this way to these kinds of cultural texts, Butler demonstrates the ways in which the drag ball envisioned in the film serves as "an occasion for building a set of kinship relations that manage and sustain those who belong to the houses in the face of dislocation, poverty, homelessness." This "resignification of the family"—resignification itself being another term for what I described earlier as figuration—offers "a cultural elaboration of kinship that anyone outside of the privilege of the heterosexual family (and those within those 'privileges' who suffer there) needs to see, to know, and to learn from, a task that makes none of us who are outside of heterosexual 'family' into absolute outsiders to this film."[24]

Butler extends her investigation of this radical reconfiguration of kinship and of the production of new forms of belonging in her short book *Antigone's Claim: Kinship Between Life and Death* (2000). In the final lines of this text, Butler makes an argument that resonates with Hardt's and Negri's call for the imagining of new monsters: "If kinship is the precondition of the human, then Antigone is the occasion for a new field of the human, achieved through political catachresis, the one that happens when the less than human speaks as human, when gender is displaced, and kinship founders on its own founding laws. She acts, she speaks, she becomes one for whom the speech act is a fatal crime, but this fatality exceeds her life and enters the discourse of intelligibility as its own promising fatality, the social form of its aberrant, unprecedented future."[25] Antigone's "crime" against the family-state couple—the law being that which sets "a limit to the social, the subversive, the possibility of agency and change, a limit that we cling to, symptomatically, as the final defeat of our own power"—is a form of monstrosity that calls into questions the very foundations on which the social order, the law or civilization itself—"Its defenders claim that to be without such a law is pure voluntarism or radical anarchy!"—appears to be anchored.[26] While such a position is indeed "outside life as we know it"—a form of what Badiou calls the void or uncounted of a situation—it is decidedly not, Butler stresses, "necessarily a position outside of life as it must be. It provides a perspective on the symbolic constraints under which livability is established, and the question becomes: Does it also provide a critical perspective by which the very terms of livability might be rewritten, or indeed, written for the first time."[27] In this way, the particularity of struggles for new forms of kinship take on what Badiou calls proper universal dimensions, promising to transform the status quo utterly.

Jameson, too, has highlighted the utopian charge of the representation in capitalism of even traditional forms of extended kinship. He argues that one of the most interesting aspects of a mass cultural text like *The Godfather* is to be located "in the fantasy message projected by the title of this film, that is, in the family itself, seen as a figure of collectivity and as the object of Utopian longing, if not as Utopian envy."[28] However, the dilemma with such representations of an "alien collectivity" is that they can rapidly degenerate into forms of nostalgia, projecting "an image of social reintegration by way of the patriarchal and authoritarian family of the past."[29] Badiou also calls into question the contemporary revalorization of the traditional family structure—"as the century draws to a close, the family has once more become a consensual and practically unassailable value"—which he sees as a fundamental block to any repeating of a modernist project of the production of "the new man" who "is envisioned in opposition to all enveloping forms as well as to all predicates."[30] Butler acknowledges our time as one "in which the family is at once idealized in nostalgic ways within various cultural forms, a time in which the Vatican protests against homosexuality [and more recently, I might add, artificial reproductive technologies[31]] not only as an assault on the family but also on the notion of the human, where to become human, for some, requires participation in the family in the normative sense." However, she emphasizes that this moment is also one "in which kinship has become fragile, porous, and expansive," a time of the proliferation of "uncounted" forms of family and kinship that make radical resignifications possible. "What will the legacy of Oedipus be," she concludes, "for those who are formed

19 Buffy asserts "We're family," from *Buffy the Vampire Slayer* (originally broadcast November 7, 2000).

in these situations, where positions are hardly clear, where the place of the father is dispersed, where the place of the mother is multiply occupied or displaced, where the symbolic in its stasis no longer holds?"[32] What makes works like *Buffy* and Butler's *Parable* novels so powerful is the way in which they figure this void, both drawing on the utopian content of the extended family and then inflecting it in new, politically radical directions.[33]

There is a moment early in the *Buffy* series' fifth season in an episode appropriately entitled "Family" when this act of monstrous resignification or figuration is made explicit. The character Tara, Willow's partner before her murder at the climax of the series' penultimate season, reveals that on their twentieth birthdays all the women in her family turn into "demons." She thus needs to return to her biological family because they are the only ones who can contain this evil. All this turns out to be a lie, constructed and perpetuated by the men of the family to control the powers of the women. (This foreshadows, as we shall see momentarily, the climax of the series.) In the final confrontation with Tara's brother and father, where Buffy and her community refuse to let them take Tara away, the following exchange occurs (figure 19):

TARA'S FATHER: "We are her blood kin! Who the hell are you?"
BUFFY: "We're family."

The opposition set into play here, that between "blood kin" and "family," is crucial, for it in one swoop replaces, as Butler argues, "the blood tie as the basis for kinship with consensual affiliation."[34] Butler goes on to note, "We might see new kinship in other forms as well, ones where consent is less salient than the social organization of need."[35] In her more recent work, Butler further argues, "If we understand kinship as a set of practices that institutes relationships of various kinds which negotiate the reproduction of life and the demands of death, then kinship practices will be those that emerge to address fundamental forms of human dependency, which may include birth, child rearing, relations of emotional dependency and support, generational ties, illness, dying, and death (to name a few)."[36] This redefines kinship as "a kind of *doing*, one that does not reflect a prior structure, but that can only be understood as an enacted practice."[37] Moreover, when these new "modes of intimate association produce sustaining webs of relationships, they constitute a 'breakdown' of traditional kinship that displaces the presumption that biological and sexual relations structure kinship centrally."[38]

It is both this displacement of traditional "presumptions" and an increasing expansion and radicalization of new forms of queer consensual kinship that subsequently unfolds in the *Buffy* series. Buffy's biological mother is killed off later in the fifth season (and the episode, "The Body," immediately following this event is one of the most harrowing portrayals in the history of television of a community's coming to grips with the reality and banal everyday details of unexpected death); the substitute father figure, Giles, is moved to a minor advisory role; and the demons and former murderers Anya and Spike become central members of the community of affiliation. The series even adds, as its central characters become older, a younger sister for Buffy who, while ultimately declared to be quite literally Buffy's blood kin — she is an artificial being, a disguise for a dangerous mystical key, created out of Buffy's blood — only unnaturally enters the "family" as an adolescent and who is then reared by Buffy and her new family.[39] Moreover, other networks of elective kinship are hinted at. Early in the final season, for example, we are presented with a flashback sequence of the moment when Anya, represented as a powerful and outspoken woman in a traditional rural community, begins her millennium-long rampage as a demon of vengeance against faithless lovers. The demon who recruits her notes that his group, too, "forms a family of sorts."

The importance in the show's imaginary of these kinships of affiliation was also stressed in an important episode entitled "Normal Again" that aired late in what turned out to be the incredibly rich, daring, and psychologically complex penultimate season of 2001–2. In an episode that recalls the hallucinogenic science fiction of Philip K. Dick, Buffy is surreptitiously given a drug that either tricks her into believing or, conversely, enables her to recognize—as in the tradition of the fantastic, as the genre has been defined by Tzetvan Todorov, we are in the end left suspended equally between both options—that she is in a mental hospital and that her entire existence as the slayer in Sunnydale is in fact a psychotic fantasy.[40] She is then presented with the option of either returning at long last to the "real" world, and rejoining her still intact nuclear family (reinserting her in Deleuze and Guattari's Oedipal territorialization "Mommy-Daddy-me"), or of retreating once again, and perhaps forever, into the "fantasy" community of affiliation that surrounds her in Sunnydale. In the end, Buffy chooses the latter: if this is madness, then it is still, the episode suggests, a far better place to be than her, and by extension our, "real" world.

But the interesting question here is, in fact, exactly what would Buffy give up in leaving Sunnydale; or to put the same question another way, what is the bond that sutures this artificial kinship structure together? The beginnings of an answer emerge when we turn our attention once again to Butler's novels. A number of critics have already commented on the ways in which the series' central character, Lauren Olamina, constructs a new form of collectivity akin to that which we see in the *Buffy* series. This community is also one forged in crisis as the characters band together for survival on a perilous journey from Lauren's middle-class, gated community outside Los Angeles up into the still sparsely settled wilds of Northern California:

> Somehow, we've reached our new home—Bankole's land in the coastal hills of Humboldt County. The highway—U.S. 101—is to the east and north of us, and Cape Mendocino and the sea are to the west. A few miles south are state parks filled with huge redwood trees and hoards of squatters. The land surrounding us, however, is as empty and wild as any I've seen. It's covered with dry brush, trees, and tree stumps, all far removed from any city, and a long, hilly walk from the little towns that

line the highway. There's farming around here, and logging, and just plain isolated living. According to Bankole, it's best to mind your own business and not pay too much attention to how people on neighboring plots of land earn a living.[41]

Tom Moylan notes that in this way, Butler is able

to posit a politicizing process that produces a vulnerable but viable utopian alternative by the end of the first book in the series. In what [Raffaella] Baccolini would term its "multi-oppositional" diversity of classes, genders, sexualities, races, ages, abilities, and experiences, Lauren's Earthseed community captures the best qualities of the identity politics of the 1980s even as it reconfigures the entire tendency within the emerging alliance politics of the 1990s. In doing so, it suggests a possible model for an oppositional movement that is fundamentally and insistently diverse yet strategically united, one able to generate a level of totalizing analysis and coordinated action that can challenge the entire socioeconomic system of the transnational corporations.[42]

However, Moylan goes on to argue that the subsequent *Parable of the Talents* fails to fulfill this initial promise, as Butler retreats into a narrative vision that "draws more heavily on the personal and theological side of her intertextual resources, and thereby reduces the acuity of her historical analysis and political speculation."[43]

Parable of the Talents opens in the colony formed by Lauren and her fellows, highlighting its brief period of viability before it is brutally destroyed by a fundamentalist Christian group that is able to seize control of the frayed federal government and to forcibly reimpose on the nation-state a normative patriarchal and heterosexist family structure. Lauren's infant daughter Larkin is taken from her, and on her escape from the fundamentalist reeducation camp, Lauren begins a long and desperate quest to find her lost child. However, in what for many readers is a surprisingly unexpected turn, Lauren soon abandons this quest and instead turns her attention to recruiting participants for what she names the "Earthseed" project. Earthseed will involve the building of interstellar ships that will allow colonists to travel to and settle other worlds in our galaxy. She is successful, and the movement flourishes, devouring more and more of

Lauren's energies. Decades pass, and when she finally meets her now adult daughter, it is evident that any bond between them has disappeared. The young woman, renamed Asha, declares the "Christian American" uncle who raised her to be "like a father to me."[44] And of her biological mother she notes, "all that she did, she did for Earthseed. I did see her again occasionally, but Earthseed was her first 'child,' and in some ways her only 'child'" (PT, 404).

Moylan argues that the vision we get here represents a retreat from the charged oppositional vision of the utopian enclave seen at the end of the first and the beginning of the second books and devolves into a merely "alternative," if indeed not a mystical, vision. Moreover, he suggests that the "usefully self-reflexive critique" offered by Asha's narrative remains undeveloped (the plot of Parable of the Talents unfolds through alternating "excerpts" from Lauren's contemporary diary and a memoir written by Asha years after her now famous mother's death). However, while I take Moylan's critique to be a powerful one of a certain (and indeed, perhaps most immediately available) New Age–style reading of the novel, I believe that there are still present much more radical resources in the text, ones that become evident when we switch our interpretive register to a more properly figurative one. Indeed, from this perspective, I would suggest the inverse conclusion: it is the utopian enclave of Parable of the Sower that the final novel marks as merely alternative, and the Earthseed project that is the figure for a truly radical totalizing politics.

There are three crucial elements of the work that a figurative interpretation brings to the surface. First, what becomes so painful for many readers in Asha's narrative is precisely the way it reverses the conventional hierarchy of blood and consensual affiliation that serves as the foundation for our dominant notions of kinship. If indeed Earthseed is Lauren's "first" and "only child," it is a child that appears to Asha as a monster: "You're a cult leader," she tells her mother in their first adult meeting, drawing on one of our current dominant myths of unnatural kinship (PT, 403). In expressing this view, Asha becomes a stand-in for the readers of the text, who like her, are formed within a patriarchal community that sees blood kinship as the only "natural" form, and all other relationships as monstrous. (Butler further explores these forms of unnatural alternative kinship in her final novel, Fledgling [2005], a classically utopian speculation on the forms of family formed by vampires and a critical reworking of some of the central strands of the *Harry Potter* series.) It is precisely in such monstrosity that its radical potential lies.

Second, in her vision of the destruction both of the middle-class gated suburban enclave of Lauren's youth *and* of the community she later founds in Northern California, Butler unequivocally rejects any kind of enclave politics that would attempt to found an alternative community outside the dominant global order. In this critique of utopian communalism, Butler's text resonates in some fascinating ways with the devastating public rejoinder to Étienne Cabet printed in the September 1847 issue of *Kommunistische Zeitschrift*, the official newspaper of the recently founded Communist League to which Karl Marx and Friedrich Engels belonged and for whom they would shortly write their most well-known work, *Manifest der Kommunistischen Partei*, the *Communist Manifesto* (1848). The essay was written in response to Cabet's call in the May 1847 issue of *Le populaire* for a group of his followers to travel with him to the western United States and found a new community based on the principles he had outlined in his hugely influential utopia, *Voyage en Icarie* (1840).[45] After outlining both the troubling effects such a project would have on the European communist movement ("It would encourage thousands of discouraged communists to leave our cause, however. The proletariat would probably suffer in misery that much longer as a consequence"), and the various hardships the ill-prepared communitarians would (and did indeed) face, the author concludes, "Moreover, we have not yet mentioned the persecution to which the Icarians, if they wished to remain in contact with the outside society (*la société extérieure*), would probably, indeed nearly certainly, be exposed in America. . . . Brothers, remain in the fight for our old Europe (*notre vieille Europe*), work and struggle here, because it is only in Europe where there already exists all the elements for the establishment of a community of wealth, and this community will be established here or it will be nowhere (*sera établie ici ou ne le sera nulle part*)."[46] By pointing toward the direct assault on and the ultimate incorporation of the community outside the existing world (the Icarian community) by *la société extérieure*, the capitalist order — something that did in fact tragically happen to the Icarian colonists[47] — the author also emphasizes that the formation of the nowhere, of the true utopian community (*nulle part*, no where, a term often used as a synonym for utopia), can occur only through the transformation of the *totality* of the world that already exists here (*ici*). This in effect short-circuits Cabet's vision of a spatial "delinking" from the totality of the present, pointing out its anti-utopian consequences and replacing it with a vision of the realization of utopia located in *time*, one that comes about only through direct human praxis: "no where" in effect becomes "now here," a concept not unrelated to Walter Benjamin's revolutionary *Jetztzeit*. This notion is then echoed in the celebrated closing lines of Marx and Engel's manifesto: "The Communists disdain to conceal their views and aims. They openly declare that their ends can be attained only by the forcible overthrow of *all existing* social conditions. Let the ruling classes tremble at a Communistic revolution. The proletarians have nothing to lose but their chains. They have a *world* to win."[48] And it would be this vision of a struggle between the bourgeoisie and the proletariat for "a world," now expanded to a global horizon, as necessary precursor to the formation of communist utopia that would serve as one of the central axioms in Marx's great notebook manuscript, *Grundrisse* (1857–58).

Moreover, what for Marx still remains a baleful process of the incorporation of the exterior by the interior is for Hardt and Negri, in our now truly global capitalism, completed: "The spatial configuration of inside and outside itself, however, seems to us a general and foundational characteristic of modern thought. In the passage from modern to postmodern and from imperialism to Empire there is progressively less distinction between inside and outside."[49] It is precisely this collapse of the distinction between inside and outside that, for Hardt and Negri, inaugurates a new revolutionary temporality in the present. The opposition that both the author of the letter to Cabet on the one hand and Hardt and Negri on the other set into play here—between utopian space (enclaves) and a revolutionary utopian temporality (the totality transformed)—is also staged in Butler's two *Parable* novels: for the Earthseed project is precisely one whose aim is the establishment not simply of a new community somewhere outside the dominant order but of the birth, or winning, of a new world. (This insight offers us a way as well to read one of the other great science fiction visions of the 1990s, Kim Stanley Robinson's *Mars* trilogy.) In short, the staging of the closure of space offered in the letter, Hardt's and Negri's book, and Butler's novel, ignites a dynamic temporality. Might we in this way read the Earthseed project as nothing less than a figure for the supreme event of revolution?

Of this project, Lauren offers the following comment:

"That's what Earthseed was about," I said. "I wanted us to understand what we could be, what we could do. I wanted to give us a focus, a goal, something big enough, complex enough, difficult enough, and in the end, radical enough to make us become more than we ever have been. We keep falling into the same ditches, you know? I mean, we learn more and more about the physical universe, more about our own bodies, more technology, but somehow, down through history, we go on building empires of one kind or another, then destroying them in one way or another. We go on having stupid wars that we justify and get passionate about, but in the end, all they do is kill huge numbers of people, maim others, impoverish still more, spread disease and hunger, and set the stage for the next war. And when we look at all of that in history, we just shrug our shoulders and say, well, that's the way things are. That's the way things always have been." (PT, 358)

This passage is interesting for a number of reasons, not the least of them being the way it appears prophetic of our current situation. In the concluding notes of the passage, Butler effectively distances this vision from the end-of-history mentality evident both in such well-known dystopias as George Orwell's *Nineteen Eighty-Four* and in the fantasies of neoliberal free-market ideologists. Each is grounded in a bleak ideological vision of the cyclical nature of history and of the immutability of a vicious and selfish human nature. (Margaret Thatcher's infamous declaration, "There is no alternative," offers a temporal closure to parallel the spatial one of global capitalism; and Badiou argues that the "genuine consensual fetish" of democracy produces a similar closure effect in the realm of radical political intervention: "Everywhere in the world, democracy is the true subjective principle — the rallying point — of liberal capitalism."[50])

However, it is the first part of the above passage — wherein Lauren describes Earthseed as "something big enough, complex enough, difficult enough, and in the end, radical enough to make us become more than we ever have been" — that most interests me here. Lauren goes on to argue that what makes humans different from other "animals" is that "we can choose: We can go on building and destroying until we either destroy ourselves or destroy the ability of our world to sustain us. Or we can make something more of ourselves. We can grow up" (PT, 358). She later points out that "fulfilling the Destiny is a long-term, expensive, uncertain project—or rather it's hundreds of projects. Maybe thousands. And with no guarantees of anything" (*PT*, 359). The problem, she notes, is that the reigning paradigms for action—the governmental (politics) and the business (economics)—are all geared toward the short-term and the immediately profitable. "The truth is, preparing for interstellar travel and then sending out ships filled with colonists is bound to be a job so long, thankless, expensive, and difficult that I suspect that only a religion could do it. . . . it will take something as essentially human and as essentially irrational as religion to keep them focused and keep it going—for generations if it takes generations" (*PT*, 359–60).

This equation of religion with a universal project of collective human transformation is not original to Butler (indeed, Jameson points out that perhaps we should understand religion precisely as a figuration of Marxism). Moreover, her description of the commitment that such a project requires—the following out of the fundamental maxim, "Do not give up"—also resonates in some powerful ways with what Badiou describes as the "fidelity" central to any truth process, or Event. Badiou, too, argues that "all the parameters of the doctrine of the event are thus laid out in Christianity."[51] Moreover, his paradigmatic example of a fidelity is that of one of the founders of Christianity, Saint Paul, who in Badiou's reading is "not a Saint or Apostle . . . but . . . a subjective figure of primary importance."[52] Such fidelity, Badiou argues, is "that which lends consistency to the presence of some-one in the composition of the subject induced by the process of this truth."[53] This person "belongs to the truth process as one of its foundations" and is thus "simultaneously himself, nothing other than himself, a multiple singularity recognizable among all others, and in excess of himself."[54] Such a description I think wonderfully grasps what occurs in the two series under examination here in the central figures of Buffy and Lauren: both maintain their subjective consistency through an unwavering fidelity to a Truth Event, Lauren's Earthseed project and Buffy's project as the Chosen One, the Slayer (an event often referred to in the series in the religious language of a "calling," and something Buffy "did not ask for," echoing Badiou's point that an Event, and hence the entrance "into the composition of a subject of truth[,] can only be something that *happens to you*").[55]

Moreover, such fidelity is not only that which holds together the consistency of the individual subject. Indeed, it is precisely the fidelity to a common project that draws together the radical new forms of elective kinship we see at work in these two texts. Badiou notes, "All equality is that of belonging together to a work. Indubitably, those participating in a truth procedure are coworkers in its becoming."[56] Or as Peter Hallward puts it, "This shared fidelity is the basis for a subjective community or being-together with no other criteria of inclusion than fidelity itself. . . . The only community consistent with truth would be a 'communism of singularities,' a community of 'extreme particularity.' Nothing is more opposed to the truth of community than a knowledge of communitarian substance."[57] Such a model of a community based on fidelity to a Truth Event, in the face of the terrible opprobrium of the dominant order, is also what we witness, I would argue, in both the drag ball and the figure of Antigone, and it is this that makes them such powerful examples for Butler. Interestingly, all of this would suggest that the only real subject in Badiou's specific sense, the one who becomes more than mere animal, is in fact the queer subject (and all of the subjects forming the community of singularities on *Buffy* are in this sense queer subjects).

Asha explains it this way in terms of her particular fidelity: "But the Church wasn't only a religion. It was a community—my community. I didn't want to be free of it. That would have been—had been—impossibly lonely. Everyone needs to be part of something" (*PT*, 378). Similarly, the projects embodied in the figures of Buffy and Lauren are more than goals for the future; they are the foundation of the community itself. For Badiou, however, Asha's fidelity, as that of any fundamentalist order, differs from that of either Lauren or Buffy in that it lacks a proper universal dimension. It is thus the form of "Evil" that he calls a "simulacrum or terror," a fidelity that "regulates its break with the situation not by the universality of the void, but by the closed particularity of an abstract set [*ensemble*] (the 'Germans' or the 'Aryans'). . . . the community and the collective are the unnameables of political truth: every attempt 'politically' to name a community induces a disastrous Evil."[58]

At this point, too, we can finally explain precisely why Buffy in the episode "Normal Again" discussed earlier "chooses" her life as a slayer, with all the potential hardships and struggle that it involves, over the security of "reality." For Buffy to give up her role as slayer—something she is tempted with at numerous places during the course of the series' run—

would in fact mean that she would, in Badiou's sense, cease to be a subject. Moreover, the community, or family—one in which she is at once inserted, which she composes, and which exceeds her—would also dissolve. In Badiou's terms, this would prove a fundamental ethical failure: "To fail to live up to a fidelity is Evil in the sense of *betrayal*, betrayal in oneself of the Immortal that you are."[59] In a way that resonates with the "Normal Again" episode, Badiou goes on to point out that "the denial of the Immortal in myself is something quite different from an abandonment, a cessation: I must always convince myself that the Immortal in question *never existed*, and thus rally to opinion's perception of this point— opinion, whose whole purpose, in the service of interests, is precisely this negation."[60]

There would at this point seem to be a significant difference between the projects outlined in the novels and television series under discussion here, a difference that is part of the very "ideology of the form" of television itself, and hence a potential site of recontainment of the radical energies set into play in *Buffy*. For while Earthseed, as I have argued above, stands in as a figure for the project of *creating* a new world, *Buffy's* battle against evil seems to be one that cannot be won, and which thereby only aims at keeping history open in *this* world. *Buffy* would then seem to deploy the same sacrificial logic of the conspiracy narrative form—wherein the individual opponent of the conspiracy sacrifices her or his "life" to the struggle with the conspiracy (which thereby comes to define their very subjectivity itself).[61] However, in a brilliant self-reflexive move, *Buffy* makes this dilemma one of the central topics of its concluding season, and in a magnificent final episode, we are presented with a vision of a truly revolutionary Event, an overturning of the repetitious naturalized law of a patriarchal order as old as human history itself that, we learn, had regulated the power of the slayers by determining that only a single Chosen One could exist at any time. The uncounted "potential slayers" across the globe thus occupy the "eventual site," the void within the situation of just such a patriarchal order, and the climactic scene of their coming to consciousness of their own agency represents one of the truly utopian moments of recent television history. *Buffy's* monologue at this juncture, which again resonates in some productive ways with Badiou's language, is worth reproducing in full:

20 Sunnydale becomes the void, from the final episode of *Buffy the Vampire Slayer* (originally broadcast May 20, 2003).

So here's the part where you make a choice. What if you could have the power now? "In every generation, one slayer is born," because a bunch of men who died thousands of years ago made up that rule. They were powerful men. This woman here [pointing to Willow] is more powerful than all of them combined. So I say we change the rules. I say my power should be our power. Tomorrow, Willow will use the power of the scythe to change our destiny. From now on, every girl in the world who might be a slayer *will* be a slayer. Every girl who could have the power, *will* have the power; can stand up, *will* stand up. Slayers, every one of us. Make your choice—are you ready to be strong?"

With this Event—and the accompanying invitation for a fidelity to it—we open up onto a world that the show itself acknowledges cannot be represented as much as "experienced." In the final scene of the series, the central characters stare out onto the literal void that had been, until now, the site of the law of the fathers, repetition, and "knowledge," that of Sunnydale itself (figure 20). This void then serves as a sign of the radical openness of their own futures. When Buffy's friend Xander exclaims that they had "saved the world," Willow corrects him, "No, we *changed* the world." She then asks Buffy what they are going to do next; to which Buffy responds only with an enigmatic smile.[62]

Here, then, we arrive at the most significant lessons that we can take from these extended narratives. Without fidelity to the universal truth content of the revolutionary event, new forms of collectivity will never come into being. But such a commitment, more then prefacing the realization of any such community, always already marks its achievement. And it is precisely such monstrosity that enables us to enact what Badiou calls the fundamental ethical maxim, "Keep going!" Fidelity to such a maxim will serve both as a way of acknowledging the authenticity of the radical projects emerging from the historical moment under examination throughout my book and as the best way of continuing their legacy in what is our new situation, making us all generations in a single and ever growing family.

Introduction **THE PRESENT AS A MOMENT OF DANGER**

1 Walter Benjamin, "On the Concept of History," in Benjamin, *Selected Writings*, 396.

2 Löwy, *Fire Alarm*, 94.

3 Walter Benjamin, *Arcades Project*, 638.

4 For a related discussion, see Hegeman, "Naïve Modernism."

5 See Buck-Morss, *Dialectics of Seeing*, esp. chap. 2.

6 Benjamin, *Arcades Project*, 698.

7 Badiou, *Century*. Although for Badiou the century ends in 1989, and hence would not include this last period.

8 Benjamin, "On the Concept of History," 397. Santner, "Miracles Happen."

9 Löwy, *Fire Alarm*, 115.

10 Morris, *Too Soon Too Late*, 26.

11 I discuss Jameson's periodizing concepts in more detail in my "Periodizing Jameson."

12 Denning, *Culture in the Age of Three Worlds*.

13 Davis, "'Fordism' in Crisis." The link between the periodizing projects of Benjamin and Jameson can also be seen in Jameson's discussion of Benjamin's method of the constellation in his *Late Marxism*, 49–58. The latter text should be read as Jameson's own "epistemo-critical prologue" to the periodizing investigation of his *Postmodernism*.

14 Jameson, *Singular Modernity*, 62.

15 Žižek, *Tarrying with the Negative*, 22–27.

16 Jameson, *Singular Modernity*, 24.

17 Ibid., 64.

18 Jameson writes of the calls for the return to or the reinvention of an aesthetic "canon": "The term and concept has the advantage of proposing an alliance between the older philologists (if there are any left), who have a genuine historical interest in and commitment to the past, and the newer aesthetes who are the true ideologists of some (late) modern" (*Singular Modernity*, 179). For the distinction between "activist" and "normative" formalisms—a distinction that parallels Jameson's differentiation of high and late modernisms—see Levinson, "What Is New Formalism?" And for a discussion of the relationship between the antitheoretical turn and the intensified nativism of the post-9/11 period, see Simpson, *9/11*.

19 Also see Fredric Jameson, "Periodizing the 60s," in Jameson, *Ideologies of Theory*, 2:178–208.

20 See Gilles Deleuze, *Cinema 1*, xiv; and Jameson, *Postmodernism*, esp. 125–26. And for a related project, see Žižek, *Looking Awry*.

21 Jameson, *Ideologies of Theory*, 1:ix.

22 Benjamin, *Origin of German Tragic Drama*, 162.

23 Žižek, *Parallax View*, 101.

24 Benjamin, *Origin of German Tragic Drama*, 177, 223. Also see the fine discussions of Benjamin's vision of allegory in Hansen, "Formalism and Its Malcontents"; and Wilkens, "Towards a Benjaminian Theory." Wilkens's discussion of "Benjamin's concern for the social context from which allegory emerges" (285–86) is of particular value for us here.

25 Jameson, *Singular Modernity*, 28.

26 I discuss this notion of genre and genre formation in more depth in *Imaginary Communities*, 4–10, 27–34.

27 Benjamin, *Origin of German Tragic Drama*, 44.

28 Watkins, *Throwaways*, 7.

29 Butler, *Antigone's Claim*, 74.

One **THE TWO DEATHS OF THE 1990S**

1 Benjamin, *Arcades Project*, 544.

2 Also see the discussion of Benjamin's "On the Concept of History" in Žižek, *Sublime Object of Ideology*, 136–55.

3 Jameson, "Politics of Utopia," 40. Also see my *Imaginary Communities*.

4 Spiegelman, *In the Shadow of No Towers*, 1.

5 For further discussion, see Wills, *Witches and Jesuits*.

6 Ibid., 15.

7 Fraser, *Faith and Treason*, 103.

8   Leggatt, *William Shakespeare's "Macbeth,"* 8.

9   Derrida, *Limited Inc*, 7, 10.

10 Derrida, *Rouges*, 103.

11 Retort, *Afflicted Powers*, 52, 80. Also see Dawson and Schueller, *Exceptional State*.

12 Badiou, *Ethics*, 41.

13 Hallward, *Badiou*, xxv, 114.

14 Žižek, "From Purification to Subtraction," 179.

15 Badiou, *Ethics*, 51–52.

16 In a related way, Jean Baudrillard argues, "The collapse of the Twin Towers is unimaginable, but that is not enough to make it a real event." See Baudrillard, "L'Esprit du Terrorisme," 413.

17 For a discussion of the conditions that make such qualifying statements necessary, and for the reasons why they are inevitably misunderstood, see Butler, *Precarious Life*, esp. chap. 1. Also see the essays collected in Hauerwas and Lentricchia, "Dissent from the Homeland."

18 Žižek, *Sublime Object of Ideology*, 61. And also see the discussion of repetition in modern culture in Jameson, *Signatures of the Visible*, 17–21.

19 Žižek, *Sublime Object of Ideology*, 135.

20 Lacan, *Seminar of Jacques Lacan*, 212.

21 Jameson, "Dialectics of Disaster," 302–3.

22 For a wide-ranging discussion of culture in the United States in the years following the end of the Cold War, see Ventura, "Cultural Logic of the United States."

23 Harvey, *New Imperialism*, 17. Also see the important refinement of Harvey's analysis in Arrighi, "Hegemony Unravelling"; and the similar analysis in Retort, *Afflicted Powers*, 9.

24 For a discussion of this nearly forgotten event, see Susan Willis, "What Goes Around Comes Around," in Willis, *Portents of the Real*, 49–69.

25 Pinkerton, "Tuesday's Act Was Not about Nothing." For an effective critique of these newfound attitudes, see Willis, *Portents of the Real*.

26 Willis, *Portents of the Real*, 25.

27 See the Resolution of Colorado House of Representatives, September 4, 2008.

28 Churchill, "'Some People Push Back'"; a revised version was published in Churchill, *On the Justice of Roosting Chickens*, 5–37. Also see Ross Birrell's discussion of the gift economy of the suicide bomber, "The Gift of Terror."

29 Žižek, *Tarrying with the Negative*, 194.

30 And for a related effort to periodize U.S. politics, see Chollet and Goldgeier, *America between the Wars*.

31 Jameson, *Singular Modernity*, 28.

32 Ibid., 29.

33 Ibid., 81.

34 Žižek, *Sublime Object of Ideology*, 135. Lacan notes in the seminar's conclusion, "Someone among you has baptized the topology that I have sketched out for you this year with the apt and somewhat humorous phrase, the zone between-two-deaths." Lacan, *Seminar of Jacques Lacan*, 320.

35 Edmundson, *Nightmare on Main Street*. Also see the insightful discussion of Edmundson's book in Hegeman, "Haunted by Mass Culture."

36 Lacan, *Seminar of Jacques Lacan*, 295.

37 Blake, "Marriage of Heaven and Hell," 174–76.

38 Žižek, *Parallax View*, 4.

39 Žižek, "Afterword," 231.

40 See Foucault, "Different Spaces"; and Casarino, *Modernity at Sea*. One of the great 1990 filmic stagings of the heterotopia of the prison, with special relevance to our discussion here, is Frank Darabont's *The Shawshank Redemption* (1994), a film I discuss in my essay "Learning to Live in History."

41 Cavell, *Pursuits of Happiness*, 126–27.

42 Žižek, *Parallax View*, 62.

43 Doug Henwood gives a graphic representation of the popular rise of the concept, charting the dramatic increase in the latter half of the decade in the number of articles published in the *New York Times* and the *Washington Post* containing the term *globalization*. See Henwood, *After the New Economy*, 146.

44 Jameson discusses this point in relationship to the concept of postmodernism in *Postmodernism*, xiii–xiv.

45 Denning, *Culture in the Age of Three Worlds*, 11. Also see Denning's first chapter, "Globalization and Culture: Process and Epoch," 17–34.

46 See Richard T. Griffiths, History of the Internet.

47 Benjamin, *Arcades Project*, 152.

48 Ibid., 26.

49 Hardt and Negri, foreword, xvi. Also see Hardt and Negri, *Empire*; Hardt and Negri, *Multitude*; Denning, "A Global Left? Social Movements in the Age of Three Worlds," in Denning, *Culture in the Age of Three Worlds*, 35–50; and Harvey, *New Imperialism*, 160–79.

50 See Israel, *Radical Enlightenment*.

51 Another indication of this shift is the resurgence of interest in the question of ontology, most significantly in Badiou's *L'être et l'eventment* (1988). In his exchange with Derrida, Negri calls for a "new — post-deconstructive — ontology." Negri, "Specter's Smile," 12. Also, however, see Derrida's reply printed in the same volume, "Marx & Sons," 213–69; and Leavey, "A Marrano's Smile."

52 Koolhaas and Mau, *S, M, L, XL*, 510.

53 For an introductory overview of some of these projects in Berlin, with a periodization identical to my own, see Imhoff and Krempel, *Berlin Architecture 2000*.

54 See Lukács, *Defence of "History and Class Consciousness,"* esp. 55; and my "Ken MacLeod's Permanent Revolution."

55 Grassian, "Passing into Post-ethnicity," 317–18. Thanks to Daniel Bell for alerting me to this essay.

56 For one powerful alternative to this reading of 9/11, see Butler, *Precarious Life*.

57 Žižek, *Tarrying with the Negative*, 175. For discussions of the fragility of this new order, see Hardt and Negri, *Multitude*; Todd, *After the Empire*; and Arrighi, "Hegemony Unravelling."

58 Jameson, "Dialectics of Disaster," 303.

59 See, for example, the comments of Badiou on the antiglobalization movement and on Hardt and Negri's work in Badiou, "Beyond Formalisation," 125–26.

60 Benjamin, *Arcades Project*, 10, 463.

61 Imhof and Krempel, *Berlin Architecture 2000*, 106–8.

62 Julian Wolfreys, "Trauma, Testimony, Criticism," 137.

63 Daniel Libeskind, qtd. in ibid., 138.

64 Hawthorne, "Living with Our Mistake." For a further discussion of the debates over the rebuilding of the site, see David Simpson, "The Tower and the Memorial: Building, Meaning, Telling," in Simpson, *9/11*, 55–85.

65 Walter Benjamin, "The Work of Art in the Age of its Technological Reproducibility," in Benjamin, *Selected Writings*, 269.

66 Derrida, *Specters of Marx*, 28. For a discussion of the figurative work of the religious and messianic elements of the film, see Jameson, "Iconographies of Cyberspace"; and finally, for a brilliant iconoclastic reading of the film that takes Agent Smith, the spokesperson for the Matrix, as the figure for a radically other "inconceivable, contraceivable" posthuman future, and Neo as the figure for the drive for the reproduction of the status quo, see Kimball, "Conceptions and Contraceptions of the Future," a revised version of which is now in *The Infanticidal Logic of Evolution and Culture*, 261–83.

67 Jameson, *Archaeologies of the Future*.

68 I have in mind here Siegfried Kracauer's classic reading of the film in *From Caligari to Hitler*, 162–64, which I will discuss further in chapter 6. For further discussion of the recontainment dynamic, see Jameson, *Signatures of the Visible*, 25–29.

69 Žižek, "Ideology Reloaded."

70 Moreover, a significant shift occurs in the figure of the Matrix in the interlude between the first and second films. In the first film the Matrix is a figure of the all-encompassing network of global capitalism and humanity, a figure for those exploited by the machine. This relationship is inverted in the series of animated short films, *Animatrix*, released between the first and second films. In two of the shorts in particular, which show the origins of the world of the films, we learn that it was originally the machines who were exploited, denigrated, and denied basic rights by the first human world, and that it is the humans who are responsible for the permanent cloud cover encircling the planet.

An earlier version of this essay was published in *Amerikastudien/American Studies* 49, no. 1 (2004): 51–63.

1 Jameson, *Singular Modernity*, 28.

2 DeLillo, *Underworld*, 465; hereafter cited parenthetically in the text as *U*.

3 For a discussion of Jameson's notion of cognitive mapping as a narrative practice, see my "Periodizing Jameson" and chapter 7 of the current volume. For a reading of paranoia as a theme in *Underworld*, see Knight, "Everything Is Connected."

4 Conrad, *Lord Jim*, 63.

5 DeLillo, *White Noise*, 281.

6 Jameson, foreword to *The Postmodern Condition*, xx.

7 I discuss the alternate history form and its relationship to the historical novel in "The Last Bomb"; and "Learning to Live in History."

8 See Fredric Jameson's classic analysis of the waning of historicity in postmodernism in his *Postmodernism*, chap. 1.

9 Georg Lukács, *Historical Novel*, 49.

10 Georg Lukács, "Walter Scott and the Historical Novel," in Lukács, *Marxism and Human Liberation*, 161–62. Also see Lukács, *Historical Novel*, 42.

11 Lukács, "Walter Scott," 167. Also see Lukács, *Historical Novel*, 48.

12 Lukács, *Historical Novel*, 54.

13 Deleuze, *Cinema 1*, 212.

14 For a discussion of images of waste management in DeLillo's fiction, see Merrill, "Abject Americans."

15 Deleuze, *Cinema 1*, 212–13.

16 Ibid., 214–15.

17 For a discussion of the influence of Godard on DeLillo's early fiction, see Osteen, *American Magic and Dread*, chap. 1.

18 DeLillo, *White Noise*, 289.

19 DeLillo, "Everything under the Bomb."

20 For a discussion of the novel's vision of artists and the work of art, see Osteen, *American Magic and Dread*, esp. 245–60; and Merrill, "Abject Americans."

21 In *Mao II*, a novel published when the collapse of the Soviet Union was imminent, we get the following exchange already presaging the "first" end of the Cold War:

> "I already have the World Trade Center."
> "And it's already harmless and ageless. Forgotten-looking. And think how much worse."
> "What?" she said.
> "If there was only one tower instead of two." (40)

22 Baudrillard, *Symbolic Exchange and Death*, 69.

23 Ibid., 69–70.

24 Ibid., 69.

25 For a general overview of the game, see "Shot Heard 'Round the World (Base-ball)."

26 For discussions of some of these figures and their role in the architecture and thematic structure of the novel, see Osteen, *American Magic and Dread*, chap. 8.

27 The phrase "paranoid style in American politics" comes from the title of Richard Hofstadter's classic 1964 essay, qtd. in Harvey, *New Imperialism*, 49.

28 Headline qtd. in Osteen, *American Magic and Dread*, 217; see also DeLillo, *Underworld*, 668. In a 1998 interview, DeLillo notes of seeing the two head-lines side by side: "It was quite stunning. I didn't know what they meant. I didn't know that there was a connection, nor that there had to be a connec-tion. But I do know that I've never begun a book after such a direct source of stimulation. When I began writing *White Noise*, it was because I felt a sort of hum in the air. But this was so immediate and striking. I felt the power of history. No other way to put it." DeLillo, "Everything under the Bomb," 33.

29 Žižek, *Sublime Object of Ideology*, 61. I discuss the role of this kind of repetition in the formation of a new literary genre in *Imaginary Communities*, 31–32.

30 Žižek, *Sublime Object of Ideology*, 62.

31 DeLillo directly acknowledges this in his 9/11 novel, *Falling Man* (2007):

> He said, "It still looks like an accident, the first one. Even from this dis-tance, way outside the thing, how many days later, I'm standing here think-ing it's an accident."
> "Because it has to be."
> "It has to be," he said.
> "The way the camera sort of shows surprise."
> "But only the first one."
> "Only the first," she said.
> "The second plane, by the time the second plane appears," he said, "we're all a little older and wiser." (135)

32 Žižek, *Welcome to the Desert of the Real*, 15.

33 Hardt and Negri, *Multitude*, 24.

Three **REPETITIONS AND REVISIONS IN *TERMINATOR***

An earlier version of this essay was published in *The Missing Link* 9, no. 3 (1991): 14–16; and in *LiberArte: La revista virtual del Colegio de Artes Liberales, Universidad San Francisco de Quito* 1, no. 1 (2005).

1 Blitz and Krasniewicz, *Why Arnold Matters*, viii.

2 Ibid., 87.

3   For a complete timeline of the Doomsday Clock since its inception in 1947, see Bulletin of Atomic Scientists.

4   Jameson, *Fables of Aggression*, 82.

5   T. K. Jones, deputy undersecretary of defense for strategic and theater nuclear forces, research, and engineering, qtd, in *Los Angeles Times*, January 16, 1982, available online at www.cdi.org/issues/nukef&f/nukequo.html.

6   Bulletin of Atomic Scientists Doomsday Clock, 2007.

7   Qtd. in Blitz and Krasniewicz, *Why Arnold Matters*, xiv.

8   Marx, *Marx-Engels Reader*, 597.

9   See, for example, Nagy, "Secret behind the Sanctions."

10 Fredric Jameson, "Reification and Utopia in Mass Culture," in Jameson, *Signatures of the Visible*, 25.

11 For some of the classic discussions of this work in the film, see Kracauer, *From Caligari to Hitler*, 162–64; and Huyssen, "Vamp and the Machine." Also see Petro, *Joyless Streets*.

12 See Jeffords, *Hard Bodies*; and Willis, *High Contrast*.

13 Ellison, *I Have No Mouth*, 28.

14 Ibid., 41–2.

15 For a contrast of the Dick novel and the film, see Peter Fitting, "Futurecop." Also see Žižek, *Tarrying with the Negative*, 9–15, 40–42.

16 I take the notion of the genre's "spatialization of time" from Rose, *Alien Encounters*. Also see Suvin, *Metamorphoses of Science Fiction*, 73–74.

17 See Penley, "Time Travel."

18 Žižek, *Sublime Object of Ideology*, 57–58.

19 Penley, "Time Travel," 117.

20 See Ross, *Strange Weather*; and Willis, *High Contrast*. Willis discusses the link between *Thelma and Louise* and *Terminator 2*.

21 For a discussion of the film's reconstruction of the nuclear family, see Willis, *High Contrast*, 118–20; and Pfeil, "Home Fires Burning."

22 Kimball, "Conceptions and Contraceptions of the Future," 88. Another version of this essay now appears in his *Infanticidal Logic of Evolution and Culture*, 261–83.

23 Kimball, "Conceptions and Contraceptions," 87.

24 See Jameson's discussion of the film and its use of motifs from the work of A. E. Van Vogt in Fredric Jameson, "The Space of SF: Narrative in Van Vogt," in Jameson, *Archaeologies of the Future*, 314–27.

25 Willis, *High Contrast*, 121.

26 For a further discussion of Schwarzenegger's use of these catchphrases and the image of the Terminator in his campaign, see Blitz and Krasniewicz, *Why Arnold Matters*, esp. chap. 7.

27 Willis, *High Contrast*, 122.

28 For the full text of the first draft script of this scene, see www.geocities.com/Hollywood/Makeup/4303/terminator.html (accessed September 8, 2008).

29   A similar vision is at work in the equally utopian conclusion to a more recent catastrophe film, *The Day after Tomorrow* (2004, dir. Roland Emmerich),
a work I will take up briefly in chapter 6, note 54.

30   For a useful discussion of Carl Schmitt's periodizing concept of the *nomos*, see
the essays collected in Rasch, "World Orderings." And for a discussion of the
way the enemy's faces—if not the Levinasian "face"—has been imagined, see
the final chapter of Butler, *Precarious Life*.

31   Also see Giovanni Arrighi's discussion of the shifting logics of U.S. "protection" in "Hegemony Unravelling—2."

32   Badiou, *Ethics*, 43.

33   Ibid., 41.

34   Jameson, *Marxism and Form*, 244–45.

35   Qtd. in Blitz and Krasniewicz, *Why Arnold Matters*, 99.

36   Benjamin, *Allegorien kultureller Erfahrung*, 160. Also see Agamben, *State of Exception*.

Four   **REMAKING THE UNITED STATES IN *CAPE FEAR***

1   For some recent discussions, see Horton and McDougal, *Play It Again, Sam*;
Forrest and Koos, *Dead Ringers*; and Verevis, "Remaking Film."

2   Arnzen, "Same and the New," 189.

3   Jameson, *Signatures of the Visible*, 38.

4   Leitch, "Twice-Told Tales," 147. The relationship between the three texts that
I will examine here resembles that modeled by Leitch in the case of James M.
Cain's novel *Double Indemnity* (1943), Billy Wilder's film adaptation (1944),
and Lawrence Kasdan's remake, *Body Heat* (1981). I thank John Hartzog for
first alerting me to this essay.

5   Indeed, both the novel and James R. Webb's original screenplay are noted
in the film's credits, a departure from the practice of most remakes, which,
Leitch points out, are often averse to acknowledging their predecessors.
Scorsese also uniquely highlights his film's status as a remake by employing a
number of the actors, albeit in new roles, from the first film version.

6   MacDonald, *Executioners*, 159; further references to this work are cited parenthetically in the text as *EX*.

7   Among the classic mappings of the dialectic of conformity and rebellion in
the 1950s were the popular works of the psychiatrist Robert Linder, whose
titles alone reveal their concerns: *Rebel without a Cause* (1944); *Prescription
for a Rebellion* (1952); and *Must You Conform?* (1955). Two useful discussions
of this phenomenon can be found in Ehrenreich, *Hearts of Men*; and Schaub,
American Fiction in the Cold War.

8   See Edelman, *No Future*. I discuss Edelman's insights further in chapter 6.

9   Lévi-Strauss, *Elementary Structures of Kinship*, 478–97. Also see Rubin's classic
"Traffic in Women."

10   Sedgwick, *Between Men*.

11   For a discussion of this operation in noir fiction, see Jameson, "On Raymond Chandler."

12   The narrative erasure of the working class similarly takes place in Sam's biography. In a chapter chronicling the couple's first encounter while students at the University of Pennsylvania, we are informed that Sam began his climb to middle-class respectability from the ranks of the "laboring classes" (*EX*, 64).

13   For the now classic discussion of the role of "germophobia" and metaphors drawn from immunology in the cultural debates of the decade, see Ross, *No Respect*, chap. 2.

14   Jameson, *Political Unconscious*, 166. Also see Jameson's introduction and the essays collected together in Greimas, *On Meaning*. I use the Greimasian rectangle in *Imaginary Communities*, chaps. 5 and 6; and I explore this device in more detail, and especially Jameson's changing deployment of it, in "Greimas avec Lacan."

15   Jameson, *Political Unconscious*, 47.

16   Agamben, *State of Exception*, 3–4.

17   This linking of feminization and conformity in the wider cultural imagination of the late 1950s is provocatively analyzed by Barbara Ehrenreich in her *Hearts of Men*, esp. chap. 3, "Early Rebels: The Gray Flannel Dissidents."

18   The text also pays much attention to the "primitive" qualities of children: after listening to a vengeful rant by his son Jamie, Sam observes, "At eleven civilization is still a thin coating. Underneath all is savage" (*EX*, 47). While the contemporary currency of this idea can be confirmed by looking no farther than the phenomenal success of William Golding's first novel *Lord of the Flies* (1954)—followed by an equally interesting, if less well-known, romanticization of the primitive, *The Inheritors* (1955)—Sam's statements resonate more immediately with the observation of the best-selling sociologist David Riesman that in modern society, "boys can be boys only from [ages] six to ten." Riesman qtd. in Ehrenreich, *Hearts of Men*, 35.

19   Norman Mailer, "The White Negro: Superficial Reflections on the Hipster," in *Advertisements for Myself*, 341. The essay was originally published in the summer 1957 issue of *Dissent*. Further references to this work are cited parenthetically in the text as WN.

20   Schaub points out that in this imagined "wedding of the white and the black," it is the African American who is placed in the role of the wife (Schaub, *American Fiction in the Cold War*, 155).

21   Ibid., 162.

22   For his groundbreaking discussion of the role "stars" play in the discursive economy of the film text, see Dyer, *Stars*; and Dyer, *Heavenly Bodies*. For an account of Mitchum's first arrest, see Friedrich, *City of Nets*, 389–91.

23   The link between the film narrative and desegregation is also briefly suggested in Hoberman, "Sacred and Profane."

24 Chafe, *Unfinished Journey*, 160.

25 Ibid., 157.

26 The idea of a Southern "rape complex" is described in W. J. Cash's 1941 classic *Mind of the South*, qtd. in Sundquist, *To Wake the Nations*, 410.

27 Likewise in *The Executioners*, the crime of rape places its victim in an impossible double bind. In the final chapter, Sam reflects that his wife is "one of the rarest of women. . . . Woman of grace and spirit, pride and delicacy. And once again he thought of the nightmare thing that had so nearly happened to her. A duller spirit might have survived the crime without too much emotional damage, but Carol never. It would have broken her utterly and forever" (*EX*, 157). In other words, either she will be mentally and physically destroyed by the assault or find herself numbered among the world's "duller spirits."

28 Kojève, *Introduction to the Reading of Hegel*, 14–15.

29 The film itself was shot in southern Florida, another New South location originally attractive to Hollywood because of its weak organized labor presence.

30 Loukides, "Hostile Redneck," 95.

31 For another discussion of the theme of reading in the film, see Arnzen, "Same and the New," 182–86.

32 Cook, "Scorsese's Masquerade."

33 Slavoj Žižek has commented critically on the superficiality of the film's psychoanalytic structure in *Tarrying with the Negative*, 67. However, Žižek ignores the degree to which the film self-consciously acknowledges its reliance on this psychoanalytical paradigm, and hence the way it further develops a pastiche of a narrative mode associated with the culture of the 1950s.

34 See Freud, "Screen Memories."

35 For a discussion of the relationship between Thompson's original film and *Psycho*, as well as between Scorsese's remake and a number of other "minor" Hitchcock films, see Robert P. Kolker, "Algebraic Figures: Recalculating the Hitchcock Formula," in Horton and McDougal, *Play It Again, Sam*, 39–50.

36 For a significant theorization of postwar U.S. economic development, see the work of the regulationist school, especially Aglietta, *Theory of Capitalist Regulation*; Lipietz, *Mirages and Miracles*; and Boyer, *Regulation School*. For further discussions that draw on the regulationist model of these economic changes and their cultural consequences, see Murray, "Life after Henry (Ford)"; Harvey, *Condition of Postmodernity*; Davis, *City of Quartz*; "Post Fordism"; and Smith, *Millennial Dreams*. Finally, also see Harrison and Bluestone, *Great U-Turn*.

37 For the classic discussion of this private leisure space, see Lefebvre, *Critique of Everyday Life*.

38 Watkins, *Throwaways*, 45.

39 Ibid., 45–46.

40 See the discussion of "immaterial labor" in Hardt and Negri, *Empire*, 289–300; as well as my following chapter.

41 Watkins, *Throwaways*, 48.

42 Ibid., 55.

43 See Hobbs, *Mark Lombardi*. The cover image of the catalogue is of his work "George W. Bush, Harken Energy, and Jackson Stephens, ca. 1979–90" (5th version), 1999.

44 For the indispensable introduction to the structural transformations that produced the riots, see Davis, *City of Quartz*, as well as his follow-up essays reprinted in *Dead Cities*.

45 Watkins, *Throwaways*, 7.

<p>*Five* **NATURALISM, DYSTOPIA, AND POLITICS**</p>

An earlier version of this essay was published in *Dark Horizons: Science Fiction and the Dystopian Imagination*, ed. Tom Moylan and Raffaella Baccolini (London: Routledge 2003), 167–85.

1   Bloch, *Principle of Hope*, 223.

2   Jameson, *Political Unconscious*, 193. Jameson's point of reference here is Goode, "Gissing, Morris, and English Socialism." And finally, also see Thompson, *William Morris*.

3   Bellamy, *Looking Backward*, 194.

4   For a significant discussion and application of a dialectical theory of genre as a way of understanding the development of these forms in history, see McKeon, *Origins of the English Novel*.

5   Moylan, *Scraps of the Untainted Sky*, 133.

6   Ibid., 188.

7   Ibid., 195.

8   Ibid., 190; my emphasis.

9   Ibid., 189.

10 Žižek, "Georg Lukács as the Philosopher of Leninism," 164.

11 Moylan, *Scraps of the Untainted Sky*, 188.

12 Ibid., 195–96.

13 Jameson, *Political Unconscious*, 99.

14 Moylan, *Scraps of the Untainted Sky*, 307.

15 For further discussion, see my "The Occluded Future: *Red Star* and *The Iron Heel* as 'Critical Utopias,'" in Wegner, *Imaginary Communities*, 99–146.

16 See my "A Map of Utopia's 'Possible Worlds': Zamyatin's *We* and Le Guin's *The Dispossessed*," in Wegner, *Imaginary Communities*, 147–82.

17 Orwell, *Collected Essays*, 329–30; my emphasis.

18 For a discussion of Orwell's admiration of Gissing's work, see Shelden, *Orwell*, 359.

19 Orwell, *Collected Essays*, 430.

20 Sargent, "Three Faces," 9.

21 Mannheim, *Ideology and Utopia*, 235. Mannheim maintains that the conservative mentality is first and foremost a form of counterutopia, its primary

antagonist being "the liberal idea which has been translated into rationalistic terms. Whereas in the latter, the normative, the 'should' is accentuated in experience, in conservatism the emphasis shifts to existing reality, the 'is'" (234–35). More important, Mannheim argues, "The time-sense of this mode of experience and thought is completely opposed to that of liberalism. Whereas for liberalism the future was everything and the past nothing, the conservative mode of experiencing time found the best corroboration of its sense of the determinateness in discovering the significance of the past, in the discovery of time as the creator of value. . . . Consequently not only is attention turned to the past and the attempt made to rescue it from oblivion, but the presentness and immediacy of the whole past becomes an actual experience" (235). Such an outlook can still be described as "utopian" because, as are the other three mentalities, it, too, "is incongruous with the state of reality within which it occurs": the conservative mentality maintains this ideal of the full self-presence of the past in the present precisely in a moment when the possibility of such an unbroken continuity begins to disappear—that is, in a moment of dramatic historical upheaval (192). Also see my "Modernity, Nostalgia, and the Ends of Nations in Orwell's *Nineteen Eighty-Four*," in Wegner, *Imaginary Communities*, 183–228.

22   Williams, *George Orwell*, 79.

23   The relationship of the superhero form to dystopian fiction is an area ripe for investigation. For some recent critical expressions of the genre that interrogate this relationship, one might look at Alan Moore, Dave Gibbons, and John Higgins's graphic novel, *The Watchmen*; Frank Miller's brilliant *The Dark Knight Returns*, as well as its sequel, by Miller and Lynn Varley, *The Dark Knight Strikes Again*, a text that is also interesting for making the movement into dystopia proper; and the Joss Whedon television series, *Buffy the Vampire Slayer* and *Angel* (Whedon also produces a comic series, *Fray*, that moves the Buffy universe into the SF territory of dystopia). For a discussion of Whedon's work, see chapter 8.

24   Jameson, *Postmodernism*, 286. For Jameson's discussion of cyberpunk as "dirty realism," see his *Seeds of Time*, 150–59.

25   See Lefebvre, *Production of Space*, 326.

26   Certeau, *Practice of Everyday Life*, 91–92.

27   Ibid., 93, v.

28   See Kipnis, "(Male) Desire and (Female) Disgust: Reading *Hustler*." Kipnis acknowledges the limits of this discourse in the final pages of her essay. And for a classic discussion of populism in the United States, see Kazin, *Populist Persuasion*.

29   Morris, *Too Soon Too Late*, 128. For a subtle dialectical defense of the political possibilities made available by the "view from above," published in the same year as the release of these two films, see the introduction to Robbins, *Feeling Global*, 1–9. And finally, see Žižek, "A Leninist Gesture Today."

30 See Palahniuk, *Fight Club*, 12–15, 203–5.

31 Hardt and Negri, *Empire*, 290.

32 For a list of some useful introductions to the regulationist school of political economy and their theorizations of Fordism and post-Fordism, see chapter 4, note 36.

33 Giroux, "Brutalized Bodies and Emasculated Politics," 36.

34 See, for example, Georg Lukács, "Idea and Form in Literature," in Lukács, *Marxism and Human Liberation*, 109–31.

35 Hardt and Negri, *Empire*, 293.

36 Jameson, *Political Unconscious*, 189.

37 Žižek, "Afterword," 258.

38 See Badiou, *Century*; Žižek, *Puppet and the Dwarf*; and Jameson, *A Singular Modernity*.

39 See Freud, "Uncanny."

40 Giroux, "Brutalized Bodies and Emasculated Politics," 36, 37.

41 Roland Barthes also emphasizes the alienation experienced by the critic of myth in ways that resonate with our discussion here: "This harmony justifies the mythologist but does not fulfill him: his status still remains basically one of being excluded. Justified by the political dimension, the mythologist is still at a distance from it. His speech is a metalanguage, it 'acts' nothing; at the most it unveils — or does it? To whom? His task always remains ambiguous, hampered by its ethical origins." Barthes, *Mythologies*, 156.

42 For a useful analysis of the central characters' hybridity and the relationship of this to Jarmusch's archival revisionist project, see Nieland, "Graphic Violence."

43 London, *Call of the Wild*, 87.

44 Auerbach, *Male Call*, 112–13.

45 Ibid., 108.

46 Ibid., 110–11.

Six **A NIGHTMARE ON THE BRAIN OF THE LIVING**

An earlier version of this essay was published in *Rethinking Marxism* 12., no. 1 (2000): 65–86.

1 Hegel, *Philosophy of Right*, 13.

2 Fukuyama, "End of History," 3. Also see Fukuyama's book-length development of these ideas, *End of History and the Last Man*.

3 Fukuyama, "End of History," 8. Also see Kojeve, *Introduction to the Reading of Hegel*.

4 Ibid., 9.

5 Fukuyama, "Reply to My Critics," 24, 22, 27.

6 Fukuyama, "End of History," 14.

7 Ibid., 13.

8 Ibid., 18.

9 For a discussion of the original reception of the film, particularly in light of the looming presidential elections, see Rogin, *Independence Day*, esp. chap. 1.

10 Jameson, "Actually Existing Marxism," 38.

11 For an intellectual history of the end-of-history thesis from Hegel through Fukuyama, see Anderson, "Ends of History."

12 Many of the most significant responses, along with a new essay by Derrida, are now reprinted in Sprinker, *Ghostly Demarcations*.

13 Derrida, *Specters of Marx*, 48; hereafter cited parenthetically in the text as SM.

14 Jameson, "Marx's Purloined Letter," 59.

15 Although also see Derrida's reservations concerning Benjamin's project in "Marx & Sons," 249–55.

16 Derrida refers to Althusser's project in SM, 89–90. For some of Derrida's other thoughts on Althusser's work, see the interview in Kaplan and Sprinker, *Althusserian Legacy*, 183–231.

17 Marx, *Contribution to the Critique of Political Economy*, 21. Also see the discussion of the problem of representing utopia in Jameson, *Archaeologies of the Future*, esp. 105–69.

18 Barthes, *Mythologies*, 146.

19 Ibid., 147. Also now see Alain Badiou's related discussion of the form of evil he names "disaster" in his *Ethics*, 71–87.

20 For further discussion of this context see Löwy, *Fire Alarm*.

21 Montag, "Spirits Armed and Unarmed," 72.

22 Ibid., 73.

23 A similar gendered anxiety is evident in Benjamin's theses: "The historical materialist leaves it to others to be drained by the whore called 'Once upon a time' in historicism's bordello. He remains in control of his powers — man enough to blast open the continuum of history." Walter Benjamin, "On the Concept of History," in Benjamin, *Selected Writings*, 396. Also see Petro, *Joyless Streets*, esp. 57–74.

24 Benjamin, "On the Concept of History," 395.

25 This recalls another Derrida text of this moment, *Archive Fever*.

26 Marx, *Eighteenth Brumaire of Louis Bonaparte*, 15; and Benjamin, "On the Concept of History," 392.

27 Marinetti, "Founding and Manifesto of Futurism," 43.

28 Benjamin, "On the Concept of History," 391.

29 Balibar, *Philosophy of Marx*, 99. Also see Žižek's discussion of the difference between Derrida's and Lacan's notion of the "act" in *Did Somebody Say Totalitarianism*, 152–60.

30 Horkheimer and Adorno, *Dialectic of Enlightenment*, 256.

31 Spivak, "Ghostwriting," 71. Of Benjamin's last work, Susan Buck-Morss similarly argues, "During this period he wrote the *Geschichtsphilosophische Thesen*,

eighteen theses on the concept of history which marked a retreat from politi-cal commitment and a return to the language of theology as the only remain-ing refuge for the ideal of the revolution." Buck-Morss, *Origins of Negative Dialectics*, 162.

32 Balibar, *Philosophy of Marx*, 15. Also see Jameson's discussion of Derrida's re-flections on the role of religion in Marx's thought in "Marx's Purloined Let-ter," 53–55.

33 Benjamin, "On the Concept of History," 392. I would suggest a similar bind is present in another contemporary science fiction film, *Star Trek: First Contact* (1996, dir. Jonathan Frakes). For while this film could be read as an endorse-ment of the vision of a socialist utopia—indeed, the film carefully works to distinguish its ideal of future postcapitalist collectivities from Cold War fan-tasies of the totalitarian menace, here embodied in the terrifying Borg—the film introduces so many messianic caesuras (an early twenty-first century war, in which, as in *Independence Day*, all of the old cities are destroyed; the crew of the Enterprise; the angelic Vulcans who arrive in the film's waning moments; and even the Borg themselves), each of which appears as an appar-ently indispensable midwife to such a future, that the passage from our world into the new place occurs seemingly without, and indeed almost in spite of, the actions of people living and acting in the present.

34 Jameson, *Postmodernism*, 309.

35 Indeed, Fukuyama writes, "Clearly, the vast bulk of the Third World remains very much mired in history, and will be a terrain of conflict for many years to come." Fukuyama, "End of History," 15.

36 For a useful discussion of the Jewish–African American alliance figured in the film, see Rogin, *Independence Day*, 45–50. For a further discussion of the Crown Heights events, see Shapiro, *Crown Heights*.

37 Laclau and Mouffe, *Hegemony and Socialist Strategy*, 128.

38 I discuss this process further in Wegner, *Imaginary Communities*, 109–10. This last dimension is absent in the conclusion of Steven Spielberg's 2005 adap-tation of Wells's novel, a fact made even more interesting given the film's repeated allegorical references to the events of September 11, 2001, an "in-vasion" of the United States that had the very consequences Wells foresaw.

39 Leinster, "First Contact," 35. Also see the useful discussion of the story in Huntington, *Rationalizing Genius*, 116–19.

40 Edelman, "The Future Is Kid Stuff," 21, 23. For Edelman's further development of these ideas, also see his *No Future*.

41 Rogin, *Independence Day*, 66. Rogin suggests a similar option is offered to the character of Steven Hiller in the figure of his flying partner, Captain Jimmy Wilder (Harry Connick Jr.).

42 For the concept of the "vanishing mediator," see Jameson, "The Vanishing Mediator; or, Max Weber as Storyteller," in *The Ideologies of Theory*, 2:3–34; and Žižek, *Tarrying with the Negative*, 226–37.

43 I would like briefly to point out an additional level of mediation that takes place by way of the film's vision of the destruction of the U.S. metropolitan centers. The trope of the blasted urban landscape has long served in the science fiction imaginary, as Andrew Ross among others has pointed out, as a figure for white middle-class anxieties about what are understood to be the irredeemable "race capitals" of the inner cities. See Ross, *Strange Weather*, 146. By clearing away these zones of "obsolescence"—to deploy the figure developed by Evan Watkins, which I discussed in more detail in chapter 4—the film imaginatively sets free an African American middle class, represented here by Smith's character Steven Hiller, from its traditional bonds to this population. Thus, as I noted earlier, the film's placement of Hiller in Los Angeles is no coincidence:, for in doing so, the film neatly dissolves any link between this "rising" middle class and the "anarchic" forces of the 1992 uprising.

44 Qtd. in Walter Benjamin, "The Work of Art in the Age of Its Technological Reproducibility," in Benjamin, *Selected Writings*, 269.

45 See Heidegger, "Question Concerning Technology."

46 Jameson, *Postmodernism*, 35.

47 Lyotard, Postmodern Condition, 4–5.

48 Jameson, "Marx's Purloined Letter," 29.

49 See Agamben, *State of Exception*.

50 Harvey, *New Imperialism*, 191–92.

51 Rushdie, *Fury*, 23.

52 See Ali, *Clash of Fundamentalisms*, especially his discussion of the contrast between the neoliberal end-of-history thesis of Fukuyama and the neoconservative clash-of-civilizations thesis of Samuel P. Huntington, 272–75 and 281–84. I take the idea that September 11 represented a shift from a neoliberal to neoconservative hegemony from Harvey's *New Imperialism*.

53 Kracauer, *From Caligari to Hitler*, 164.

54 There is another interesting link between Lang and the makers of *Independence Day*: for just as Lang's later films, *M* (1931) and *Das Testament des Dr. Mabuse* (1933), in their allegorical critique of fascism can be read as apologies for the vision in *Metropolis* so enthusiastically embraced by the Nazis (Joseph Goebbels reportedly admired the film and later invited Lang to serve as the director of the German film industry), so, too, does Emmerich's post-9/11 ecological disaster film, *The Day After Tomorrow* (2004), in effect "remake" *Independence Day* to undo the earlier film's endorsement of a U.S.-dominated global order. In this later film, we see figured, in a striking image of the planet after the onset of the new Ice Age, the entire northern hemisphere frozen in a massive sheet of ice, and the U.S. government, along with the hordes of "illegal immigrants" that had followed them south, reduced to the status of the "guests" of Mexico. A similar trajectory might be traced out in the development of George Lucas's vision between the original *Star Wars* (1977)—a film that even provided the Reagan administration with the popular title of its costly and

ultimately unworkable space missile defense program—and its most recent and final "prequel," *The Revenge of the Sith* (2005).

55 Montag, "Spirits Armed and Unarmed," 80.

56 Žižek, *Welcome to the Desert of the Real*, 152–53.

57 Gramsci, *Selections from the Prison Notebooks*, 9.

58 Ibid., 334. Also see the important footnote to this passage concerning Gramsci's use of the term "elite."

59 Robbins, *Feeling Global*, 32–36.

60 Gramsci, *Selections from the Prison Notebooks*, 10.

61 For some significant discussions of this aspect of Marx's later work, see Balibar, *Philosophy of Marx*, esp. chap. 4; Ross, *The Emergence of Social Space*, 21–25; and Dunayevskaya, *Rosa Luxemburg*.

62 See the group's Web site at 911scholars.org.

63 Žižek, Afterword, 225.

Seven **FIGURES OF THE MULTITUDE IN THE *FOREVER* TRILOGY**

An earlier version of this essay was published in *World Bank Literature,* ed. by Amitava Kumar (Minneapolis: University of Minnesota Press, 2003): 280–96.

1 Jameson, "Cognitive Mapping," 347.

2 Ibid. Jameson again uses this formulation in his essay "Periodizing the 60s," where he notes, "Althusser's proposal seems the wisest in this situation: . . . the historian should reformulate her vocation—not any longer to produce some vivid representation of History 'as it really happened,' but rather to produce the *concept* of history." Fredric Jameson, "Periodizing the 60s," in Jameson, *Ideologies of Theory*, 2:180.

3 Jameson, "Cognitive Mapping," 356.

4 Kumar, "World Bank Literature," 197. Also see Kumar, *World Bank Literature*, in which an earlier version of the present chapter also appears. And for further discussion of the concept, see Benjamin, *Invested Interests*.

5 Kumar, "World Bank Literature," 203.

6 Moretti, "Conjectures on World Literature," 54. For the attempt to develop a new model of literary study adequate to this reality, what Moretti calls "distant reading" (see note 26 below), see his *Graphs, Maps, Trees*.

7 Kumar, "World Bank Literature," 203.

8 For the importance of an attention to different levels of spatial scale in a reconceived critical cultural studies, see Harvey, *Spaces of Hope*, esp. chap. 5; and Smith, "Homeless/Global."

9 Jameson, *Postmodernism*, 403.

10 Harvey, *Spaces of Hope*, 69.

11 See Harvey, *New Imperialism*, esp. chap. 5.

12 For a further discussion of the history of the concept of Americanization, see Wegner, "Pretty Woman Goes Global."

13 Harvey, *Spaces of Hope*, 68. And now see his discussion of the strategy of "accumulation by dispossession" in *New Imperialism*, chap. 4.

14 Jameson, *Postmodernism*, 321.

15 Jameson, "Third-World Literature," 69. For a useful overview of the debate surrounding the essay, see Neil Lazarus, "Fredric Jameson on 'Third-World Literature': A Qualified Defence," in Kellner ad Homer, *Fredric Jameson*, 42–61; and the essays by Ian Buchanan and Imre Szeman in Irr and Buchanan, *On Jameson*, 173–88, 189–211.

16 Jameson, *Political Unconscious*, 106.

17 Jameson, "Third-World Literature," 65.

18 Ibid., 88.

19 For Jameson's specific acknowledgment of the class content of postmodern culture, see *Postmodernism*, 407.

20 Louis Althusser, "Ideology and Ideological State Apparatuses (Notes towards an Investigation)," in Althusser, *Lenin and Philosophy*, 162. I explore the relationship between Jameson's and Lacan's tripartite schemas, as well as that found in Henri Lefebvre's monumental *The Production of Space*, in "Horizons, Figures, and Machines"; and in *Imaginary Communities*, chap. 1.

21 Jameson, *Postmodernism*, 54.

22 Ibid., 38.

23 Jameson, *Geopolitical Aesthetic*, 155.

24 Ibid., 3–4.

25 Kumar, "World Bank Literature," 199.

26 Moretti offers a similar, and what will be for U.S. literary scholars a particularly scandalous, observation about the necessarily collective nature of a revitalized project of world literature studies: "Literary history will quickly become very different from what it is now: it will become 'second hand': a patchwork of other people's research, *without a single direct textual reading*." Moretti, "Conjectures on World Literature," 57.

27 Many of these essays, including those cited below, now have been collected in the second part of Jameson, *Archaeologies of the Future*. I discuss this book and Jameson's theorizations of science fiction more generally in my essay "Jameson's Modernisms; or, the Desire Called Utopia."

28 Fredric Jameson, "Progress versus Utopia; or, Can We Imagine the Future?" in Jameson, *Archaeologies of the Future*, 288–89. I further discuss Jameson's thoughts about utopia in my "Horizons, Figures, and Machines"; and I explore this central modern generic institution in much greater depth in *Imaginary Communities*.

29 Jameson, "Progress versus Utopia," 287. Jameson discusses the link of SF and detective fiction on page 288 of this essay. Jameson's earliest investigation

of the spatial mapping operations of popular literary genres is to be found in his "On Raymond Chandler." However, whereas science fiction's mapping scale has been from its earliest days that of the global, in Chandler's work it remains constrained to the local urban and national horizons, a limit whose constitutive function Jameson explores further in his more recent "The Synoptic Chandler," in Copjec, *Shades of Noir*, 33–56.

30 Jameson, "Progress versus Utopia," 288.

31 Jameson, *Postmodernism*, 283.

32 Mark Rose has similarly stressed that in this genre "fictions of time are drawn by the force of a kind of inner linguistic gravity until they collapse into fictions of space." Rose, *Alien Encounters*, 127.

33 Fredric Jameson, "Science Fiction as a Spatial Genre," in Jameson, *Archaeologies of the Future*, 313. This, too, suggests the roots of modern science fiction in the older tradition of the prose romance, whose spatial mapping dimensions Jameson discusses in *Political Unconscious*, 112.

34 Fredric Jameson, "Generic Discontinuities in SF: Brian Aldiss' *Starship*," in Jameson, *Archaeologies of the Future*, 265.

35 Fredric Jameson, "After Armageddon: Character Systems in *Dr. Bloodmoney*," in Jameson, *Archaeologies of the Future*, 360–61.

36 Fredric Jameson, "The Space of Science Fiction: Narrative in A. E. Van Vogt," in Jameson, *Archaeologies of the Future*, 323.

37 Haldeman, *The Forever War*, 236, 76.

38 Ibid., 208.

39 Ibid., 273.

40 Ibid., 274.

41 Ibid., 276.

42 Jameson, *Postmodernism*, 54.

43 I explore a similar dilemma manifest in Ursula K. Le Guin's *The Dispossessed* (1974), one of the great utopian narratives contemporary with *The Forever War*, in *Imaginary Communities*, chap. 5.

44 Haldeman, *Forever Peace*, hereafter cited parenthetically in the running text as FP.

45 See Haldeman, *The Forever War*, 16–17. For a recent discussion of the representation in *The Forever War* of the technologically augmented soldier's body, with special attention to the questions of gender raised by this figuration, see Hantke, "Surgical Strikes and Prosthetic Warriors."

46 Jameson, *Seeds of Time*, 158.

47 Ibid., 158–59.

48 For an important discussion of the relationship between cyberpunk and the economic, political, and social restructurings of the 1980s, see Moylan, "Global Economy, Local Texts." Moylan points out that the major protagonists in Gibson's celebrated cyberpunk trilogy—*Neuromancer* (1984), *Count Zero* (1986), *Mona Lisa Overdrive* (1988)—are figures of a significant labor sector of

a then emergent post-Fordist economy: "A smaller, but growing, number of skilled professional-managerial-technical workers who individually contract with corporations (and governments) for limited term, relatively high-paid tasks" (191). Moylan's essay also contains a useful early bibliography of other critical engagements with cyberpunk fiction.

49 There is a deep family resemblance between Haldeman's image of information technologies and the older science fiction figure of telepathy: Jameson notes, "In this case — the theme of telepathy — the material signifier expresses and conceals the utopian fantasy of a genuinely collective set of social relationships, in which the individual subject or ego — a historical result of the development of commerce and capitalism — is again dissolved in its monadic isolation and returned to its ground as a nexus of human relationships and a transmission point for collective relationships." Jameson, "Science Fiction as a Spatial Genre," 300. Peter Fitting, in a brilliant survey of the shifts in the thematic configurations of Anglo-American science fiction from the 1930s through the late 1970s, suggests something similar about the utopian charge of the figure of telepathy in such classic works as Theodore Sturgeon's *More Than Human* (1953); however, Fitting goes on to point out political limits to this image, similar to the ones I suggested at work in Haldeman's earlier figure of the collective Man: "It is also clear that the final phase of the first model — the 'spontaneous' development of telepathy — was a dead end, an alternative which took any possibility for change or improvement out of human hands." Fitting, "The Modern Anglo-American SF Novel," 65.

50 Žižek, *Looking Awry*, 35.

51 Jameson, *Seeds of Time*, 63. I discuss Marin's work in more detail in *Imaginary Communities*, chap. 2, and in my following chapter in the present work. Jameson's classic discussion of Marin's *Utopiques: Jeux d'espaces* (1974) is to be found in "Of Islands and Trenches: Neutralization and the Production of Utopian Discourse," in *Ideologies of Theory*, 2:75–101. Jameson first demonstrates the productivity of his joining of Marin's concept of neutralization and A. J. Greimas's semiotic rectangle as a way of mapping contemporary architectural practice in *Seeds of Time*, esp. 132–33 and 194–95. He further develops the significance of the place of the neutral term for any understanding of the production of utopian imaginaries in *Archaeologies of the Future*, 178–81. I discuss this move, and its relevance for a reconsideration of dialectical thought more generally, in my "Greimas avec Lacan."

52 Žižek, *Parallax View*, 121.

53 Jameson, "Lacan and the Dialectic," 376. A related vision of the Imaginary of late capitalism is outlined in Žižek, *Tarrying with the Negative*, 219–26, an argument I discuss in more detail in "Greimas avec Lacan."

54 Žižek, *Tarrying with the Negative*, 96, 97.

55 Ibid., 22. Hegel, *Hegel's Science of Logic*, 642.

56 Jameson makes a similar point in his call to distinguish terrorism from what

he names "disruption as Novum, as restructuration and the unexpected blasting open of habits, as the lateral side-door which suddenly opens onto a world of transformed human beings." Jameson, *Archaeologies of the Future*, 232.

57 Hardt and Negri, *Empire*, 62.

58 Ibid., 103. Also see Hardt and Negri's follow-up volume, *Multitude*.

59 Balibar, *Spinoza and Politics*, 98.

60 Ibid., 95.

61 Ibid., 124.

62 Ibid., 96.

63 Spinoza, *Ethics*, 238.

64 Ibid., 209–10.

65 Balibar, *Spinoza and Politics*, 97.

66 Ibid., 98.

67 Derrida, "University Without Condition," 236.

68 Horkheimer and Adorno, *Dialectic of Enlightenment*, 199. Eve Kosofsky Sedgwick comes to a similar conclusion about the family likeness between current attacks on university scholarship, anti-Semitism, and queer bashing in her powerful essay, "Queer and Now," in Sedgwick, *Tendencies*, esp. 17–20.

69 Bruce Robbins writes, "The point would be both to defend the social welfare state and, as much as possible, to extend it outward—for example toward residents who are noncitizens." Robbins, *Feeling Global*, 36. Jameson maintains, "Today, speaking at least from the perspective of the United States, but also, I venture to say, from that of the Europe of the European Union countries, the most urgent task seems to me the defense of the welfare state and of those regulations and entitlements that have been characterized as barriers to a completely free market and its prosperities." Fredric Jameson, "Lenin and Revisionism," in Budgen, Kouvelakis, and Žižek, *Lenin Reloaded*, 69.

70 Haldeman, *Forever Free*, 34.

71 Ibid., 254.

72 Ibid., 266.

73 Ibid., 267.

74 Ibid., 277.

75 Adorno, *Minima Moralia*, 112. See also Jameson, *Late Marxism*, 101–2; and Jameson, *Archaeologies of the Future*, 172–75.

Eight **WE'RE FAMILY**

1 Žižek, *Ticklish Subject*, 216–17.

2 Ibid., 221.

3 Ibid.

4 Ibid., 221–22.

5 Ibid., 222.

6 Badiou, *Ethics*, 101.

7 "Consequently, to *repeat* Lenin does not mean a *return* to Lenin. To repeat
  Lenin is to accept that Lenin is dead, that his particular solution failed, even
  failed monstrously, but that there was a utopian spark in it worth saving. To
  repeat Lenin means that one has to distinguish between what Lenin actually
  did and the field of possibilities that he opened up, the tension in Lenin between what he effectively did and another dimension one might call what was
  'in Lenin more than Lenin himself.'" Žižek, "Plea for Leninist Intolerance,"
  566. Also see Žižek, "Afterword"; and Budgen, Kouvelakis, and Žižek, *Lenin
  Reloaded*. Also see Deleuze, *Difference and Repetition*.
8 Hardt and Negri, *Empire*, 367–68.
9 Ibid., 368.
10 Ibid., 52.
11 Hardt and Negri, "Globalization and Democracy," 330. Also see their *Multitude*, 194.
12 Rose, *Alien Encounters*, 32.
13 Butler, *Antigone's Claim*, 74.
14 Armstrong, *How Novels Think*, 145–46.
15 Wilcox and Lavery, *Fighting the Forces*, 218.
16 See Harvey, *New Imperialism*; and Harvey, *Brief History of Neoliberalism*, esp.
  81–85.
17 I offer a more extended discussion of Marin's work in *Imaginary Communities*.
18 Badiou, *Ethics*, 41.
19 Ibid., 51–52.
20 See Jameson, *The Geopolitical Aesthetic*.
21 Morris, *Too Soon Too Late*, 155.
22 Ross, *Emergence of Social Space*, 25, 123–24.
23 Feldman, *Formations of Violence*, 204, 264.
24 Butler, *Bodies That Matter*, 137.
25 Butler, *Antigone's Claim*, 82.
26 Ibid., 21.
27 Ibid., 55.
28 Jameson, *Signatures of the Visible*, 32.
29 Ibid., 33.
30 Badiou, *Century*, 66.
31 See Pontifical Academy for Life Tenth General Assembly, "Final Communique."
32 Butler, *Antigone's Claim*, 22–23, also see 69.
33 And now for a related reading of the figuration of new forms of collectivity
  in one of the other landmark texts of the period, Arundhati Roy's *The God of
  Small Things* (1997), see Benjamin, *Invested Interests*, 165–88.
34 Butler, *Antigone's Claim*, 74.
35 Ibid.

36 Butler, *Undoing Gender*, 102–3.

37 Ibid., 123.

38 Ibid., 26.

39 One of my contentions in this chapter is that the *Buffy* series, to develop these kinds of complex figurations *across* various episodes, transgresses the fundamentally discontinuous and episodic structure characteristic of most television series. *Buffy*, rather, deploys the logic of "world continuity" that is first developed in the comic book narrative form. Joss Whedon, the series creator, is a noted fan and practitioner of the medium (he was also involved in *The X-Men* series) and has produced both the comic book series *Fray*, which projects the *Buffy* mythos in a future dystopian setting, and now continues the Buffy series itself in the comic book format with 2007's *Buffy: Season Eight*.

40 Todorov, *Fantastic*, 25.

41 Butler, *Parable of the Sower*, 281.

42 Moylan, *Scraps of the Untainted Sky*, 237.

43 Ibid., 238.

44 Butler, *Parable of the Talents*, 403; hereafter cited parenthetically in the text as PT.

45 Louis Marin, in the final chapter of *Utopiques* from which I cite this essay, claims that it was written by Marx himself. However, the essay is in its original form unsigned. There is no other indication in his writings or correspondence that would suggest Marx's authorship, and it may have been composed by the issue's editor Karl Schapper. For an English translation of the entire issue of *Kommunistische Zeitschrift*, the only issue of the paper published, see Ryazanoff, *Communist Manifesto*, 286–318.

46 Qtd. in Marin, *Utopiques*, 349, 350; and Marin, *Utopics*, 277, 278.

47 I discuss Cabet and the fate of the community in "Here or Nowhere," 122–23.

48 Marx and Engels, *Marx-Engels Reader*, 500.

49 Hardt and Negri, *Empire*, 186–87.

50 Badiou, "Beyond Formalisation," 127.

51 Qtd. in Hallward, *Badiou*, 108.

52 Badiou, *Saint Paul*, 1. Žižek offers this interesting reading of the foundational importance of the fourth truth procedure, love (after science, art, and politics), in Badiou's thought: "What is encompassed by this fourth procedure is not just the miracle of love, but also psychoanalysis, theology, and philosophy itself (the *love* of wisdom). Is not love, then, Badiou's 'Asiatic mode of production' — the category into which he throws all truth-procedures which do not fit the other three modes? This fourth procedure also serves as a kind of underlying formal principle or matrix of all procedures (which accounts for the fact that, although Badiou denies religion the status of a truth-procedure, he nonetheless claims that Saint Paul was the first to deploy the very formal matrix of the Truth-Event)." Žižek, *Parallax View*, 406n28.

53 Badiou, *Ethics*, 44.

54 Ibid., 45.

55 Ibid., 51.

56 Badiou, *Saint Paul*, 60.

57 Hallward, *Badiou*, xxvi, 26.

58 Badiou, *Ethics*, 74, 86.

59 Ibid., 71. Moreover, the series completes Badiou's sequence of three forms of evil in its final season when it shows Buffy becoming increasingly rigid in her views and unwilling to recognize the value of her comrades' assessments of their rapidly evolving situation. In Badiou's terms we could say that Buffy has fallen into the trap of identifying "a truth with total power," the form of evil he names "*disaster*." Badiou writes, "Every absolutization of the power of a truth organizes an Evil. Not only does this Evil destroy the situation (for the will to eliminate opinion is, fundamentally, the same as the will to eliminate, in the human animal, its very animality, i.e. its being), but it also interrupts the truth-process in whose name it proceeds, since it fails to preserve within the composition of its subject, the duality [*duplicité*] of interests (disinterested-interest and interest pure and simple)" (*Ethics*, 71, 85). Such an evil takes its most devastating real-world form in Stalinism (which then crucially differs from fascist "terror").

60 Ibid., 79.

61 See Wegner, "Beat Cops of History."

62 The plot line of the series has now been continued in comic-book form in Whedon, *Buffy the Vampire Slayer*.

Adorno, Theodor. *Minima Moralia: Reflections from a Damaged Life*. Trans. E. F. N. Jephcott. London: Verso, 1978.

Agamben, Giorgo. *State of Exception*. Trans. Kevin Attell. Chicago: University of Chicago Press, 2005.

Aglietta, Michel. *A Theory of Capitalist Regulation: The US Experience*. Trans. David Fernbach. New York: Verso, 1987.

Ali, Tariq. *The Clash of Fundamentalisms: Crusades, Jihads, and Modernity*. New York: Verso, 2002.

Althusser, Louis. *Lenin and Philosophy and Other Essays*. Trans. Ben Brewster. New York: Monthly Review Press, 1971.

Anderson, Perry. "The Ends of History." In *A Zone of Engagement*, 279–375. New York: Verso, 1992.

Armstrong, Nancy. *How Novels Think: The Limits of Individualism from 1719–1900*. New York: Columbia University Press, 2005.

Arnzen, Michael A. "The Same and the New: *Cape Fear* and the Hollywood Remake as Metanarrative Discourse." *Narrative* 4, no. 2 (1996): 175–94.

Arrighi, Giovanni. "Hegemony Unravelling." *New Left Review*, no. 32 (2005): 23–80.

———. "Hegemony Unravelling—2." *New Left Review*, no. 33 (2005): 108–13.

Auerbach, Jonathan. *Male Call: Becoming Jack London*. Durham: Duke University Press, 1996.

Badiou, Alain. 1988. *Being and Event*. Trans. Oliver Feltham. New York: Continuum, 2005.

———. "Beyond Formalisation: An Interview." *Angelaki* 8, no. 2 (2003): 111–36.

———. *The Century*. Trans. Alberto Toscano. Malden, M.A.: Polity, 2007.

———. *Ethics: An Essay on the Understanding of Radical Evil*. Trans. Peter Hallward. New York: Verso, 2001.

———. *Saint Paul: The Foundation of Universalism*. Trans. Ray Brassier. Stanford: Stanford University Press, 2003.

Balibar, Étienne. *The Philosophy of Marx*. Trans. Chris Turner. New York: Verso, 1995.

———. *Spinoza and Politics*. Trans. Peter Snowdon. New York: Verso, 1998.

Barthes, Roland. *Mythologies*. 1957. Trans. Annette Lavers. New York: Hill and Wang, 1972.

Baudrillard, Jean. "L'Esprit du Terrorisme." Trans. Michel Valentin. *South Atlantic Quarterly* 101, no. 2 (2002): 403–15.

———. *Symbolic Exchange and Death*. Trans. Iain Hamilton Grant. London: Sage, 1993.

Bellamy, Edward. *Looking Backward, 2000–1887*. 1888. New York: New American Library, 1960.

Benjamin, Bret. *Invested Interests: Capital, Culture, and the World Bank*. Minneapolis: University of Minnesota Press, 2007.

Benjamin, Walter. *Allegorien kultureller Erfahrung: Ausgewählte Schriften 1920–1940*. Ed. Sebastian Kleinschmidt. Leipzig: Reclam, 1984.

———. *The Arcades Project*. 1982. Trans. Howard Eiland and Kevin McLaughlin. Cambridge: Harvard University Press, 1999.

———. *The Origin of German Tragic Drama*. Trans. John Osborne. London: New Left Books, 1977.

———. *Selected Writings*. Vol. 4, *1938–1940*. Ed. Howard Eiland and Michael W. Jennings. Cambridge: Belknap, 2003.

Birrell, Ross. "The Gift of Terror: Suicide-Bombing as *Potlach*," www.spar wasserhq.de/Index/HTMLjan5/jesper2.htm (accessed September 16, 2008).

Blade Runner. Dir. Ridley Scott. Warner Brothers, 1982.

Blake, William. "The Marriage of Heaven and Hell." In *William Blake's Illuminated Books*. Vol. 3, *The Early Illuminated Books*. London: William Blake Trust, Tate Gallery, 1993.

Blitz, Michael, and Louise Krasniewicz. *Why Arnold Matters: The Rise of a Cultural Icon*. New York: Basic Books, 2004.

Bloch, Ernst. *The Principle of Hope*. Trans. Neville Plaice, Stephen Plaice, and Paul Knight. Oxford: Blackwell, 1986.

Boyer, Robert. *The Regulation School: A Critical Introduction*. Trans. Craig Charney. New York: Columbia University Press, 1990.

Buck-Morss, Susan. *The Dialectics of Seeing: Walter Benjamin and the Arcades Project*. Cambridge: MIT Press, 1989.

———. *The Origins of Negative Dialectics: Theodor W. Adorno, Walter Benjamin, and the Frankfurt Institute*. New York: Free Press, 1977.

Budgen, Sebastian, Stathis Kouvelakis, and Slavoj Žižek, eds. *Lenin Reloaded: Toward a Politics of Truth,* Durham: Duke University Press, 2007.

Buffy the Vampire Slayer. Seasons 1–7. DVD. Twentieth Century Fox Television, 2002–2004.

Bulletin of Atomic Scientists. Doomsday Clock, www.thebulletin.org/minutes-to-midnight/timeline.html (accessed June 25, 2008).

Butler, Judith. *Antigone's Claim: Kinship between Life and Death*. New York: Columbia University Press, 2000.

———. *Bodies That Matter: On the Discursive Limits of "Sex."* New York: Routledge, 1993.

———. *Precarious Life: The Powers of Mourning and Violence*. New York: Verso, 2004.

———. *Undoing Gender*. New York: Routledge, 2004.

Butler, Octavia E. *Dawn*. New York: Warner Books, 1987.

———. *Fledgling*. New York: Seven Stories Press, 2005.

———. *Parable of the Sower*. 1993. New York: Warner Books, 1995.

———. *Parable of the Talents*. New York: Warner Books, 1998.

Cape Fear. Dir. J. Lee Thompson. Universal Pictures, 1962.

Cape Fear. Dir. Martin Scorsese. Universal Pictures, 1991.

Casarino, Cesare. *Modernity at Sea: Melville, Marx, Conrad in Crisis*. Minneapolis: University of Minnesota Press, 2002.

Cash, W. J. *The Mind of the South*. 1941. New York: Vintage, 1969.

Cavell, Stanley. *Pursuits of Happiness: The Hollywood Comedy of Remarriage*. Cambridge: Harvard University Press, 1981.

Certeau, Michel de. *The Practice of Everyday Life*. Trans. Steven Rendall. Berkeley: University of California Press, 1984.

Chafe, William H. *The Unfinished Journey: America since World War II*. New York: Oxford University Press, 1986.

Chollet, Derek, and James Goldgeier. *America Between the Wars: From 11/9 to 9/11*. New York: Public Affairs, 2008.

Churchill, Ward. *On the Justice of Roosting Chickens: Reflections on the Consequences of U.S. Imperial Arrogance and Criminality*. Oakland: AK Press, 2003.

———. " 'Some People Push Back:' On the Justice of Roosting Chickens." Kersplebedeb, http://www.kersplebedeb.com/mystuff/s11/churchill.html (accessed September 17, 2008).

Conrad, Joseph. *Lord Jim*. New York: Penguin, 1989.

Cook, Pam. "Scorsese's Masquerade." *Sight and Sound* 1, no. 12 (1992):14–15.

Davis, Mike. *City of Quartz: Excavating the Future in Los Angeles*. New York: Verso, 1990.

———. *Dead Cities and Other Tales*. New York: New Press, 2002.

———. "'Fordism' in Crisis: A Review of Michel Aglietta's *Régulation et crises: L'expérience des États-Unis*." *Review* 2, no. 2 (1978): 207–69.

Dawson, Ashley, and Malini Johar Schueller, eds. *Exceptional State: Contemporary U.S. Culture and the New Imperialism*. Durham: Duke University Press, 2007.

The Day after Tomorrow. Dir. Roland Emmerich. Twentieth Century Fox, 2004.

Deleuze, Gilles. *Cinema 1: The Movement-Image*. Trans. Hugh Tomlinson and Barbara Habberjam. Minneapolis: University of Minnesota Press, 1986.

DeLillo, Don. "Everything under the Bomb." *Guardian*, January 10, 1998, 33.

———. *Falling Man*. New York: Scribner, 2007.

———. *Mao II*. New York: Penguin, 1991.

———. *Underworld*. New York: Scribner, 1997.

———. *White Noise*. New York: Penguin, 1986.

Denning, Michael. *Culture in the Age of Three Worlds*. New York: Verso, 2004.

Derrida, Jacques. *Archive Fever: A Freudian Impression*. Trans. Eric Prenowitz. Chicago: University of Chicago Press, 1996.

———. *Difference and Repetition*. Trans. Paul Patton. New York: Columbia University Press, 1994.

———. *Limited Inc*. Evanston, Ill.: Northwestern University Press, 1988.

———. "Marx & Sons." In *Ghostly Demarcations: A Symposium on Jacques Derrida's Specters of Marx*, ed. Michael Sprinker, 213–69. New York: Verso, 1999.

———. *Rouges: Two Essays on Reason*. Trans. Pascale-Anne Brault and Michael Naas. Stanford: Stanford University Press, 2005.

———. *Specters of Marx: The State of the Debt, the Work of Mourning, and the New International*. Trans. Peggy Kamuf. New York: Routledge, 1994.

———. "The University without Condition." In *Without Alibi*, ed. and trans. Peggy Kamuf, 202–37. Stanford: Stanford University Press, 2002.

Dunayevskaya, Raya. *Rosa Luxemburg, Women's Liberation, and Marx's Philosophy of Revolution*. 2nd ed. Urbana: University of Illinois Press, 1991.

Dyer, Richard. *Heavenly Bodies: Film Stars and Society*. New York: St. Martin's, 1986.

———. *Stars*. London: British Film Institute, 1979.

Edelman, Lee. "The Future Is Kid Stuff: Queer Theory, Disidentification, and the Death Drive." *Narrative* 6, no. 1 (1998): 18–30.

———. *No Future: Queer Theory and the Death Drive*. Durham: Duke University Press, 2004.

Edmundson, Mark. *Nightmare on Main Street: Angels, Sadomasochism, and the Culture of the Gothic*. Cambridge: Harvard University Press, 1997.

Ehrenreich, Barbara. *The Hearts of Men: American Dreams and the Flight from Commitment*. Garden City, N.Y.: Anchor, 1983.

Ellison, Harlan. *I Have No Mouth and I Must Scream*. New York: Pyramid, 1967.

Escape from LA. Dir. John Carpenter. Paramount Pictures, 1996.

Feldman, Allen. *Formations of Violence: The Narrative of the Body and Political Terror in Northern Ireland*. Chicago: University of Chicago Press, 1991.

Fight Club. Dir. David Fincher. Twentieth Century Fox, 1999.

Fitting, Peter. "Futurecop: The Neutralization of Revolt in *Blade Runner*." *Science Ficton Studies*, no. 43 (1987): 340–54.

———. "The Modern Anglo-American SF Novel: Utopian Longing and Capitalist Cooptation." *Science Fiction Studies*, no. 17 (1979): 59–76.

Forrest, Jennifer, and Leonard R. Koos, eds. *Dead Ringers: The Remake in Theory and Practice*. Albany: State University of New York Press, 2001.

Foucault, Michel. "Different Spaces." In *Essential Works of Foucault, 1954–1984*, vol. 2, *Aesthetics, Methods, and Epistemology*, ed. James D. Faubion, 175–85. New York: New Press, 1998.

Fraser, Antonia. *Faith and Treason: The Story of the Gunpowder Plot*. New York: Doubleday, 1996.

Freud, Sigmund. "Screen Memories." In *The Standard Edition of the Complete Psychological Works*, vol. 3, ed. and trans. James Strachey, 47–69. London: Hogarth, 1963.

———. "The Uncanny." In *The Standard Edition of the Complete Psychological Works*, vol. 17, ed. and trans. James Strachey, 219–56. London: Hogarth, 1964.

Friedrich, Otto. *City of Nets: A Portrait of Hollywood in the 1940's*. New York: Harper and Row, 1986.

Fukuyama, Francis. "The End of History?" *National Interest*, 1989, 3–18.

———. *The End of History and the Last Man*. New York: Free Press, 1992.

———. "A Reply to My Critics." *National Interest*, 1989–90, 21–28.

Ghost Dog. Dir. Jim Jarmusch. Channel Four Films, 1999.

Giroux, Henry A. "Brutalized Bodies and Emasculated Politics: *Fight Club*, Consumerism, and Masculine Violence." *Third Text*, no. 53 (2000–2001): 31–41.

Goode, John. "Gissing, Morris, and English Socialism," *Victorian Studies* 12, no. 2 (1968): 201–26.

Gramsci, Antonio. *Selections from the Prison Notebooks*. Ed. and trans. Quintin Hoare and Geoffrey Nowell Smith. New York: International Publishers, 1971.

Grassian, Daniel. "Passing into Post-ethnicity: A Study of Danzy Senna's *Caucasia*." *Midwest Quarterly* 47, no. 4 (2006): 317–35.

Greimas, Algirdas Julien. *On Meaning: Selected Writings in Semiotic Theory*. Trans. Paul J. Perron and Frank H. Collins. Minneapolis: University of Minnesota Press, 1987.

Griffiths, Richard T. History of the Internet, Internet for Historians (and Just about Everyone Else), www.let.leidenuniv.nl/history/ivh/chap2.htm (accessed September 17, 2008).

Groundhog Day. Dir. Harold Ramis. Columbia Pictures, 1993.

Haldeman, Joe. *Forever Free*. New York: Ace, 1999.

———. *Forever Peace*. 1997. New York: Ace, 1998.

——. *The Forever War*. 1974. New York: Harper Collins, 2003.

Hallward, Peter. *Badiou: A Subject to Truth*. Minneapolis: University of Minnesota Press, 2003.

Hansen, Jim. "Formalism and Its Malcontents: Benjamin and de Man on the Function of Allegory." *New Literary History* 35, no. 4 (2005): 663–83.

Hantke, Steffen. "Surgical Strikes and Prosthetic Warriors: The Soldier's Body in Contemporary Science Fiction." *Science Fiction Studies* no. 76 (1998): 495–509.

Hardt, Michael, and Antonio Negri. *Empire*. Cambridge: Harvard University Press, 2000.

——. Foreword to *Another World Is Possible: Popular Alternatives to Globalization at the World Social Forum*, ed. William F. Fisher and Thomas Ponniah, xvi–xix. New York: Zed, 2003.

——. "Globalization and Democracy." In *Democracy Unrealized: Documenta 11, Platform 1*, ed. Okwui Enwezoe et al., 323–36. Ostfildern-Ruit, Germany: Hatje Cantz, 2002.

——. *Multitude: War and Democracy in the Age of Empire*. New York: Penguin, 2004.

Harrison, Bennett, and Barry Bluestone. *The Great U-Turn: Corporate Restructuring and the Polarization of America*. New York: Basic Books, 1990.

Harvey, David. *A Brief History of Neoliberalism*. Oxford: Oxford University Press, 2005.

——. *The Condition of Postmodernity: An Enquiry into the Origins of Cultural Change*. Oxford: Blackwell, 1989.

——. *The New Imperialism*. Oxford: Oxford University Press, 2005.

——. *Spaces of Hope*. Berkeley: University of California Press, 2000.

Hauerwas, Stanley, and Frank Lentricchia, eds. "Dissent from the Homeland: Essays after September 11." Special issue, *South Atlantic Quarterly* 101, no. 2 (2002).

Hawthorne, Christopher. "Living with Our Mistake: Is New York About to Choose the Wrong Proposal for Rebuilding the World Trade Center?" www .slate.com/id/2079228 (accessed September 16, 2008).

Hegel, G.W.F. *Hegel's Philosophy of Right*. Trans. T. M. Knox. Oxford: Oxford University Press, 1967.

——. *Hegel's Science of Logic*. Trans. A. V. Miller. Amherst, N.Y.: Humanity, 1999.

Hegeman, Susan. "Haunted by Mass Culture." *American Literary History* 12, nos. 1–2 (2000): 298–317.

——. "Naïve Modernism and the Politics of Embarrassment." In *Discipline and Practice: The (Ir)resistibility of Theory*, ed. Stefan Herbrechter and Ivan Callus, 154–77. Lewisburg, Penn.: Bucknell University Press, 2004.

Heidegger, Martin. "The Question Concerning Technology." In *Basic Writings*, ed. David Farrell Krell, 283–317. New York: Harper and Row, 1977.

Henwood, Doug. *After the New Economy*. New York: New Press, 2003.

Hobbs, Robert. *Mark Lombardi: Global Networks*. New York: Independent Curators International, 2003.

Hoberman, J. "Sacred and Profane." *Sight and Sound* 1, no. 10 (1992): 8–11.

Horkheimer, Max, and Theodor Adorno, *Dialectic of Enlightenment*. Trans. John Cumming. New York: Continuum, 1972.

Horton, Andrew, and Stuart Y. McDougal, eds. *Play It Again, Sam: Retakes on Remakes*. Berkeley: University of California Press, 1998.

Huntington, John. *Rationalizing Genius: Ideological Strategies in the Classic American Science Fiction Short Story*. New Brunswick, N.J.: Rutgers University Press, 1989.

Huyssen, Andreas. "The Vamp and the Machine: Fritz Lang's *Metropolis*." In *After the Great Divide: Modernism, Mass Culture, Postmodernism*, 65–81. Bloomington: Indiana University Press, 1986.

Imhoff, Michael, and Léon Krempel. *Berlin Architecture 2000: A Guide to New Buildings from 1989 to 2001*. Petersberg, Germany: Michael Imhoff, 2001.

Independence Day. Dir. Roland Emmerich. Twentieth Century Fox, 1996.

Irr, Caren, and Ian Buchanan, eds. *On Jameson: From Postmodernism to Globalization*. Albany: State University of New York Press, 2006.

Israel, Jonathan I. *Radical Enlightenment: Philosophy and the Making of Modernity, 1650–1750*. Oxford: Oxford University Press, 2001.

Jameson, Fredric. "Actually Existing Marxism." In *Marxism Beyond Marxism*, ed. Saree Makdisi, Cesare Casarino, and Rebecca E. Karl, 14–54. New York: Routledge, 1996.

———. *Archaeologies of the Future*. New York: Verso, 2005.

———. "Cognitive Mapping." In *Marxism and the Interpretation of Culture*, ed. Cary Nelson and Lawrence Grossberg, 347–57. Urbana: University of Illinois Press, 1988.

———. "The Dialectics of Disaster." *South Atlantic Quarterly* 101, no. 2 (2002): 297–304.

———. *Fables of Aggression: Wyndham Lewis, the Modernist as Fascist*. Berkeley: University of California Press, 1979.

———. Foreword to *The Postmodern Condition: A Report on Knowledge*, by Jean-François Lyotard. Trans. Geoff Bennington and Brian Massumi, vii–xxi. Minneapolis: University of Minnesota Press, 1984.

———. *The Geopolitical Aesthetic: Cinema and Space in the World System*. Bloomington: Indiana University Press, 1992.

———. "The Iconographies of Cyberspace." *Polygraph*, no. 13 (2001): 121–27.

———. *The Ideologies of Theory: Essays, 1971–1986*. Vol.1, *Situations of Theory*. Minneapolis: University of Minnesota Press, 1989.

———. *The Ideologies of Theory: Essays, 1971–1986*. Vol. 2, *The Syntax of History*. Minneapolis: University of Minnesota Press, 1989.

———. "Lacan and the Dialectic: A Fragment." In *Lacan: The Silent Partners*, ed. Slavoj Žižek, 365–97. New York: Verso, 2006.

———. *Late Marxism: Adorno; or, The Persistence of the Dialectic*. New York: Verso, 1990.

———. *Marxism and Form: Twentieth-Century Dialectical Theories of Literature*. Princeton: Princeton University Press, 1971.

———. "Marx's Purloined Letter." In *Ghostly Demarcations: A Symposium on Jacques Derrida's "Specters of Marx,"* ed. Michael Sprinker, 26–67. New York: Verso, 1999.

———. "On Raymond Chandler." *Southern Review* 6, no. 3 (1970): 624–50.

———. *The Political Unconscious: Narrative as a Socially Symbolic Act*. Ithaca: Cornell University Press, 1981.

———. "The Politics of Utopia." *New Left Review*, no. 25 (2004): 35–54 .

———. *Postmodernism; or, The Cultural Logic of Late Capitalism*. Durham: Duke University Press, 1991.

———. *Seeds of Time*. New York: Columbia University Press, 1994.

———. *Signatures of the Visible*. New York: Routledge, 1990.

———. *A Singular Modernity: Essay on the Ontology of the Present*. New York: Verso, 2002.

———. "The Synoptic Chandler." In *Shades of Noir: A Reader*, ed. Joan Copjec, 33–56. New York: Verso, 1993.

———. "Third-World Literature in the Era of Multinational Capitalism." *Social Text*, no. 15 (1986): 65–88.

Jeffords, Susan. *Hard Bodies: Hollywood Masculinity in the Reagan Era*. New Brunswick, N.J.: Rutgers University Press, 1994.

Kaplan, E. Ann, and Michael Sprinker, eds. *The Althusserian Legacy*. New York: Verso, 1993.

Kazin, Michael. *The Populist Persuasion: An American History*. New York: Basic Books, 1995.

Kellner, Douglas, and Sean Homer, eds. *Fredric Jameson: A Critical Reader*. New York: Palgrave Macmillan, 2004.

Kimball, A. Samuel. "Conceptions and Contraceptions of the Future: *Terminator 2, The Matrix*, and *Alien Resurrection*." *Camera Obscura* 50 (2002): 69–107.

———. *The Infanticidal Logic of Evolution and Culture*. Newark: University of Delaware Press, 2007.

Kipnis, Laura. "(Male) Desire and (Female) Disgust: Reading *Hustler*." In *Ecstasy Unlimited: On Sex, Capital, Gender, and Aesthetics*, 219–241. Minneapolis: University of Minnesota Press, 1993.

Knight, Peter. "Everything Is Connected: *Underworld*'s Secret History of Paranoia." In *Critical Essays on Don DeLillo*, ed. Hugh Ruppersburg and Tim Engles, 282–301. New York: Hall, 2000.

Kojève, Alexandre. *Introduction to the Reading of Hegel: Lectures on the "Phenomenology of the Spirit."* Trans. James H. Nichols Jr. Ithaca: Cornell University Press, 1980.

Koolhaas, Rem, and Bruce Mau. *S, M, L, XL: Office for Metropolitan Architecture.* Ed. Jennifer Sigler. New York: Monacelli Press, 1995.

Kracauer, Siegfried. *From Caligari to Hitler: A Psychological History of the German Film.* Princeton: Princeton University Press, 1947.

Kumar, Amitava, ed. *World Bank Literature.* Minneapolis: University of Minnesota Press, 2003.

———. "World Bank Literature: A New Name for Post-colonial Studies in the Next Century." *College Literature* 26, no. 3 (1999): 195–204.

Lacan, Jacques. *The Seminar of Jacques Lacan, Book VII: The Ethics of Psychoanalysis, 1959–1960.* Trans. Dennis Porter. New York: W. W. Norton, 1992.

Laclau, Ernesto, and Chantal Mouffe. *Hegemony and Socialist Strategy: Towards a Radical Democratic Politics.* New York: Verso, 1985.

Leavey, John, Jr. "A Marrano's Smile: Taking On — Several Protocols to an Armistice." Unpublished MS.

Lefebvre, Henri. *The Critique of Everyday Life.* Vol. 1. Trans. John Moore. New York: Verso, 1991.

———. *The Production of Space.* Trans. Donald Nicholson-Smith. Oxford: Blackwell, 1991.

Leggatt, Alexander, ed. *William Shakespeare's "Macbeth": A Sourcebook.* London: Routledge, 2006.

Leinster, Murray. "First Contact." *Astounding Science Fiction* 35, no. 3 (1945): 7–35.

Leitch, Thomas M. "Twice-Told Tales: The Rhetoric of the Remake." *Literature/Film Quarterly* 18, no. 3 (1990): 7–67.

Lévi-Strauss, Claude. *The Elementary Structures of Kinship.* Trans. James Harle Bell, John Richard von Sturmer, and Rodney Needham. Boston: Beacon, 1969.

Levinson, Marjorie. "What Is New Formalism?" *PMLA* 122, no. 2 (2007): 558–69.

Lipietz, Alain. *Mirages and Miracles: The Crisis of Global Fordism.* Trans. David Macey. New York: Verso, 1987.

London, Jack. *The Call of the Wild, White Fang, and Other Stories.* New York: Oxford, 1998.

Loukides, Paul. "The Hostile Redneck and the American Dream." In *Beyond the Stars: Stock Characters in American Popular Film,* ed. Loukides and Linda K. Fuller, 90–96. Bowling Green, Ohio: Bowling Green State University Popular Press, 1990.

Löwy, Michael. *Fire Alarm: Reading Walter Benjamin's "On the Concept of History."* Trans. Chris Turner. New York: Verso, 2005.

Lukács, Georg. *A Defence of "History and Class Consciousness": Tailism and the Dialectic.* Trans. Esther Leslie. New York: Verso, 2000.

———. *The Historical Novel.* Trans. Hannah and Stanley Mitchell. Lincoln: University of Nebraska Press, 1983.

———. *Marxism and Human Liberation,* ed. E. San Juan Jr. New York: Dell, 1973.

Lyotard, Jean-François. *The Postmodern Condition: A Report on Knowledge.* Trans.

Geoff Bennington and Brian Massumi. Minneapolis: University of Minnesota Press, 1984.

MacDonald, John D. *The Executioners*. Greenwich: Fawcett, 1957.

Mailer, Norman. *Advertisements for Myself*. New York: Putnam's Sons, 1959.

Mannheim, Karl. *Ideology and Utopia: An Introduction to the Sociology of Knowledge*. Trans. Louis Wirth and Edward Shils. New York: Harcourt Brace Jovanovich, 1936.

Marin, Louis. *Utopics: The Semiological Play of Textual Spaces*. Trans. Robert A. Vollrath. Atlantic Highlands, N.J.: Humanities Press International, 1984.

————. *Utopiques: Jeux d'espace*. Paris: Éditions de Minuit, 1973.

Marinetti, F. T. "The Founding and Manifesto of Futurism." In *Selected Writings*, 39–44. Trans. R. W. Flint and A. A. Coppotelli. New York: Farrar, Strauss and Giroux, 1972.

Mars Attacks! Dir. Tim Burton. Warner Brothers, 1996.

Marx, Karl. *A Contribution to the Critique of Political Economy*. Trans. S. W. Ryazanskaya. New York: International Publishers, 1970.

————. *The Eighteenth Brumaire of Louis Bonaparte*. New York: International Publishers, 1964.

Marx, Karl, and Friedrich Engels. *The Marx-Engels Reader*. Ed. Robert C. Tucker. New York: W. W. Norton, 1978.

The Matrix. Dir. Laurence Wachowski and Andrew Wachowski. Warner Brothers, 1999.

The Matrix Reloaded. Dir. Laurence Wachowski and Andrew Wachowski. Warner Brothers, 2003.

The Matrix Revolutions. Dir. Laurence Wachowski and Andrew Wachowski. Warner Brothers, 2003.

McKeon, Michael. *The Origins of the English Novel, 1600–1740*. Baltimore: Johns Hopkins University Press, 1987.

Merrill, Derek. "Abject Americans: Waste, Obsolescence, and Strategies of Recycling in Twentieth Century Literature." PhD diss., University of Florida, 2006.

Metropolis. Dir. Fritz Lang. UFA and Paramount Pictures, 1926.

Miller, Frank. *The Complete Frank Miller Batman*. Stamford, Conn.: Longmeadow, 1989.

Miller, Frank, and Lynn Varley. *The Dark Knight Strikes Again*. New York: DC Comics, 2001–2.

Montag, Warren. "Spirits Armed and Unarmed: Derrida's *Specters of Marx*." In *Ghostly Demarcations: A Symposium on Jacques Derrida's "Specters of Marx*," ed. Michael Sprinker, 68–82. New York: Verso, 1999.

Moore, Alan, Dave Gibbons, and John Higgins. *The Watchmen*. New York: Warner Books, 1987.

Moretti, Franco. "Conjectures on World Literature." *New Left Review*, 2nd ser., no. 1 (2000): 54–68.

————. *Graphs, Maps, Trees: Abstract Models for a Literary Theory*. New York: Verso, 2005.

Morris, Meaghan, *Too Soon Too Late: History in Popular Culture*. Bloomington: Indiana University Press, 1998.

Moylan, Tom. "Global Economy, Local Texts: Utopian/Dystopian Tension in William Gibson's Cyberpunk Trilogy." *Minnesota Review*, nos. 43–44 (1995): 182–97.

————. *Scraps of the Untainted Sky: Science Fiction, Utopia, Dystopia*. Boulder, Colo.: Westview, 2001.

Murray, Robin. "Life after Henry (Ford)." *Marxism Today* 32, no. 10 (1988): 8–13.

Nagy, Thomas J. "The Secret behind the Sanctions: How the U.S. Intentionally Destroyed Iraq's Water Supply." *Progressive*, September 2001, 22–25.

Negri, Antonio. "The Specter's Smile." In *Ghostly Demarcations: A Symposium on Jacques Derrida's "Specters of Marx,"* ed. Michael Sprinker, 3–16. New York: Verso, 1999.

Nieland, Justus. "Graphic Violence: Native Americans and the Western Archive in *Dead Man*." CR: *The New Centennial Review* 1, no. 2 (2001): 171–200.

Nietzsche, Friedrich. *Basic Writings of Nietzsche*, ed. and trans. Walter Kaufmann. New York: Modern Library, 1968.

Orwell, George. *The Collected Essays, Journalism, and Letters*. Vol. 4, *In Front of Your Nose, 1945–1950*. Ed. Sonia Orwell and Ian Angus. New York: Harcourt, Brace and World, 1968.

————. *Nineteen Eighty-Four*. New York: Harcourt, Brace, 1949.

Osteen, Mark. *American Magic and Dread: Don DeLillo's Dialogue with Culture*. Philadelphia: University of Pennsylvania Press, 2000.

Palahniuk, Chuck. *Fight Club*. New York: Henry Holt, 1996.

Penley, Constance. "Time Travel, Primal Scene, and the Critical Dystopia." In *Alien Zone: Cultural Theory and Contemporary Science Fiction*, ed. Annette Kuhn, 116–27. New York: Verso, 1990.

Petro, Patrice. *Joyless Streets: Women and Melodramatic Representation in Weimar Germany*. Princeton: Princeton University Press, 1989.

Pfeil, Fred. "Home Fires Burning: Family *Noir* in *Blue Velvet* and *Terminator 2*." In *Shades of Noir*, ed. Joan Copjec, 227–59. New York: Verso, 1993.

Phone Booth. Dir. Joel Schumacher. Twentieth Century Fox, 2003.

Pinkerton, James P. "Tuesday's Act Was Not about Nothing." *Newsday*, September 16, 2001.

Pontifical Academy for Life Tenth General Assembly. "Final Communique on 'The Dignity of Human Procreation and Reproductive Technologies: Anthropological and Ethical Aspects,'" February 21, 2004, www.vatican.va/roman_curia/pontifical_academies/acdlife/documents/rc_pont-acd_life_doc_20040316_x-gen-assembly-final_en.html (accessed September 16, 2008).

"Post-Fordism: Flexible Politics in the Age of Just-in-Time Production." Special section, *Socialist Review* 21, no. 1 (1991): 53–153.

Punk: Attitude. Dir. Don Letts. Capital Entertainment, 2005.

Rabelais, François. *Gargantua and Pantagruel*. Trans. J. M. Cohen. London: Penguin, 1955.

Rasch, William, ed. "World Orderings: Confronting Carl Schmitt's *The Nomos of the Earth*." Special issue, *South Atlantic Quarterly* 104, no. 2 (2005).

"Resolution of Colorado House of Representatives, February 2, 2005." Kersplebedeb, http://www.kersplebedeb.com/mystuff/s11/churchill_hor.html (accessed Sept. 11, 2008).

Robbins, Bruce. *Feeling Global: Internationalism in Distress*. New York: New York University Press, 1999.

Retort. *Afflicted Powers: Capital and Spectacle in a New Age of War*. New ed. New York: Verso, 2006.

Rogin, Michael. *Independence Day; or, How I Learned to Stop Worrying and Love the Enola Gay*. London: British Film Institute, 1998.

Rose, Mark. *Alien Encounters: Anatomy of Science Fiction*. Cambridge: Harvard University Press, 1981.

Ross, Andrew. *Strange Weather: Culture, Science, and Technology in the Age of Limits*. New York: Verso, 1991.

Ross, Kristin. *The Emergence of Social Space: Rimbaud and the Paris Commune*. Minneapolis: University of Minnesota Press, 1988.

Rubin, Gayle. "The Traffic in Women: Notes on the 'Political Economy' of Sex." In *Toward an Anthropology of Women*, ed. Rayna R. Reiter, 157–210. New York: Monthly Review Press, 1975.

Rushdie, Salman. *Fury*. New York: Random House, 2001.

Ryazanoff, D., ed. *The Communist Manifesto of Karl Marx and Friedrich Engels*. New York: Russell and Russell, 1963.

Santner, Eric L. "Miracles Happen: Benjamin, Rosenzweig, Freud, and the Matter of the Neighbor." In *The Neighbor: Three Inquiries in Political Theology*, by Slavoj Žižek, Santner, and Kenneth Reinhard, 76–133. Chicago: University of Chicago Press, 2005.

Sargent, Lyman Tower. "The Three Faces of Utopianism Revisited." *Utopian Studies* 5, no. 1 (1994): 1–37.

Schaub, Thomas Hill. *American Fiction in the Cold War*. Madison: University of Wisconsin Press, 1991.

Sedgwick, Eve Kosofsky. *Between Men: English Literature and Homosocial Desire*. New York: Columbia University Press, 1985.

———. *Tendencies*. Durham: Duke University Press, 1993.

Shapiro, Edward S. *Crown Heights: Blacks, Jews, and the 1991 Brooklyn Riot*. Lebanon, N.H.: Brandeis University Press, 2006.

Shelden, Michael. *Orwell: The Authorized Biography*. New York: Harper Collins, 1991.

"Shot Heard 'Round the World (Baseball)." *Wikipedia*, en.wikipedia.org/wiki/

Baseball%27s_Shot_Heard_%27Round_the_World (accessed September 16, 2008).

Simpson, David. *9/11: The Culture of Commemoration*. Chicago: University of Chicago Press, 2006.

The Simpsons: The Complete Eighth Season. DVD. Twentieth Century Fox Television, 2006.

Six Feet Under: The Complete Series. DVD. HBO, 2006.

Smith, Neil. "Homeless/Global: Scaling Places." In *Mapping the Futures: Local Cultures, Global Change*, ed. Jon Bird et al., 87–119. New York: Routledge, 1993.

Smith, Paul. *Millennial Dreams: Contemporary Culture and Capital in the North*. New York: Verso, 1997.

Spiegelman, Art. *In the Shadow of No Towers*. New York: Pantheon, 2004.

Spinoza, Benedict de. *The Ethics and Other Works*. Ed. and trans. Edwin Curley. Princeton: Princeton University Press, 1994.

Spivak, Gayatri Chakravorty. "Ghostwriting." *Diacritics* 25, no. 2 (1995): 65–84.

Sprinker, Michael, ed. *Ghostly Demarcations: A Symposium on Jacques Derrida's "Specters of Marx."* New York: Verso, 1999.

Star Trek: First Contact. Dir. Jonathan Frakes. Paramount Pictures, 1996.

Sundquist, Eric J. *To Wake the Nations: Race in the Making of American Literature*. Cambridge: Belknap, 1993.

Suvin, Darko. *Metamorphoses of Science Fiction: On the Poetics and History of a Literary Genre*. New Haven: Yale University Press, 1979.

The Terminator. Dir. James Cameron. Orion Pictures, 1984.

Terminator 2: Judgment Day. Dir. James Cameron. Tri-Star Pictures, 1991.

Terminator 3: The Rise of the Machines. Dir. Jonathan Mostow. Warner Brothers, 2003.

"The Terminator Saga." www.geocities.com/Hollywood/Makeup/4303/terminator.html (accessed September 16, 2008).

Thompson, E. P. *William Morris: Romantic to Revolutionary*. Rev. ed. New York: Pantheon, 1977.

Titanic. Dir. James Cameron. Paramount Pictures, 1997.

Todd, Emmanuel. *After the Empire: The Breakdown of the American Order*. Trans. C. Jon Delogu. New York: Columbia University Press, 2003.

Todorov, Tzvetan. *The Fantastic: A Structural Approach to a Literary Genre*. Trans. Richard Howard. Ithaca: Cornell University Press, 1975.

Total Recall. Dir. Paul Verhoeven. Tri-Star Pictures, 1990.

Ventura, Patricia. "The Cultural Logic of the United States in the Globalization Era." PhD diss., University of Florida, 2003.

Verevis, Constantine. "Remaking Film." *Film Studies*, no. 4 (summer 2004): 87–103.

Watkins, Evan. *Throwaways: Work Culture and Consumer Education*. Stanford: Stanford University Press, 1993.

Wegner, Phillip E. "The Beat Cops of History; or, The Paranoid Style in American Intellectual Politics." *Arizona Quarterly*. Forthcoming.

——. "Greimas avec Lacan; or, From the Symbolic to the Real in Dialectical Theory." Unpublished manuscript.

——. "Here or Nowhere: Utopia, Modernity, and Totality." In *Utopia Method Vision: The Use Value of Social Dreaming*, ed. Tom Moylan and Raffaella Baccolini, 113–29. Oxford: Peter Lang, 2007.

——. "Horizons, Figures, and Machines: The Dialectic of Utopia in the Work of Fredric Jameson." *Utopian Studies* 9, no. 2 (1998): 58–73.

——. *Imaginary Communities: Utopia, the Nation, and the Spatial Histories of Modernity*. Berkeley: University of California Press, 2002.

——. "Jameson's Modernisms; or, the Desire Called Utopia." *Diacritics* 37, no. 4 (2009): 2–20.

——. "Ken MacLeod's Permanent Revolution: Utopian Possible Worlds, History, and the *Augenblick* in the 'Fall Revolution' Quartet." In *Red Planets: Marxism, Science Fiction, Fantasy*, ed. Mark Bould and China Miéville. London: Pluto, 2009.

——. "The Last Bomb: Historicizing History in Terry Bisson's *Fire on the Mountain* and Gibson and Sterling's *The Difference Engine*." *Comparatist*, no. 23 (1999): 141–51.

——. "Learning to Live in History: Alternate Historicities and the 1990s in *The Years of Rice and Salt*." In *Mapping the Unimaginable: Kim Stanley Robinson and the Critics*, ed. William Burling. New York: MacFarland, 2009.

——. "Periodizing Jameson." In *On Jameson: From Postmodernism to Globalization*, ed. Caren Irr and Ian Buchanan, 241–80. Albany: State University of New York Press, 2006.

——. "The Pretty Woman Goes Global; or, Learning to Love 'Americanization' in *Notting Hill*." *Genre* 38, no. 3 (2006): 309–26.

Whedon, Joss, et al. *Buffy the Vampire Slayer: Season 8*. Milwaukie, Oreg.: Dark Horse Comics, 2007.

Whedon, Joss, Karl Maline, and Andy Owens. *Fray*. Milwaukie, Oreg.: Dark Horse Comics, 2003.

Wilcox, Rhonda V., and David Lavery, eds. *Fighting the Forces: What's at Stake in Buffy the Vampire Slayer?* Lanham, Md.: Rowman and Littlefield, 2002.

Wilkens, Matthew. "Towards a Benjaminian Theory of Dialectical Allegory." *New Literary History* 37, no. 2 (2006): 285–98.

Williams, Raymond. *George Orwell*. New York: Columbia University Press, 1971.

Willis, Sharon. *High Contrast: Race and Gender in Contemporary Hollywood Films*. Durham: Duke University Press, 1997.

Willis, Susan. *Portents of the Real: A Primer for Post-9/11 America*. New York: Verso, 2005.

Wills, Garry. *Witches and Jesuits: Shakespeare's Macbeth*. New York: Oxford University Press, 1995.

Wolfreys, Julian. "Trauma, Testimony, Criticism: Witnessing, Memory, and Responsibility." In *Introducing Criticism at the Twenty-First Century*, ed. Wolfreys, 126–48. Edinburgh: Edinburgh University Press, 2002.

Žižek, Slavoj. "Afterword: Lenin's Choice." In *Revolution at the Gates: Selected Writings from February to October 1917*, by V. I. Lenin, ed. Žižek, 167–336. New York: Verso, 2002.

———. "From Purification to Subtraction: Badiou and the Real." In *Think Again: Alain Badiou and the Future of Philosophy*, ed. Peter Hallward, 165–81. New York: Continuum, 2004.

———. "Georg Lukács as the Philosopher of Leninism." In *A Defence of "History and Class Consciousness": Tailism and the Dialectic*, by Georg Lukács, 151–82. Trans. Esther Leslie. New York: Verso, 2002.

———. "Ideology Reloaded." *In These Times* 27, no. 16 (2003): 23–25.

———. *Did Somebody Say Totalitarianism? Five Interventions in the (Mis)use of a Notion*. New York: Verso, 2001.

———. "A Leninist Gesture Today: Against the Populist Temptation." In *Lenin Reloaded: Toward a Politics of Truth*, ed. Sebastian Budgen, Stathis Kouvelakis, and Žižek, 74–98. Durham: Duke University Press, 2007.

———. *Looking Awry: An Introduction to Jacques Lacan through Popular Culture*. Cambridge: MIT Press, 1991.

———. *The Parallax View*. Cambridge: MIT Press, 2006.

———. "A Plea for Leninist Intolerance." *Critical Inquiry* 28, no. 2 (2002): 542–66.

———. *The Puppet and the Dwarf: The Perverse Core of Christianity*. Cambridge: MIT Press, 2003.

———. *The Sublime Object of Ideology*. New York: Verso, 1989.

———. *Tarrying with the Negative: Kant, Hegel, and the Critique of Ideology*. Durham: Duke University Press, 1993.

———. *The Ticklish Subject: The Absent Center of Political Ontology*. New York: Verso, 1999.

———. *Welcome to the Desert of the Real*. New York: Verso, 2002.

Davis, Mike, 4, 229 n. 36, 230 n. 44

Dawn (Butler), 200

Dawson, Ashley, 221 n. 11

Day after Tomorrow (Emmerich), 227 n. 29, 235–36 n. 54

Days of Eclipse (Sokurov), 172

Dead Man (Jarmusch), 13, 22, 133, 232 n. 42

death drive, 24, 63, 153–54

Degrees of Shame (Wolf), 173

Delany, Samuel, 36

Deleuze, Gilles, 6, 46–48, 196, 202, 207, 241 n. 7

DeLillo, Don, 224 n. 14, 227 n. 17; *Americana*, 47; *Falling Man*, 225 n. 31; *Libra*, 44; *Mao II*, 51, 224 n. 21; *Players*, 51; *Underworld*, 10, 22, 25, 43–59, 224 n. 3, 225 n. 28; *White Noise*, 43–44, 47–48, 225 n. 28

Deliverance (Boorman), 107

Demolished Man (Bester), 202

De Niro, Robert, 11, 85, 106

Denning, Michael, 4, 33, 222 n. 45, 222 n. 49

Depp, Johnny, 133

Derrida, Jacques, 18, 21, 23, 25, 34, 141, 147–49, 151, 161, 163–64, 191–92, 222 n. 51, 233 n. 12, 233 n. 15, 233 n. 25, 233 n. 29, 234 n. 32; *Specters of Marx*, 13, 137, 139–40, 142–46, 150, 154, 158, 162, 233 n. 16

desegregation, 22, 99–100, 102–4, 161, 200, 228 n. 23

desire: containment of, 67–68, 84, 99, 122, 154, 157, 231 n. 28; for escape, 50, 69, 126; gender and, 77–78, 103, 109; incest and, 90, 109; messianic, 13, 80, 149–50, 161–62; for narrative, 44; for ontological purity, 142, 149; radical political, 41, 68–70, 72, 119–20, 131–32, 149–50, 154, 157, 231 n. 28; for repetition, 37

detective fiction, 91, 174, 228 n. 11, 237–38 n. 29

DeVito, Danny, 61

dialectics, 239 n. 51; bad side of, 142–43, 149; complement to, 172, 227 n. 7; dialectical sequence, 62, 83; literary history and, 118, 121, 230 n. 4; periodization and, 2, 4–5, 48; view from above and, 231 n. 29. *See also* *Aufhebung*; contradiction; master-slave dialectic; negation

dialectics at a standstill, 2, 38

DiCaprio, Leonardo, 30

Dick, Philip K., 207; *Do Androids Dream of Electric Sheep?*, 70, 226 n. 15; *Dr. Bloodmoney*, 175; "Faith of Our Fathers," 141; *Time Out of Joint*, 174; *Ubik*, 177

dirty realism, 124, 182, 188, 231 n. 24

Disch, Thomas M., 176

Dispossessed, The (Le Guin), 230 n. 16, 238 n. 43

Diva (Beineix), 171

Divine Comedy (Dante), 44

Do Androids Dream of Electric Sheep? (Dick), 70, 226 n. 15

Dr. Bloodmoney (Dick), 175

Dr. Strangelove, 63, 156

Dog Day Afternoon (Lumet), 171

Dole, Bob, 140

Donnelly, Ignatius, 125

Doomsday Clock, 63–64, 226 n. 3

Doonesbury, 78

Double Indemnity (Cain), 227 n. 4

Double Indemnity (Wilder), 227 n. 4

doubling, 18, 21, 29, 52, 58, 71, 82–83, 125, 129–31, 176, 192. *See also* repetition

Douglas, Illeana, 85

Dove, Rita, 36

Dracula (Stoker), 198

drag, 110–11, 153, 203, 214

Dreiser, Theodore, 120

Goldblum, Jeff, 146

Gold Coast (Robinson), 119

Goldgeier, James, 221 n. 30

Golding, William, 228 n. 18

Goode, John, 230 n. 2

gothic, 197–98

Gramsci, Antonio, 70, 163–64, 191, 236 n. 58

Grasian, Daniel, 35–36

Gravity's Rainbow (Pynchon), 36

Greengrass, Paul, 59

Greimas, A. J., 93–94, 187–89, 228 n. 14, 239 n. 51, 239 n. 53

Greimasian semiotic rectangle, 93–94, 187–89, 239 n. 51

Griffiths, Richard T., 222 n. 46

Grin without a Cat, A (Marker), 23

Groundhog Day (Ramis), 9, 29, 31–32

Grundrisse (Marx), 211

grunge, 35

Gunpowder Plot, 19–21

Guy Fawkes Day, 19

Haldeman, Joe, 190–92; *Forever Free*, 14, 22, 193–94; *Forever Peace*, 14, 22, 166, 176–89, 194; *The Forever War*, 14, 22, 176–79, 182–83, 193–94, 238 n. 45; "None So Blind," 177

Hallward, Peter, 214

Hamilton, Linda, 64

Hankte, Steffan, 238 n. 45

Hansen, Jim, 220 n. 24

Hardt, Michael, 14, 59, 203, 223 n. 57, 223 n. 59; *Empire*, 34, 128–29, 189–90, 196–97, 211, 222 n. 49, 229 n. 40

Harry Potter series, 210

Harvey, David, 25, 166, 168–71, 176, 182, 201, 221 n. 23, 222 n. 49, 229 n. 46, 235 n. 52, 236 n. 8, 237 n. 13, 241 n. 16

Harwell, Ernie, 43

hauntology, 13, 23, 142, 149

Hawthorne, Christopher, 39

He, She, and It (Piercy), 119

Hegel, G. W. F., 5, 40, 105–6, 118, 139, 142–43, 149–50, 170, 189; *Phenomenology of Spirit*, 138; *The Philosophy of Right*, 137

Hegeman, Susan, 219 n. 4, 222 n. 35

Heidegger, Martin, 155

Henwood, Doug, 222 n. 43

heteronormativity, 90, 154, 178, 203, 208

heterotopia, 31, 222 n. 40

Higgins, John, 231 n. 23

High Noon (Zinnemann), 134

hipster, 11, 96–99, 106

Hiroshima, 58

His Dark Materials (Pullman), 35, 194

historical novel, 7, 10, 44–49, 224 n. 7

Hitchcock, Alfred, 58; *Psycho*, 111, 229 n. 35; *Vertigo*, 86, 112

Hitler, Adolf, 67

Hoberman, J., 228 n. 23

Hodges, Russ, 45, 59

Hoffmann, E. T. A., 131

Hofstadter, Richard, 225 n. 27

Holland, Agnieszka, 172

Hoover, J. Edgar, 45, 52–54

Horkheimer, Max, 150, 192

Houston, 156, 184

Hughes, Langston, 36

Hugo Award, 68, 176

Hulk (Lee), 40

Human Front, The (MacLeod), 73

Huntington, John, 234 n. 39

Huntington, Samuel P., 235 n. 52

Hussein, Saddam, 67, 82, 159

Hustler, 127

Huxley, Aldous, 18

Huyssen, Andreas, 226 n. 11

Icarian colony, 210, 242 n. 47

ideology, 27, 113–14, 171; desegregation and, 99; end of history and, 139, 142, 250; globalization as,

168–69, 182, 187–88, 195, 212;
mapping, 93; naturalist, 130, 135–
36; reworking, 62; Soviet, 149;
Titanic as, 29; United States and,
65–66, 74; work of, 120, 144, 157–59.
See also aesthetic ideology; fantasy;
myth
ideology of form, 121, 215
"I Have No Mouth and I Must Scream"
(Ellison), 68–71
imaginary, 7, 55, 83, 93, 123, 150, 153,
155, 161, 167, 171, 179, 188, 202, 207,
235 n. 43. *See also* Real; symbolic
Imaginary Communities (Wegner), 220
n. 26, 220 n. 3, 225 n. 29, 228 n. 14,
230 nn. 15–16, 231 n. 21, 234 n. 38,
237 n. 20, 237 n. 28, 238 n. 43, 239
n. 51, 241 n. 17
immaterial labor, 112, 128–29, 197, 229
n. 40
imperialism, 23, 147, 169, 175, 197, 203,
211
Independence Day (Emmerich), 13, 22,
29, 37, 39, 132, 139–41, 143, 145–48,
150–62, 164, 233 n. 9, 234 n. 36, 234
n. 41, 235 n. 43, 235 n. 54
Inheritors, The (Golding), 228 n. 18
intellectuals, 34, 127, 158, 162–65, 181,
183–84, 188, 191–92, 232 n. 41
Internet, 22, 33
In the Shadow of No Towers (Spiegelman), 19
Iraq, 20, 59, 67, 79, 152
Iron Heel, The (London), 121–22
Israel, Jonathan, 34

James I, 19–20
Jameson, Fredric, 34; on allegorical
encounter films, 171; on allegory,
87, 158, 167, 171–74, 202, 213, 223
n. 66, 236 n. 2; on cognitive mapping, 14, 44, 166–67, 169–74, 182,
200, 202, 224 n. 3, 228 n. 11, 238

n. 29; on cyberpunk, 124, 182, 187,
231 n. 24; on end of history, 141–42;
on genre, 7; *The Geopolitical Aesthetic*, 167, 172–73, 202; on Greimas,
93, 188, 239 n. 20; on ideology of
form, 121; on Lacan, 228 n. 14; on
late modernism, 131, 220 n. 18; on
mass culture, 6, 67, 87, 204, 221
n. 18, 223 n. 66, 223 n. 68; on narrative, 44, 224 n. 3; on naturalism,
130, 230 n. 2; periodization, vii, 4–7,
27–28, 43, 172, 219 n. 11, 219 n. 13,
220 n. 19, 236 n. 2; on postmodernism, 4–6, 141–42, 167, 169–72,
219 n. 13, 220 n. 19, 222 n. 44, 224
n. 8, 237 n. 19; *Postmodernism; or,
The Cultural Logic of Late Capitalism*,
5, 167, 170–72, 219 n. 13, 220 n. 20,
222 n. 44, 224 n. 8, 237 n. 19; on the
practico-inert, 63–64, 83–84; on
religion, 213, 234 n. 32; on science
fiction, 77, 174–76, 178, 182, 187,
200, 223 n. 66, 226 n. 24, 231 n. 24,
237 nn. 27–29, 238 n. 33, 239 n. 49;
A Singular Modernity, 4–5, 220 n. 18;
on terrorism, 37, 239–40 n. 56;
on third world literature, 169–71,
237 n. 15; "Third World Literature
in the Era of Multinational Capitalism," 169–70, 174, 237 n. 15; on
totalization, 168; on transcoding,
6, 220 n. 20; on utopia, 18, 67, 118,
202, 204, 233 n. 17, 239–40 n. 56; on
vanishing mediator, 234 n. 42; on
welfare state, 192, 240 n. 69
Jarmusch, Jim: *Dead Man*, 13, 22, 133,
232 n. 42; *Ghost Dog*, 12–13, 22, 124,
132–35
Jaws (Spielberg), 171
jazz, 96, 103
Jazz (Morrison), 44
Jeffords, Susan, 68
Jetée, La (Marker), 70

post-Fordism, 111, 124, 129, 158, 229 n. 36, 232 n. 32, 239–40 n. 48. *See also* immaterial labor

postindustrial economy, 12, 46, 111–12, 124, 128, 168

postmodernism, 4–5, 14, 33–34, 170–72, 177, 222 n. 44, 224 n. 8, 237 n. 19

Postmodernism; or, The Cultural Logic of Late Capitalism (Jameson), 5, 167, 170–72, 219 n. 13, 220 n. 20, 222 n. 44, 224 n. 8, 237 n. 19

practico-inert, 64, 69–70, 84

prefiguration, 19, 22, 29, 37, 86, 143, 160, 167, 175, 179

primitive, 77, 89, 95–96, 125, 176, 228 n. 18

Project for the New American Century, 14, 25, 139, 160–61

Psycho (Hitchcock), 111, 229 n. 35

psychoanalysis, 24, 89, 109–10, 131, 229 n. 33

Pullman, Bill, 145

Pullman, Philip, 35, 194

punk, 35

Punk: Attitude (Letts), 35

Punxsutawney, 32

Pynchon, Thomas, 36, 44

Quaid, Randy, 146

queerness, 97, 153–54, 198, 206, 214, 240 n. 68

Rabelais, François, 195, 197

race, 11, 88, 99, 101–3, 179, 235 n. 43; discrimination and, 100; positioning and, 106, 109, 113–15, 146, 203, 208; representations of, 68, 73, 113; violence and, 13, 133

Rage against the Machine, 40

Rashomon (Kurosawa), 134

Reagan, Ronald, 62–64, 100, 119, 161, 183, 187, 235 n. 54

Real, 3, 9, 23–24, 28, 35–36, 54, 57, 83,

131, 148, 163, 186, 188–89, 202. *See also* Event; imaginary; symbolic

Red Badge of Courage, The (Crane), 179

Reeves, Keanu, 39

remake, 7, 11, 13, 22, 62, 70, 87–88, 106, 109, 227 n. 1, 227 nn. 4–5, 229 n. 35, 235 n. 54

repetition: beginnings and, 10, 17, 28, 36–40, 54–59, 81, 142, 202, 215–16; commemoration and, 38–39; compulsion for, 28, 32, 62, 130, 141–42; events as, 9, 21–22, 24–25, 28, 32; genres and, 225 n. 29; mass culture and, 221 n. 18; meaning of, 21–22, 24–25; periods and, 7; remarriage as, 31–32; repeating, 196, 204, 241 n. 7; as return to past, 5; as revision, 10, 64–65, 79, 81–83; urbanization and, 126. *See also* doubling

resignification, 203–5

Retort collective, 23, 221 n. 23

return of the repressed, 12, 28, 86, 111

Revenge of the Sith (Lucas), 236 n. 54

revolution: as break, 2, 40–41, 143–44, 146, 148, 157, 164–65, 202, 211, 215, 217; conservative, 161; fidelity to, 189, 217; Marxism and, 3, 13, 143–44; modernity and, 196–97; project of, 41, 66, 128, 184, 196–97; representation of, 122–24, 148–49, 191, 234 n. 31; threat of, 68, 156

Riesman, David, 93, 228 n. 18

Rimbaud, Arthur, 202

Roadside Picnic (Strugatsky and Strugatsky), 178

Robbins, Bruce, 34, 164, 192, 231 n. 29, 240 n. 69

Robinson, Kim Stanley: *Gold Coast*, 119; *Mars* trilogy, 35, 211; *Pacific Edge*, 35; *Years of Rice and Salt*, 35, 44–45

Rodia, Sabato, 55

181; information and, 14, 33, 66, 157–58, 181–83, 239 n. 49; liberation and, 188; military, 65–66, 68, 72–74, 133, 154, 158–59, 176, 178, 180, 238 n. 45; reproductive, 204

television, 2, 9, 15, 29, 68, 86, 107, 130, 197–98, 206, 215, 242 n. 39

Terminator, The (Cameron), 10, 22, 29, 39, 60, 62–66, 68–72, 83–84, 155–56

Terminator 2: Judgment Day (Cameron), 11, 29, 37, 64–67, 72–75, 83, 156, 226 nn. 20–21

Terminator 3: Rise of the Machines (Mostow), 11, 22, 63, 75–83

terrorism, 19, 21–22, 29, 37, 58, 76, 81–82, 125–26, 128, 179, 189, 239–40 n. 56

Terrorizer, The (Yang), 172

Testament des Dr. Mabuse, Das (Lang), 235 n. 54

Thatcher, Margaret, 29, 119, 161, 212

Thelma and Louise (Scott), 73, 226 n. 20

theory, 5–6, 34, 138, 141, 163, 165, 168, 196, 220 n. 18

third world, 91, 156, 158, 169–72, 174, 234 n. 35, 237 n. 15

third world literature, 169–72, 174, 237 n. 15

"Third-World Literature in the Era of Multinational Capitalism" (Jameson), 169–70, 174, 237 n. 15

Thompson, E. P., 230 n. 2

Thompson, Fred Dalton, 109

Thompson, J. Lee, 11, 87, 110, 229 n. 35

Thomson, Bobby, 52–53, 55

Thoreau, Henry David, 18

throwaways, 12, 88, 111–16, 124

time-loop paradox, 11, 70–71, 73, 79. *See also* narrative; science fiction

Time Machine, The (Wells), 175

Time Out of Joint (Dick), 174

Titanic (Cameron), 9, 29–31

Todorov, Tzvetan, 207

Toomer, Jean, 36

totalitarianism, 96–97, 156, 162, 192, 234 n. 33

totality, 15, 45–46, 48, 138, 167–68, 170–72, 177, 183, 189, 210–11

Total Recall (Verhoeven), 66, 183

transcoding, 6

trauma, 7, 24, 26, 39, 54, 57–58, 83, 185–86, 198

Trudeau, Garry, 78

Twelve Monkeys (Gilliam), 70

Twins (Reitman), 61

Tykwer, Tom, 83

Ubik (Dick), 177

Ugly Swans, The (Strugatsky and Strugatsky), 178

Underworld (DeLillo), 10, 22, 25, 43–59, 224 n. 3, 225 n. 28

United Nations, 19

United 93 (Greengrass), 27, 59

university, 184, 191–92, 200

urbanization, 34, 46, 73, 91, 96, 103, 106, 124, 126–27, 132, 146–48, 154, 182, 188, 235 n. 43, 238 n. 29

Utopia (More), 7, 18–19, 201

utopianism, 2, 155, 227 n. 29; atrophy of imagination and, 72; in *Buffy*, 215; conservative, 123, 230–31 n. 21; in cyberpunk, 182; dialectical image of, 38; dystopia and, 118–25; enclave and, 209–11; family as, 204–5, 209–11; in *Forever Peace*, 184, 187, 191, 193–94; as genre, 8, 18–19, 35, 118–25, 152, 174–75, 178, 201–2, 220 n. 26, 234 n. 33, 238 n. 43, 237 n. 28, 239 n. 49; horizon and, 23, 38, 122, 125, 178; mass culture and, 67–68; minimal difference and, 194; of 1960s, 23; in *Parable* novels, 208–11; as place between two deaths, 30–32; politics and, 8, 34, 119–20, 157, 241 n. 7; primitivist, 125; representa-

PHILLIP E. WEGNER is an associate professor of English at the University of Florida and the author of *Imaginary Communities: Utopia, the Nation, and the Spatial Histories of Modernity*.

Library of Congress
Cataloging-in-Publication Data

Wegner, Phillip E., 1964–
Life between two deaths, 1989–2001 :
U.S. culture in the long nineties /
Phillip E. Wegner.
p. cm. — (Post-contemporary interventions)
Includes bibliographical references and index.
ISBN 978-0-8223-4458-2 (cloth : alk. paper)
ISBN 978-0-8223-4473-5 (pbk. : alk. paper)
1. United States — Civilization — 1970–
2. United States — History — 1969–
3. Nineteen nineties.
I. Title.
II. Series: Post-contemporary interventions.
E169.12.W395 2009
973.92 — dc22
2009003276